T0366253

About "More Than a Game"

"You are from Belgium, you played for Royal Antwerp and eventually wind up teaching and coaching the beautiful game in Africa. So you decide to write a novel about your experiences, and it becomes Africa's number one bestselling book.

This is an interesting look at the way football is run, African style. Riddled by in-fighting, corruption, embezzlement of club funds and dodgy referees, this novel tells the story of one man's insurmountable odds of trying to make his former club the best team in East Africa.

In the end he learns his lessons and moves to their city rivals—like George Graham going from Arsenal to Spurs. But the great thing about the book is that it's true to life and sheds light on an unknown area of the game. That alone keeps you enthralled."

FourFourTwo

Also by Ronny Mintjens

Siri Ya Ndani

A Chief's Story
Winner of the ROC-Taiwan 40th Anniversary Writing Contest, Swaziland, 2008

A Journey through North Korea

MORE THAN A GAME

RONNY MINTJENS

For book orders, email orders@traffordpublishing.com.sg

Most Trafford Singapore titles are also available at major online book retailers.

Printed in Singapore.

ISBN: 978-1-4669-3156-5 (sc)
ISBN: 978-1-4669-3157-2 (e)

Trafford rev.: 11/27/2012

 www.traffordpublishing.com.sg

Singapore
toll-free: 800 101 2656 (Singapore)
Fax: 800 101 2656 (Singapore)

To all the children who will dream about football this evening.

"One person with a belief is equal to a force of ninety-nine who only have interests."

ONE

The Nou Camp Stadium in Barcelona, Spain, October 30ᵗʰ

Sᴇᴛᴛᴏᴏ ʜᴇʀᴇ ɪɴ ᴛʜɪs ᴍᴏsᴛ wonderful football stadium, the home of Barcelona Football Club, with more than one hundred thousand football lovers screaming around me, my thoughts start to drift. The excitement on the terraces simultaneously reflects and helps create the magic that is being weaved on the field, several rows below my comfortable seat. It doesn't matter that the evening is chilly, that the wind is picking up, and that there is a hint of rain in the air. What matters is that the atmosphere is magical. A hundred thousand people are together for an hour or two, and totally oblivious to what goes on in the world outside this concrete shell of a stadium. The city of Barcelona oozes a feel-good factor, wherever one goes, looks or listens. *"Més que un club"*, 'More than a club', is written in large letters across the main stand of this football temple.

Barcelona Football Club is an institution where the people of Catalunya find their identity, where they all feel they belong, and from where they source the strength to express their relative independence from the central government in Madrid. Across the city, youngsters get together and engage in impromptu chanting of the famous *"Barça, Barça"* battle cry. Football has that sort of an effect on people, and on this late and rather damp autumn evening in the shadows of the Sagrada Familia, footballing perfection is near. What is being displayed on the field is poetry, pure poetry. Poetry against a green background, you could say. Just that around these parts, they call it *'tiki taka'*.

FC Barcelona are making cold meat of Sevilla FC. They are leading 4-0 through goals by Argentina's superstar Lionel Messi and Spain's goal-poacher David Villa. By the end of the match, Brazilian defender Dani Alves has completed the rout. FC Sevilla are condemned to return to the south of the country with a 5-0 trashing, and to try to regroup for the return match in a couple of months' time. But there is much more to see than just the goals. Each move, each pass, each offensive combination and each defensive action is well rehearsed, calculated and efficient. This *'tiki taka'* style of play is football at its very best, how it should be played and how it has conquered millions and millions of fans over the past century.

Sevilla FC don't play badly at all. It's just that Barcelona are in a class of their own. The style of play that they exhibit on the green carpet has won them plaudits from all over the world, and more and more expert voices have started to suggest that this could well be the greatest football team the world has ever seen. Teams from around the world try to imitate and emulate the Barça style of play, but of course it takes much more than a few talented players and a few afternoons on the training ground. Guided by my personal friend and colleague from my coaching days in Qatar, Josep 'Pep' Guardiola, they possess a near-perfect balance in the team, and the perfect blend of players, players who want to work for each other and who are all fighting for the same cause. The players are almost interchangeable, as they have been taught from a young age that there is one way forward, and they either buy into this way, or they go and try their luck elsewhere. In this club, nobody is indispensable, yet nobody can be taken out of the equation without upsetting the structure. The whole club, from the youngest junior to the most senior player, and from the tea-ladies to the President of the Board of Directors, permeates a particular culture, a style of play and a football philosophy that is simply irresistible.

The ideological and structural distance that separates FC Barcelona and Safari Sports Club, my own club in Tanzania on the East African coast, is tremendous, and can only be calculated in light years. And when I realize once more that my ambition is to achieve what Pep Guardiola is achieving, but that this simply cannot happen at Safari Sports Club because of the totally incompetent leadership, I make up my mind.

Pep Guardiola has not produced this FC Barcelona team all by himself. When he joined the club, he found a structure that had been developed over the years and that aimed at making FC Barcelona the greatest club in the world. In fact, he himself is a product of this structure. As a young apprentice, he was thrust into the Barça world, and he was taught the one way that this club believes in. When he returned years later as a coach, he found a philosophy that he had breathed his whole life, and he found the same passion and ambition that he had experienced as one of the club's most accomplished players and one of its distinguished former captains. The motor behind this ambition was the club's leadership. However, Pep must have felt that he could make a contribution towards this goal, and that is why he decided to become a part of the adventure. His influence is undeniable. He has taken the club to the zenith of two Champions' League victories, as well as three successive La Liga titles, a long list of La Liga records, and an unprecedented six-trophy haul in 2009. He has turned Barcelona into the champions of Spain, Europe and the world. Winning trophies has become a mere habit for FC Barcelona, and there are no signs that their gusto for more success is abating . . .

I sigh in pure admiration. Sitting in the Nou Camp and watching this harmony between directors and technical staff being reflected on the field of play, I start to think about my future with Safari Sports Club, back home in Dar Es Salaam. What exactly happened there, and what are the lessons for the future. Where did I want to go with this club? And was it even possible to get to where I wanted to be?

The night is getting cooler and the final whistle approaches. The action in these final minutes on the field takes a backseat, and I start to reflect on the journey so far. What has led me to this seat in the Nou Camp, and what will the future bring? I see myself again as a small child in Flanders, Belgium. I see that child grow up and become a footballer, then a coach, in Belgium, in Swaziland and ultimately in Tanzania. What were my goals in the first place?

The answer to this question is relatively straight-forward, obvious you might say, as it hadn't changed since my first day with the club. I wanted to transform Safari Sports Club into the greatest club of Tanzania and even East Africa, a club against which all other clubs would measure themselves. Not just a club that wins a title here and a cup there. No, I wanted to convert Safari Sports Club into a standard-bearer that leads the way and that would become the first East African club to unearth and fully develop the incredible talents of African players. Yes, the same talents that the whole world has been talking about for many years, but that have never materialized in any significant achievements. I wanted first place.

I've always wanted to be the best at whatever I do. As a matter of habit, I just don't settle for silver medals. In my long list of favorite sayings, somewhere near the top, you will find that "a silver medal is the prize for the first person in the long line of losers". Does anyone even remember runners-up? Can anyone recall who won the silver and bronze medals when Usain Bolt ran to gold in world-record time in the 100 metres final at the 2008 Beijing Olympics? I rest my case. But we all remember where we were when 'the Lightning Bolt' wrote history, don't we? Failure is not something I like to identify with, not something I want to be associated with, and not something I would enjoy. But at the same time I realize that the only place where 'success' comes before 'work' is in the dictionary. This competitive edge that characterizes my philosophy is a result not only of the coaching that I received when growing up in Belgium, but also of the cultivated determination that my path in life has brought.

So, was it at all possible for me to succeed in that club and achieve my goals? The answer to this question was equally easy to guess. "No, it was not possible!" Not at this club. Not at Safari Sports Club. Not after all the trials and tribulations that I experienced with the leadership. Not after seeing that, besides myself, nobody in the club wanted to plan for the longer term or even knew where the club should be heading. Not after realising that all my efforts to turn Safari Sports Club into a self-reliant, respectable and respected club had been frustrated. After all these setbacks, there was only one answer to this particular question. With Safari Sports Club I was going absolutely nowhere, and it had become impossible to talk sense into the club leaders. Our visions were miles apart, and there simply didn't seem to be any common ground. Unfortunately for the club my good ideas, almost exclusively taken from my experience with European football and my friendships with football technicians who knew the ropes, were never adopted by the incompetent and selfish 'leaders'. My ambition to improve the club was in stark contrast with their intention to siphon as much money and other benefits as possible out of the club during their three years in office, after which they would simply disappear into the sunset, never to be heard of again. Accountability, you ask? Not for these guys. And the worst part is, all this happened at the expense of the club's members, the players and the technical staff, and most importantly, at the expense of the development of the club. I willingly leave the fans out of the equation—they merit a chapter in themselves.

Dear reader, be advised that a status quo doesn't interest me. Tomorrow I want to be better than today. I want to learn more, teach more, try more and achieve more. And I will always look for opportunities to do this. We all do, don't we? It is the reason why those 'leaders' decided to get involved in the club in the first place. However, their interest was not in improving the club. Their interest was limited to improving their own social and financial status—at least in the short term. The Chairman of the club believed that he was as powerful and important as the President of the country, when in fact he was just trying to get easy money out of a football club that he could not care less about. This get-rich-quick scheme was of course much more successful than having to wait until somebody decided to stay at his dilapidated guesthouse. The 'leaders' of Safari Sports Club didn't understand, or refused to understand, that they had been elected into office in order to <u>serve</u> the club, and not in order to plunder and rob the club. Between the honest and the corrupt way of making money, which one is easier and quicker?

So, I wanted to achieve my ambitions, and my thoughts in the Catalan capital confirmed that I wouldn't be able to do this at Safari Sports Club. After one full year of investing my energy, my time, my money and my experience, I needed to look for a change for the better. Surely there were better opportunities out there.

In Dar Es Salaam, Tanzania's commercial capital and largest city, that could only mean one thing. I decided in the Nou Camp in Barcelona that I would approach the rival team, Ndovu Football Club, and ask them if they would be interested in my services and experience. I knew that this would cause some controversy because of the fierce rivalry between the two clubs and their fans. For the unsuspecting reader, let me clarify that a switch between these two clubs can only be compared to a switch between Arsenal FC and Tottenham Hotspur FC, or between Glasgow Rangers and Celtic Glasgow. It's something one only does in desperate times and after very careful consideration and a lot of soul-searching. But it happens—and it happened to me. It was a risk that I was willing to take, in pursuit of my personal ambitions. I knew that I would disappoint thousands of fans of Safari Sports Club whom I had gotten to know very well and who respected me a lot for my contributions, my perseverance despite all the frustrations, and my forthright intention to improve the club. They realized very soon that an opportunity had slipped through their club's fingers, but they also knew that the blame rested with the club's 'leadership' and with nobody else. They were clever enough to understand that you can't stop an ambitious person in their tracks. These fans understood my decision, as they were well aware of the problems that the leaders were creating for me.

And for myself? I knew immediately that changing clubs was the best option. Well, it was the only option. The opportunities for me to contribute towards the development of a Tanzanian football club were, apparently, much greater at Ndovu Football Club, and

I felt that I would personally be able to develop more as a coach. At least, this was my impression . . . Only one way to find out, of course.

And what about the rivalry? Well, rivalry between two or more clubs is a good thing, because it forces both clubs to push themselves to their level best. Nobody likes to be second best. However, for me this rivalry doesn't go as far as to 'hate' the other team. Whether as a player or as a coach, I always say that I fear no team, but that I respect all teams. Rivalry needs to be put into perspective, and to me it doesn't really make sense when somebody says : "If you belong to Safari Sports Club, then you can never belong to Ndovu Football Club, and you should hate Ndovu Football Club". I do understand that many supporters have a life-long love and passion for their favorite football club. On the other hand, I also have friends who regularly update their Facebook status and become fans of the latest team to have won the UEFA Champions' League or the FIFA World Cup . . .

In September 2012, when the Hillsborough disaster was being remembered in the United Kingdom, Sir Alex Ferguson wrote a special letter to all the fans and followers of Manchester United. The fans of Liverpool Football Club had just been exonerated of the events that led to the deaths of ninety-six football lovers on that fateful day, and Sir Alex Ferguson, whose team was to face Liverpool FC on that same weekend, asked his club's fans to show respect during the occasion. He wrote:

> "Today is about thinking hard about what makes Manchester United the best club in the world. Our rivalry with Liverpool FC is based on a determination to come out on top—a wish to see us crowned the best against a team that held that honour for so long. It cannot and should never be based on personal hatred."

I could not have said this any better, and I thank Sir Alex for illustrating my point so clearly. There is no place for hatred in football, not even when you're a Dutchman celebrating a victory against Germany or when you're a Rangers or Celtic fan getting inebriated over last Sunday's Old Firm derby.

Support and fanaticism are great, even necessary, but not at the expense of someone's feelings towards other individuals. Many a bar and many a living room around the world light up when the match that is being broadcast splits the audience or even the family right through the middle. But two hours later, all that should remain is a bit of banter and a lot of bragging—nothing more.

For players and coaches though, the situation is slightly different from that of the fans—they are merely employees of the club, and barring a few exceptions, allegiance and loyalty have become a thing of the past. Can we blame them? Can we fault them for following their ambitions (and sometimes the money) and trying to make the most out of their short careers? Is that not what every straight-thinking person would do?

When I worked for Safari Sports Club I gave 100% of my energy to Safari Sports Club every day. When I go and work for Ndovu Football Club I will give 100% of my energy to

Ndovu Football Club every day. It is just like changing jobs, and you try to do your very best each time. There's no looking back, the job lies ahead. Of course it is always nice to get one over a former club, especially when this affords one the bragging rights in the city for a couple of days—or weeks! But as soon as one allows this rivalry to dominate the season and the club's development, then the bigger picture is lost, and no development can or will take place.

After my move a lot of Safari Sports Club fans came to wish me well, and I sincerely thank them. Many of them also asked me what exactly made me decide to cross over to Ndovu Football Club, and it was—in part—to answer that question that I decided to write this book. Many people around the world often ask how a player, a coach or an official can possibly leave their club or team, and join the arch rivals . . . And how do such decisions turn out? Do we always walk off into the sunset with our ambitions fulfilled and our decisions vindicated? Well, it's possible, and I hope that my story provides answers, but at the same time I hope that it will raise questions. If this is the case, then I have fulfilled my ambition, once again.

The Republic of Tanzania should be called the Pearl of Africa. This proud nation of over forty million inhabitants has some of the world's most stunning natural sights and boasts the largest wealth of animal species on our planet. It is an open-air park that never ceases to amaze visitors. Barring some exceptions, it has some of the gentlest and most humble people one can encounter anywhere. Tanzania's potential simply can not be quantified. This country is a gift to man, and it is no coincidence that this 'cradle of mankind' is where we now find the earliest signs of human habitation and activity. Tanzania deserves that honor.

Tanzania is also a land of challenges. Throughout its history, it has confronted these challenges head-on, and this has ultimately led to the creation of a unique culture. For a foreigner living in Tanzania, it is rather easy to learn about the music, the dance, the colors and the language. Tanzanian food is a feast for the eyes and the stomach. There is an unmistakable 'joie de vivre' in this country, where smiles abound and where everyone feels welcome. There are easy paths that allow the visitor to gain a partial understanding of the culture. And then there are steep, muddy and rocky trails that lead the visitor to a deeper understanding of what makes the Swahili people tick. I decided to take the football trail—and it's as steep, muddy and rocky as you like!

Esteemed reader, let me take you to the world of Tanzanian football. A world that is unknown to most, but that is fascinating nonetheless, and that offers a very realistic and insightful glance at life in Tanzania as a whole. Let me show you how the football culture is a reflection of life in this beautiful country on the African East coast. In the shadows of Mount Kilimanjaro and on the eastern banks of the Great Rift Valley, a story is being created every day. A child is kicking a football made of old rags, and a man in a white shirt and black tie is walking around with a plastic bag. The time has come to tell their and my story . . .

TWO

Belgium, the seventies and eighties.

FOOTBALL. IT HAS BEEN A big part of my life ever since I was a small child. It's the stuff that little boys' big dreams are made of.

My earliest memories are of a little blond boy running after a black and white plastic ball. My first touches were taken in a medium-sized garden, with a small lawn in the centre and some flowers and vegetables around the edges. The fence around the garden ensured that I didn't have to sneak through the neighbors' flowers too often in order to retrieve my football from their garden. Some of these early memories are still rather vivid, probably because more often than not, a brief session of kicking that plastic ball around the garden ended in me being scolded for having just decapitated yet another beautiful flower . . . Luckily, given the shortness of the Belgian summer, these flowers never lasted long anyway, and soon enough I would be able to reclaim my football territory without having to fear eternal damnation in floral hell.

My earliest photos show me with a football at my feet, at an age when I could barely walk. It would probably not be an exaggeration to state that that black and white plastic football helped me turn into *homo erectus* long before my due date. From the day that these grainy photos were taken, football has dominated the way I spend my time on this planet. Going to school was a necessity, but I enjoyed sitting in an open-air classroom in the middle of winter. Those 'open-air' schools certainly toughen you up from a young age, and I still fondly remember the freshness of the December air, even when the temperatures outside dropped well below freezing point. My friends and I learned about the rivers and hills of our beautiful country whilst wearing woolen hats, gloves and scarves. We shivered our way through Mathematics class, comforted by the thought that the next recess was never far away. The lessons were interesting and the teachers were nice. But the highlight of each day was running after a football, a tennis ball or some other spherical object during break time, during the lunch hour or after school. Soon enough, we even agreed to get to school half an hour early in the morning, so that we could kick-start our day with a quick football match. At eight thirty, the shrill sound of the bell signaled the end of our latest world cup semi-final, but in my head the game continued well into Science or History class. I can still hear my exasperated teacher shout:

"Peter, put that ball away and take your books out of your bag! It's time to read History!"

Now I am sure that despite my young age, I thought to myself:

"Sorry teacher, I don't read History. One day, I am going to make History!"

In French class, the scolding was usually done in the language of Molière and Victor Hugo, but not quite with the same levels of polished eloquence. I was now on my way to becoming a bilingual footballer! I picked up some extra-curricular French vocabulary that would come in handy if one day I played in the European Cup final against some merciless defender of Paris Saint-Germain or Olympique Lyon.

Those books were usually sticker books that contained blue squares and lots of names and data. They also contained the names of all the First and Second Division football clubs in Belgium. Every afternoon after school I would stop at the local grocery store and buy a packet of six stickers, each carrying the photo of a first division player. The idea was then that you put that sticker in this special book, my football bible, which had all sorts of information on each of the players. These larger than life heroes quickly became household names, and just like every other young boy in the village, I dreamt of one day having my own photo on such a sticker. If in your packet you found a picture of a player whose sticker you already had in your book, then you could always exchange it with one of your friends. I spent my meager weekly allowance of 50 francs on these stickers, which I admired during the lessons. My teachers, few of them football lovers themselves, were not impressed, but after a while they wisened up and abandoned the practice of confiscating the book.

At one stage though, my French teacher thought that enough was enough, and he punished me by forcing me to translate all the players' particulars from Flemish into French. To me, this was a dream punishment. After all, translating dates of birth or the number of times a player has played for the national team isn't very difficult . . . When later that year he allowed me to use my translations in a French sports project, I knew that deep down inside he understood and admired my love for the game. One cold Saturday afternoon, when I was playing a competitive match with the school's junior team, I saw him standing quietly next to one of the poplar trees that flanked our muddy football field. When he saw that I had noticed him, he gently tipped his hat with his finger. I gladly consider him one of my first ever football soul mates.

Quarter past four was a magical time, as it meant the end of the lessons and the start of our daily football match on the school field. There were lots of matches in the park or in the street during the weekends, and of course lots of practice sessions on the training grounds in the evenings. But whenever we didn't have a competitive match or a scheduled training session, we made one up. My friends and I took a rather long time to work out that actual football matches last 90 minutes. Most of our training sessions and simple kick-abouts on the school ground lasted for three or four hours! Mobile phones did not exist yet, but nevertheless it wasn't hard to find us when we didn't get home until past our bed-time. We could easily be found on one or the other football ground in the village or at school . . . At the end of every training or impromptu kick-about, we faced the long bike ride home. Reflecting now on those days, I truly wonder when we ever got any homework done . . .

On July 11th, 2010, a Spain side primarily built around players of Barcelona FC won its first FIFA World Cup title. Deep into extra-time, Andrés Iniesta became only the 56th player in the history of the game to score in a World Cup final. It is a rather exclusive group, and of course we always have to wait for four years before twenty-six new applicants can vie for membership in the World Cup Final goal scorers' club. I dreamt of becoming a member too . . .

Like thousands of other small boys in Belgium and around the world who dream about one day emulating their football heroes and scoring the winning goal in the World Cup final, I made my way through the youth teams of a number of clubs. K. Beerschot VAV, one of the oldest and most prestigious clubs in the Flemish half of the country, took me on as a five-year old, and I remember proudly wearing the purple and white uniform that half the city of Antwerp identified with. By the time I had turned eight, it became clear that travelling 20 kilometres to the city every Wednesday afternoon was not an easy feat, so I transferred to the village team. At SK 's-Gravenwezel I found twice-a-week training sessions and quite a few of my school mates. Every year we competed for the provincial championship, and more often than not we ended up with the cup at the end of the season. Two training sessions a week was hardly enough for me, so I also joined SK Simikos. The latter was a school team which I captained for 6 years. For many years I played for two teams at the same time : the village team and the school team. They competed under different football associations (the National Football Association and the Catholic Sports Union respectively), so I was able to play in competitive leagues on Saturdays ánd on Sundays. As far as I was concerned, there were never too many games to be played. The words "football fatigue" were not part of my vocabulary!

I must have been nine or ten years old when I went to watch a Belgian First Division game for the very first time. My grandfather, himself a former Premier League player in Belgium, took me to one of the most important matches on the Belgian football calendar : the Royal Antwerp Football Club against K. Beerschot VAV. This was the big derby match of the city of Antwerp in Northern Belgium, a match that arouses—to this day—as much passion as a Barcelona versus Real Madrid match in Spain or a Young Africans Sports Club versus Simba Sports Club match in Tanzania.

At the time I was a Beerschot supporter—remember, I had been a youth player at that club, and Beerschot was at that time doing remarkably better than its red-and-white local rival. Even though I don't remember who scored the goals, I do remember that I spent most of the second half praying to God that Beerschot might score an equaliser. God must have been a fan of the Royal Antwerp Football Club, because my purple heroes lost the derby by two goals to one. What I also remember very vividly is that I spent a large part of the match looking at the players on the field and matching them up with the stickers in my book. For the first time, my heroes presented themselves as footballers made of flesh and blood . . . and rather long hair!

After this first experience of live football at the highest level, trips to the stadium became more and more frequent. The expert knowledge of my grandfather helped me a lot in starting to identify and understand the patterns of play and the intrinsic beauty of the game of football. Given the fact that my meager allowance had not increased in recent months, and since I was still spending my coins on stickers, I was grateful that my grandfather used part of his small pension to subsidize my tickets . . . At the end of a long week at school and looking forward to the weekend, I eagerly anticipated a phone call from my grandfather on Friday evening.

"Peter, I am free on Sunday afternoon. Would you like to go to the football match?"

There was a high level of monotonousness and predictability to the answer that followed, time and time again . . . My weekend routine quickly expanded to playing two matches, one on Saturday and one on Sunday, and watching a First Division match on alternative weekends. On match day, I often went to visit my grandparents in the morning, went for a kick-about in the park with my grandfather, had lunch with them, and then headed for the stadium to go and watch my sticker book heroes.

He never quite realized it, but grandpa was to have an enormous influence on my love for football. I learned so much from him, even though he never taught me. He passed his knowledge of and his love for the game on to me. He was the impersonation of the perfect guide who gave me the two things that I needed the most : roots and wings. And to top all the football excitement on the weekend, on Sunday evening grandpa and I would be glued to the small black and white television set that showed the highlights of the weekend's football action in just over thirty seconds. Blink and you miss it! The days of live match coverage were still far off, and because all the news footage was in black and white, the producers of the football segment had to indicate on the screen that "Beerschot plays from the left to the right" . . . There simply was no other way of distinguishing between the two teams playing in shades of black, grey and white . . .

Once inside the stadium on Saturday evening or on Sunday afternoon, I was also completely absorbed in the passion of the fans—the waving of the club's flags, the chanting and shouting, the 'oohs' and the 'aahs' when a chance was almost taken, and of course the unbridled joy whenever a goal was scored or a victory secured. In those early days, long before the Heysel disaster that changed the nature of stadium security and safety, the stadiums in Belgium still had a lot of standing spaces, and rival fans often mixed and mingled in the same sections of the stands. The chants were mostly funny, with here and there some cheekiness and sometimes a bit of vitriol. The weather didn't really matter. When it was hot, we stood in the sun and we enjoyed it. When it poured with rain, we stood ankle-deep in the mud and we enjoyed it just as much. And when it snowed, we all marveled at the orange football that only came out on such occasions . . .

Most fans came to the stadium to enjoy an evening or an afternoon out, to cheer and jump for two hours at all the goals, the great passes and the wonderful tackles, to scream and shout for ninety minutes at all the injustices and poor decisions made by the referees, and at the end of it all they would simply shake hands and give each other a thumbs-up.

"See you at our home ground in the Spring!"
"Sure! But first let's go to the bar and have a drink."
"Only because you insist!"

Those were the days when there were still true football fans, people who enjoyed the game for what it was and for its ability to let them forget their work in the factories or in the mines for a couple of hours. Win or lose, they all enjoyed a pint in the pub and agreed that the referee had been rubbish that afternoon. Haven't times changed a bit . . .

My interest in football has continued ever since that first derby, and has never stopped growing. During my youth I had the privilege of watching top quality international players like Robbie Rensenbrink, Arie Haan, Morten Olsen, Jan Tomaszewski and Grzegorz Lato. They fought side by side with Belgium's own heroes like Erwin Vandenbergh, Jan Ceulemans, Juan Lozano, Eric Gerets and Jean-Marie Pfaff. Great generations come around once every so often. In 1920 Belgium won gold in the Olympic football tournament, after which the country entered in some kind of a transition period . . . of sixty years! But suddenly, in the early 80s, everything fell into place. Suddenly we found ourselves with a combination of technically-gifted players and hard grafters. We balanced our national team between the steamrollers and those who could weave their magic around opposition defenses. And we suddenly started to win matches! The Red Devils mentioned above were all part of the Belgian national team that reached the final of the 1980 European championship.

In 1982, little Belgium made cold meat of the mighty Argentinians, the defending World Cup champions and now also counting Diego Armando Maradona in their ranks, in the opening match of the FIFA World Cup in Spain. Our crowning moment came when this small nation, usually safely and rather quietly tucked away in between the footballing might of Holland, Germany and France, made it all the way to the semifinals of the World Cup in Mexico in 1986. Only the brilliance and the two goals—as well as his wounded pride from the 1982 defeat—of Diego Armando Maradona denied us our place in the final . . . For his second goal, Maradona ran through the Belgian defense as if it didn't exist. He ran past four highly accomplished players who, for the past ten years, had been withstanding anything that was thrown at them at national and international level. Well off-balance after the final tackle, the Argentine captain still found the composure to tuck the ball beyond one of the best goalkeepers the world has ever seen.

We didn't blame our heroes when they couldn't stop Don Diego. They had served the nation well, and we were proud of them nonetheless. After all, a couple of days earlier Maradona had scored the greatest goal of all time by running past seven tough-tackling Englishmen, and we knew the world would remember that goal much more than the ones he scored against Belgium. Reaching the semi-finals of the 1986 World Cup showed that we had come out of our 60-year long hibernation, and it was the moment that defined everything that was great about Belgian football in the 1980s. I was privileged to be a part of that golden era.

THREE

Rewind to 1980, when two major events took place.

The oldest football club in Belgium, the Royal Antwerp Football Club (which, as you will remember, has God as one of its supporters), celebrated its one hundred years of existence. To mark this centenary, and most probably also to boost the attendances in its vast stadium, the club decided to give out free season tickets to all youths under the age of 16. Even though I was still 'officially' a Beerschot supporter, I could not possibly let such an opportunity pass. On January 2nd 1980, some school friends and I braved the snow and the cold, and cycled to the stadium office to become one of the first "Centenary Season Ticket" holders. The Bosuil Stadium on the outskirts of the city of Antwerp was at that time Belgium's biggest stadium with a capacity of 68.000 spectators. It had been the venue of several epic Belgium versus Holland matches, and was only a 15 kilometre bicycle ride away from home.

From early 1980 onwards, this stadium would become my destination every other Sunday when the Royal Antwerp Football Club played its home games. After our Sunday morning match for the village team, my friends and I would simply grab a small bag of crisps and a coke in the local canteen—courtesy of our team manager who promised us a treat every time we won—and off we'd go on our bikes to the stadium. I watched all of Antwerp's home games that season, as well as some reserves games. My friends and I never felt like traitors. We were simply there to watch the football free of charge, and during the days following a particular match, we would try and emulate some of the technical skills that we had noticed in the stadium. We were fortunate in that Antwerp had an excellent team and challenged for the league title, so there were many interesting and high quality clashes with other strong clubs like Anderlecht, Club Bruges and Standard Liège. These three clubs in particular were the standard bearers of Belgian football. They had—and still have—more financial power than the other clubs, so they were able to bring in great players from abroad. Anderlecht had a particular connection with Dutch players, and for us young boys, you can imagine the thrill of watching and screaming at footballers who had played in World Cup finals—and almost won them! With the added friendly rivalry between Belgium and Holland, the visits by Anderlecht were particularly colorful. Seeing that I was now fully occupied in the Royal Antwerp FC stadium, my grandfather soon also joined us there, and we continued to benefit from his great wisdom and his calm demeanor. "Remember, it's just a game", he used to say.

Around the same time, I also became aware that sporting rivalries mostly exist in the minds of the fans. The Royal Antwerp FC team of the early eighties, one that regularly qualified for the European Cup tournaments, had a number of players who had made their name with the cross-town rivals, K Beerschot VAV. Officially, this was not 'the right thing to do', but obviously it was being done. The players in question didn't seem too affected by the banter from the crowds, and simply got on with their task of serving their paymaster. After a couple of excellent performances, the home fans easily accepted them as one of 'their own', and their former team swiftly replaced them with new blood. No big deal, really. I remembered this many years later, when I found myself in a similar predicament.

Soon a life-changing moment arrived. During the course of the 1980-81 season I received a letter from the Royal Antwerp Football Club, inviting me for trials. One of their scouts had watched me play for my school team or for my village team, possibly during an annual Easter football tournament, and R Antwerp FC decided to have a closer look at my footballing potential. I was never told exactly where or when they had spotted me, but with the high number of matches that I played every week, I was bound to get noticed by someone, somewhere.

I had four Monday and Wednesday evening trials on an icy field, and I remember telling myself to simply do what I did best, to play my own game, to show them my ability, and to let the rest take care of itself. There were a number of trialists, and the last thing you want to do is let the nerves and the tense competition get the better of you. I must have done enough to impress the coaches because a few days later I was asked to sign for the club. Even at that young age I usually liked to think things over before making a decision, but this situation was different. This was an offer that I could not possibly refuse. This was the Royal Antwerp Football Club, one of the biggest clubs in Belgium, and certainly the biggest club in my region, asking me if I would please sign for them. They could have asked me if I would please come and cut the grass on the field and I would have done it. But no, they asked me to join their youth team set-up, and to help them compete for provincial and national honors. I jumped on my bike and I doubt that the wheels ever touched the road. I may well have left a trail of burning rubber behind me, that's how exited I was over this opportunity. Suddenly I could see my football career take shape, and I knew that I was going to develop much quicker under the guidance of some very accomplished youth coaches, many of whom had been top level players themselves. I signed as soon as I got to the stadium, and a new chapter started in my life. To the envy of many of my friends, I was now a Royal Antwerp Football Club player, and I hoped that I was on my way to greater things . . .

Club practices took place three times a week, on Monday, Wednesday and Friday evenings. The bike rides became longer, the evenings became longer too, and again, I have no recollection of when or where the homework got done. I did however always keep in mind that a football career can be short, and I never neglected the importance of a good education. With some creative time management, things seemed to work out fine. On the many cold winter evenings, we would train from 6 to 8 pm, and drink burning hot lemon tea in a plastic cup at the end of the session. We would train in tracksuits or with black cotton stockings under our shorts, and some of us even applied what we used to call 'green oil'. This herbal oil, applied to the legs and available in every local pharmacy, not only made us feel warmer, it also made us look as shiny as a Turkish oil wrestler. After training and when we had managed to pull our football boots off our frozen toes, it was time for all of us to get in the concrete communal shower—the water either freezing cold or burning hot. For some reason, maybe in an attempt to toughen us up, it was simply impossible to adjust the water temperature to a level that did not border on torture and a blatant abuse of human rights. Most evenings the changing room would steam up so much that it could easily have been mistaken for a Finnish steambath. But we did not complain. We were glad to play for this club, and we knew that it was no different from other clubs. Boot camp was probably invented in Belgian football clubs in the eighties.

The road from the stadium to my home went along a canal, and I remember how my hair, still wet from the post-training shower, used to freeze in winter while I was riding home.

Our matches against the junior sides of other national First Division clubs took place on Sunday mornings. For a young boy who was desperate to make it to the top, three practices of two hours per week didn't quite seem enough. I knew that only hard work and determination would get me into the first team, because there were hundreds of boys with the same ambition. Competition for places was intense, even in those days, and only the best and toughest would make it. I had to come up with a plan to set myself apart from the other contestants.

I started to spend countless hours by myself on the training ground. In the rain, in the wind, the snow, the mist or the occasional sunshine, I would juggle the ball for hours, kick it against the wall or shoot for goal. I believed then, as I believe now, that there is no more beautiful sound than that of a leather ball hitting the back of a net. Like the sound of a whip, followed by a soft thumb when the ball comes to rest in the corner of the goal. Audiovisual poetry. And the looks of dejection on the faces of defenders and goalkeepers who have just conceded a goal. Quite unique, isn't it?

I also believed then, as I believe now, that there is no substitute for practice. No matter how talented one is, it's only the practice that brings one closer to perfection. And for those of us who have been gifted with no more than a mediocre level of skill or talent, practice becomes even more essential. I never counted the hours that I practiced, but when I get the chance to look back upon my youth and do some calculations, I am sure that there will not be a big discrepancy between the hours spent practicing football and the hours spent sleeping. As for the hours spent doing homework . . . that's another story altogether. Some years later I came across one of Bruce Lee's great sayings : "I fear not the man who has practiced ten thousand kicks once. I fear the man who has practiced one kick ten thousand times." I could not agree more, except that I would have preferred a more accurate translation of the verb 'fear'.

So I found myself on the training ground at least once a day, be it at school or in the village. Sometimes I found a couple of friends to play with, but as time passed, most of them seemed to need more and more time to complete their homework . . . With only one football and nobody to go fetch it when it went in the net, and occasionally over the bar, I had to come up with a strategy in order to minimise the time wasted on collecting the ball. So I started to aim all my shots at the crossbar. And sure enough, more and more often the ball would rebound off the crossbar and come back—more or less—to where I was standing. Practical problems required practical solutions . . . I found this to be an excellent way to sharpen my shooting accuracy, and I would recommend it to any aspiring footballer. As Bruce Lee wisely told us, you can never take too many shots in practice.

It was quite clear that by now my passion for football was starting to become something akin to an obsession. The hours on the training ground were supplemented by a lot of reading on the topic. I literally devoured books on great clubs and players, on the history of the game and on how to play it. I would study the skills and techniques of the world's leading players and coaches until deep into the night, and tried to imitate and emulate them during my next training sessions.

Being unable to buy too many books because of a lamentable shortage of pocket money, I quickly became the most frequent visitor to the local libraries. One of the best-stocked libraries that I could find was located halfway between the stadium and my home. So even when the evening trainings ended at 8 pm, there was no guarantee that I would be home before 11 pm. More often than not, I made a halfway stop at the library, nodded a quick 'hello' to the librarian, and went straight to the first floor. I did check out books to take home and read well into the night, but I also thoroughly enjoyed just sitting on the heated library floor with a book about the 1974 World Cup or about the life of Edson Arantes do Nascimento. I knew all about little-known Eastern European teams such as FC Rijeka, Carl Zeiss Jena and Ujpest Dosza. It is probably fair to say that football helped me enormously with my knowledge of European geography. If a town had a football club that had achieved something in the past sixty or so years, then I probably knew where that town was . . .

Of course, in the early eighties we had no idea that ten years later Eastern Europe would suddenly become accessible and real. Until such time, it was nothing more than a distant land where the skies always seemed to be grey and where people apparently never smiled. The news that occasionally filtered through suggested that there were good footballers at the other side of the Iron Curtain, but we only really knew the statistics that the books provided us with. Those statistics kept me warm and took me to countries that, at that time, I had no hope of ever travelling to. Unless of course I ended up playing in European cup tournaments, which was precisely the motivation that I was looking for in the dusty pages of little-used library books.

By now I knew the lives and achievements of the games biggest stars, and I could give the line-ups of all the World and European Cup finals. In some cases, I may even have been able to state how many people attended the match, and who the referee was. The pronunciation of players' names was only a secondary consideration but on the field, during football matches with my friends and classmates, we all wanted to be Pelé, Johan Cruyff or Franz Beckenbauer . . .

In between all the football I also practised a few other sports. I have always thoroughly enjoyed distance running and took part in numerous half-marathons during my school and university years. I was a provincial roller skating champion in the days that we still used to go roller skating. The arrival of rollerblades and many other devices has somehow made roller skating a thing of the past, but it was certainly very popular then, and Belgium even managed to produce a number of world champions in this highly technical and highly competitive sport. The winters were cold enough to see the moats around the local castles freeze over, and we would all head for the ice and play our own version of the National Hockey League. As the fastest team sport in the world, ice hockey offers an excellent opportunity to work on your reflexes, your tactical and strategic understanding of team sport, and your strength. And when one of the players has been pushed into the bushes on the side of the moat, the occasional punch-up is a mere bonus. Swimming would have been high on my list of hobbies too, but the coaches at the club did not permit any of us to swim. "Swimming develops a very different type of muscle, completely incompatible with what you need for football!" So we didn't swim all that much. But amongst all the sports I practiced apart from football, the one that probably contributed the most to my development as a player was judo.

I practiced judo for many years and now hold a black belt. Judo was a very good supplementary sport to high-level football in that it taught me three very useful and essential skills, which I soon transferred to the way I played football, and which I now try to implement as a coach. No, I am not talking about lifting somebody off the ground and dropping him a few meters further while breaking his neck in the process. That, by the way, never happens in judo. There are very strict and clear rules in this often misunderstood sport, and injuries are almost unheard of.

During a fight, a judoka needs to be able to do three things. First and foremost, he needs to be able to exercise patience. Flying in with a wild tackle or attack will see the judoka being countered and upended on the floor. Many people comment on the fact that "nothing seems to happen in a judo match. They are just pulling and pushing each other". This is a layman's view of the sport, for what really goes on when two judokas go head to head is much more complicated. They are well aware that they can only make a move when the moment is right . . . and indeed, sometimes this moment takes a long time to arrive. Until that time, it's all about patience, focus and concentration.

Secondly, there is that right moment for an attack, and a footballer, as much as a judoka, needs to be able to identify that moment. A match, be it a judo match or a football match, is really just made up of moments. What happened two or three minutes earlier in a match does not matter two or three minutes later. Every moment is one where a player or fighter can make an offensive or a defensive decision, can show a weakness or exploit a strength—and this is where matches are won and lost. As a very old Kung Fu adage says, "there is always a weakness, just make sure you can find it when it appears". When the ball suddenly fell for Andrés Iniesta, so close to the end of extra-time in the 2010 World Cup final, he was ready to deal with it and to exploit that one weakness that the Dutch defense was guilty of. One moment was all it took for the Spanish to seal their victory, and all the earlier free-kicks, passes, tackles and throw-ins didn't matter anymore. One moment, the difference between elation and dejection. The moment that the ball hits the back of the net with that beautiful, thudding sound . . . or the moment that the opponent hits the tatami and the umpire's arm goes up to award an 'ippon' . . .

Lastly, a fighter needs to know exactly which strategy to use in the attack. Once the moment for a strike has come, an array of options may be open. It is then of extreme importance to choose the most direct and effective strategy to defeat the opponent, and to minimise the opponent's options for defense and counter-attack. Upon receiving that pass from Cesc Fabregas, Andrés Iniesta chose to take one touch to bring the ball under his control before volleying it into the Dutch net. Had he opted to dribble past the onrushing defender, the outcome may have been very different, and who is to say which way a penalty shoot-out would have gone? Top talents often defy the anticipation of their opponents, and become 'unplayable'. A common comment made by defenders about Lionel Messi is that "we pretty much know what he is going to do when he gets the ball, but we simply can't stop him from doing it" . . . Messi knows exactly which strategy to use against which defenders, and he uses it to perfection.

A football team that masters these three factors will find itself in a very strong position. Using these tactics and working very hard on the training ground, I managed to work my way further up the ranks in the Royal Antwerp Football Club. I continued reading as much as I could and hitting the crossbar as often as my schedule would allow me. I was also fortunate enough to have some very good youth coaches, including former Antwerp-player Louis Van Gaal, who went on to become the European Cup-winning coach of Ajax Amsterdam, Barcelona Football Club and Bayern Munchen FC, and who is now the coach of the Dutch national team. With coaches like him inspiring you, even many years before he went on to coaching greatness, there is no way that you will not develop a desire to learn more and more about the beautiful game.

I need to add that as a player I had a severe weakness. My right foot only helped me to run and jump, as I hardly ever kicked a ball with it. I had always trained my left foot, and the accuracy in the passes and shots that left from that foot more than made up for the lack of accuracy on the other end. Had I received that pass from Cesc Fabregas in the same position where Andrés Iniesta received it, I would probably have missed it or, at best, blasted it towards the corner flag. However, if the mirror image had presented itself and Cesc had delivered that pass to my left foot, I would have buried my shot past the Dutch keeper just as clinically as Iniesta did . . . In the early eighties, nobody told us about the need to be ambidextrous. Since 99% of the players were predominantly right-footed, those of us who relied almost exclusively on our left foot were a rare commodity, and no coach was going to interfere with that. Nowadays players are required to use both feet effectively, and there is now also more flexibility in the positions that players can occupy—tactical decisions that were unheard of in the eighties.

In those days we still played with the old-fashioned left-winger or right-winger in the style of Stanley Matthews or Garrincha. I had started to build up some sort of a reputation as a left-footed player and crosser of the ball, and it is probably fair to say that my left-footedness was a determining factor in my rise to the upper levels of the football pyramid in Belgium. I don't spend too much time wondering what would have happened if I had been 'just another' right-footed player with the limited skill that I had. It's a question that does not need to be asked nor answered. My subsequent days in football were a result of the work that I had invested in that left foot, and that was sufficient for me, thank you very much. My reputation as a left winger would soon be further enhanced in a different country and on a different continent.

FOUR

Life in the big club was good. As my team mates and I worked our way through the junior ranks, slowly but surely we could see the day of our debut in the senior team approach. Around the training grounds we would regularly meet the first team players, and those heroes from the sticker books started to become more and more real as time went by. These players, and especially the home-grown ones, also took an interest in seeing other youngsters develop and make their way through the system. After all, we were now where they had been just a few years earlier. Who was to know that one day we would share the same dressing room and celebrate our goals together? We certainly entertained the thought, and it kept us motivated to work even harder the next day!

Another notable figure around the training and match grounds was the first team coach. Whenever we spotted him near the sidelines or behind one of the goals, we all sprinted faster, kicked harder and jumped higher. We felt, and rightly so, that our way into the senior team depended to a large extent on this one man's opinion and impression of us. And as most of us had a direct rival in our youth team, someone who qualified for the same position that we hoped to occupy in the first team one day, it was not a rare occurrence to see a bone-crunching tackle or a 'loose' elbow being swung around during a practice match. In our minds, the end justified the means, and it was up to those rivals not to stand in our way when we were charging towards goal. Deep down inside, I knew that the coach, watching from under his umbrella, liked the fight and the determination that he could see in some of us.

Throughout these years, I continued to put my education first. Yes, playing football and training every evening was great. But in the eighties, football was not the proverbial goldmine that it has become. An average footballer, such as myself, could expect to earn a good income, but saving for the future was very hard. The good times as a footballer would last for as long as one played at the high level, and of course football retirement could come any day. In those days, serious injuries still meant the end of a promising career, and a premature retreat into the shadows of the club. There were ample examples of players who had met their sporting end far too soon, and who were now pretty much left to their own devices. Several of them had opened a café in their home town, but fame and glory are only temporary. They are good for the soul, but they don't feed the stomach. After a few months or years of reminiscences and commiserations, the customers would one day find a new hero to follow. Up to this day, I often wonder what has become of those players who had a decent career and who, when it ended, did not have a diploma or a career as a coach that would see them through the next phase in their life. I stuck to my guns, and only ever signed a semi-professional contract. I refused to abandon my studies, and instead tried to find a way to reconcile language study with football.

I achieved my goal of playing in the first team sooner than I had expected, and the fact that I was almost exclusively left-footed had a lot to do with that. When the Royal Antwerp Football Club's regular left wing player, an import from Yugoslavia, needed to undergo a hernia operation, the door to the first team opened for me. I took the chance with both hands and both feet, and settled in quite easily. I was primarily tasked with running up and down the left wing and providing crosses for our two strikers to finish off. Occasionally I was allowed a bit further infield and score myself, but the instructions were quite rigid. The good thing was though, they worked! The team had a very good run and continued to challenge for honors against the 'big guys' in the Belgian First Division.

Combining high-level football with university studies was not always an easy task, but my determination to obtain a degree as well as a World Cup winner's medal saw me through the difficult moments. At times both parts of my life made demands that affected the other, but there were enough understanding people to make it work. At university I was not the only student who at the same time pursued a sporting career, so the professors were quite sympathetic. And to please the university even more, those of us who played in the bigger clubs also represented our university in national and international competitions—and we delivered. The coaches in the club also understood our desire to complete our studies. In those days of course, clubs did not have the financial clout to bring in megastars from abroad. Nor did they have the TV money that is now being offered, and that allows the clubs to deal with millions, rather than thousands. No, in my day, the clubs still depended very much on developing their own players, and as soon as they spotted someone who might one day represent the club in the senior team, they did make some allowances.

There were of course restrictions and rules imposed by the club, and I am grateful to this day that they existed at that time. Drinking alcohol and smoking was strictly prohibited. For insurance reasons, we were not allowed to ride motorbikes. We received a weekly diet schedule that we were kindly forced to follow religiously. And we were told how many hours we had to sleep each night.

The drinking and smoking rules made a lot of sense. At this young age, as young adults, we were of course very easily influenced, and peer pressure existed even then. Many of our friends, at university or back in the village, started to smoke and drink—and we players were often offered a glass or a cigarette. The easy thing to do would have been to succumb to the offer and to give in to at least some of the many opportunities that offered themselves to 'be a man for once'. Coincidentally, that would also have been the stupid thing to do. Keeping the bigger picture in mind, I rejected all offers of such temptations, and have never picked up the habit of drinking or smoking. I am forever indebted and grateful to the person who drew up these rules at the club! Some of my young teammates did fall by the wayside, but to be totally honest, those of us who 'survived' did not mind this process of natural selection at all . . . one less rival every time someone suddenly stopped reporting for training!

The dietary regime was not as strict as the rules on smoking and drinking. Basically, we were allowed to eat almost anything, as long as it was not too sweet or too salty. The crisps that we used to get after our youth matches, several years earlier, were now in the no-go zone, and we were also asked to take it easy on Belgium's famed pastries and chocolate. We managed that. The direction did realize though that asking a Belgian not to eat fries with mayonnaise is tantamount to sacrilege, so nobody went that far. In fact, they offered us a weekly portion of fries in the club—at least, this allowed them to control the oil levels a little bit. In any case, we trained hard and burned more calories than we could consume. The bike rides home remained a daily feature of our training regime, so we were pretty 'sharp' to say the least.

There were still a couple of years to go before the fall of the Berlin Wall and the end of communism as we knew it in Eastern Europe. In Belgium, military service was compulsory for all healthy males. The entry age of new recruits was 18 years, but the Army authorities allowed everyone to postpone their service for as long as they were enrolled in full-time education. Of course, the day came that I graduated from university, and just a few days later, the dreaded letter arrived in my letter box. It was basically a one-way train ticket stapled to an invitation to come and serve for ten to twelve months in the armed forces. The prospect did not attract me. Thankfully, for those of us who preferred to travel and use their skills in a more productive way than shining boots and learning to fight on the battle field, there was an interesting alternative. If one was qualified and determined enough to pass a long list of examinations and interviews, then the wide world beckoned. Having finished my university studies and realizing that I had reached my personal goal of playing in the first team of the Royal Antwerp Football Club, I started to look for a new challenge. The Bosman arrest that changed the face of football forever, and that basically turned average footballers into millionaires overnight, was still some time off. I could not wait for this moment, and seized my chance to pursue another one of my passions : travel.

Foreign countries had always attracted me, and by the time I was 22 years old my wanderlust had already taken me through most of Europe, as well as across parts of Asia, North Africa and Latin America. As a child, I had also lived in the former Zaïre for half a year. I started to feel that at least a part of my life would have to be lived outside Belgium, and the opportunity presented itself in early 1989.

After a long process of tests, examinations and panel interviews, I was offered a teaching position in the beautiful Kingdom of Swaziland, Southern Africa. I will admit that

I didn't know much more about Swaziland than its location and the name of its capital, but as soon as I had been offered—and accepted—this position, I threw myself into the research on this country with the same fervor and enthusiasm that I had shown when devouring books on the European Cup competitions and on the World Cup—all those years ago. For the next few years I would be teaching languages and football in one of the most beautiful parts of the African continent.

The decision to leave my life as it was and to head for the unknown was not taken lightly. I carefully weighed the pros and the cons of interrupting and possibly compromising my football career, but eventually the desire to see the world and to contribute in the area of education won the upper hand. I also knew myself well enough to understand that my achievements in football up to that point had been down to hard graft, rather than any kind of special talent. I realized that I had gotten as far as I would get in Belgian football, and that the national team would be populated with much better players than myself for many years to come. I also told myself that I would, one day, win that elusive World Cup winner's medal as a coach . . .

Of course, I was still left with the small matter of informing my club that they would have to do without my services for a while . . . I gathered my thoughts and my courage, and went to see our Head Coach. I did not know what to expect from our meeting but as it turned out, the coach had very similar ideas to mine about peace and conflict, and about the role of the military during the Cold War years. He was one of the few former footballers fortunate enough to be able to leave Yugoslavia and pursue a professional football career in Belgium. He had played for a number of First Division clubs, and after some while he had obtained the Belgian nationality. He was very sympathetic towards my choice not to serve in the army, and he wished me the best of luck for my African adventure. I thanked him for his understanding and his support, I shook his hand, and I walked out of his office for the final time. The world beckoned.

FIVE

Swaziland, the early nineties

A FEW WEEKS LATER, I FOUND myself fastening my seat belt in window seat 34F on a plane to Johannesburg. Just before take-off for the ten-hour flight from Brussels International Airport, I remember looking out of the plane window and thinking : "Here we go! " I was ready to start a new adventure and to discover a culture that, despite all the pre-Internet era research I had been doing in the days preceding my flight, I knew very little about.

Swaziland is a stunningly beautiful country. However, tucked away between its two giant neighbors, South Africa and Mozambique, the Kingdom hardly registers on a world map. Of the many visitors who take in the highlights of South Africa, most simply complete the drive from Johannesburg or Pretoria to the Kruger National Park without realizing that they are bypassing a very scenic country. Despite its small size, Swaziland has three very distinct regions, namely the High Veld, the Middle Veld and the Low Veld. The capital, Mbabane, is located in the High Veld, and this is where I would spend the next few years of my life. Beautiful mountains, hills and valleys, with very picturesque villages and homesteads, and with a capital town just large enough to provide in our basic needs. The Apartheid era was still raging in South Africa, and Swaziland was a direct beneficiary of the international boycott affecting its neighbor. International companies, obviously eager to do business with South Africa but unable to do so directly because of the sanctions, established themselves in Swaziland, thus providing employment, income and easy access to consumer goods. When I first walked into the main supermarket in downtown Mbabane, and only had visions of my younger days in Kinshasa in mind, I could hardly believe my eyes. Spread out in front of me was everything that I could have dreamt of, and more. There wasn't all that much difference between this supermarket and a comparable one in Belgium, except that the prices here were much, much lower. I knew from that moment that life in Swaziland would be nice and comfortable.

I settled down quickly at my place of employment, and during the first week of my being there, we organized and participated in a televised football tournament. I quickly acquainted myself with my footballing colleagues, and we did rather well on the day of the tournament. We went all the way to the final, which we won, and I ended the day having scored quite a number of goals. The prize presentation was followed by a couple of interviews with local reporters and with the Swazi TV crew. And lo and behold, that evening our tournament was shown on national TV! Quite an introduction to my new home.

It is no understatement that at least three quarters of the population of Swaziland watches the local news on TV every evening. After all, with only one TV channel to watch, the choices are rather limited. So it was no surprise that someone took an interest in the footage shown from that first tournament.

A day or two after my goals were shown to the nation, I received a phone call. Would I be interested in playing for one of the local clubs? The person on the other end of the line told me that he was the father of two of my students, and that he was rather influential in one of Swaziland's biggest clubs. What he didn't tell me, but what I found out soon after, was that he was referring to Manzini Wanderers, one of the giants of Swazi football, and a club that every year competed for major honors, not just in Swaziland, but also in regional and continental tournaments. What he didn't tell me either was that the patron of Manzini Wanderers was King Mswati III, the young ruler of Swaziland. And to top it all, he didn't tell me that he was in fact the father-in-law of the King, his eldest daughter having recently become the King's third wife. No pressure son, you're just going to play for the King's team.

It was late September, and I was invited to witness my future team's next match from the team bench at the Somholo National Stadium. The Swaziland Premier League is played from February to November, and things were starting to heat up in the league. Manzini Wanderers were still in contention for the title, and the match against one of the main contenders promised to be a sizzler. Furthermore, due to the lack of stadiums that are of Premier League standard, the top division matches in Swaziland are mostly played as double-headers. So, on this gentle early Spring afternoon in the Southern hemisphere, I witnessed two matches that had a direct impact on the title race. Two duels between the four strongest teams from the two largest towns in Swaziland. At 2 pm, I witnessed the clash between Mbabane Highlanders and Denver Sundowns, and at 4.30 pm it was time for Manzini Wanderers and Mbabane Swallows to lock horns. This double-header can best be compared with watching Manchester United versus Chelsea directly followed by Manchester City versus Arsenal, all in one afternoon and in one stadium . . . and with the fans of all four teams doing verbal battle in the stands! Direct duels between the biggest clubs in the country, defending the honours of their home town, and playing in a stadium that is exactly halfway between the two towns. A treat. And as you can imagine, the stadium was packed. The atmosphere was electric and carnivalesque, with drums, horns, vuvuzelas and lots of chanting from all sides. I immediately felt at home here, and was pleased with the efforts of my future club. As I was the only white person in the stadium, of course there were some curious looks, and when I took my seat on the team's bench, a roar went up from the corner of the stands where most people were wearing maroon and white outfits.

Two days after this first glimpse of Swazi soccer at the highest level, I started to train with my new club, Manzini Wanderers. The town of Manzini is located about 40 kilometres south-east of the capital, Mbabane, and because of its affiliation with his Excellency King Mswati III, Manzini Wanderers was considered the Royal club—the Real Madrid of Swaziland! Since I had only just arrived in the country and had not had time to go car-shopping yet, I had the privilege of being collected each day for training by one of the elders of the club—the same man who had called me a couple of days earlier. So I will claim for the rest of my days that I was once driven around Swaziland by the King's father-in-law. Now there's an introduction to African hospitality!

I felt welcomed by my teammates, and I insisted from day one that they communicate with me in siSwati, the national language of Swaziland. I did not want them to have to adapt to me. Instead, I preferred to adapt to them and their culture. Our training sessions took place on a bumpy field next to the Police College in Manzini, and I soon found out why so many African players have this fantastic technique with the ball. To try and control, pass or shoot a ball that randomly bounces from left to right, or up and down, is no mean feat, but of course my teammates had never known otherwise. They had learned their football on very rough patches of open space, often playing with a 'football' made of rolled-up plastic shopping bags kept together with some strings or tape. I noticed that some of them played in football shoes that had clearly seen their best years, and this made their ease on the ball even more remarkable. The training field was surrounded by patches of tall, rank grass that stood out like spears in the twilight of the African evening. In some places the grass was taller than ourselves, and of course, during many a practice, the football would end up in the middle of what we called 'the forbidden zone'. I soon realized that none of the players ever ventured into that tall grass to retrieve the ball, but that they instead sent one of the little boys who came to watch our practices. When I asked for the reason, I was given one word only : "mamba". The presence of one of the world's most venomous and lethal snake species, the black mamba, did not really impress me, but I just had to get on with the job of training hard and integrating myself in the team as soon as possible. Come to think of it, I never saw a single black mamba, or any other snake for that matter, anywhere near our training ground. The lack of lighting around our little patch of land was, at first, also a hindrance. Training usually started around 5.30 pm and would last well into the darkness.

One evening per week our training session consisted of nothing but physical work. We had a dedicated fitness coach who sent us sprinting, squatting, skipping, hopping and doing frog jumps until we could stand up no more. Some of his methods dated back to the early days of football, maybe even to the Middle Ages . . . and it disconcerts me to know that he is still working with Premier League teams to this day! We could easily be spotted around town on the day after such a 'fitness workout' : we could barely walk, and simply getting in a car was major torture. I don't know if John Cleese or Michael Palin have ever visited Swaziland, but maybe this is where Monty Python's famous "Ministry of Silly Walks" got its inspiration . . . I did not complain however. I just took it all in my stride and reminded myself that one day retirement would be more gentle to me. Surely one day I would look back at it all and smile.

Our Head Coach, a former Malawian national team star, was a very well-travelled man who ran a building materials business during the day and imparted us with his footballing wisdom in the evenings. At the time of my arrival, he was a player-coach, and clearly a hero amongst the Manzini Wanderers' faithful. Soon though his business schedule became too much of a burden (not to mention his age), and he decided to focus exclusively on his coaching. He was a very amicable and soft-spoken person with whom I quickly established a very positive relationship. It must be said though that this coach also had his shortcomings. One evening, he was clearly not in the mood to take us through our regular training routine. He asked all the elders who had come to the training ground in pick-up trucks to ferry all the players to the other side of the town, some 10 kilometres away. Off we went, all of us huddled in the canopy of four or five different cars. It was a very cold evening, the mist was descending on the town, and suddenly we were told to get out of the cars and to run back to the training ground . . . right through the town centre! I don't know whether Pep Guardiola would get away with instructing Lionel Messi, Xavi or Andrés Iniesta to run right through the Ramblas in Barcelona, from the Columbus statue all the way to the Plaça Catalunya, as part of their training regime . . . but our coach did! Many heads turned as we passed the filling stations, the shopping centres and the bus stands. We were never told what the purpose of this little oddity was, and we never asked.

I now became more and more part of the family of the Weslians or 'emaweseli'—the local name of the club, named after the area in Manzini where the club was founded. The reporters also soon picked up on the fact that an 'umlungu', or white man, had signed for one of the country's biggest clubs. Newspaper reports started to appear on a more and more regular basis, ranging from "Weslians sign Belgian" to "New Wanderers Star set to play against Mozambican visitors".

The 1989 Premier League ended with the Weslians taking second place, and we all agreed that the next year, we would only settle for the title plus victory in a number of cup tournaments. The ambitions of the club were further highlighted when they recruited another Malawian international player, as well as a South African midfield dynamo and some of the best up-and-coming Swazi talents.

During the pre-season, we played a high number of friendly matches, both in Swaziland and abroad. I had to juggle my time between my job and my football, and the fact that there is a two-month long Christmas break in the Southern Hemisphere certainly helped my cause! We travelled to South Africa and Namibia for friendlies and training camps, and I made the most of the opportunity to see as much as I could of these beautiful countries.

My first home game with Manzini Wanderers came against Mozambican champions, Ferroviario FC. Yes indeed, in many parts of Africa, the strongest and best-funded clubs belong to major companies and organisations, and Ferroviario de Maputo, as the club of the National Railways, was no exception. Even though the civil war in Mozambique was still raging, Ferroviario were a strong and well-respected club, and the anticipation before the match was huge. The presence of thousands of Mozambican migrant workers, mainly in the mines and in the garages, had created some kind of a rivalry between the two countries, and whenever clubs or the national teams met, sparks flew.

The stadium was packed, as all our fans wanted to see their new-look team for the first time. And we did not disappoint. We all played as if we were contesting a major cup final, and by the end of the match we had crushed the Mozambicans by two goals to nothing. The media had a field day, and nobody dared bet against us taking the league title ten months later. The headline in the national newspaper the next day read "Wanderers shatter Maputo's Ferroviario". According to their reporter, "the Mozambican ensemble went into the game with their heads high only to find an uncompromising and talented Wanderers playing superior football with emphasis on ball possession and territorial advantage". He also found that the three new recruits, including myself, had "made a memorable and heroic debut for the Manzini glamour side". A bit further down in the match report, I received some personal praise for the fact that I had, apparently, "played an exciting and glowing football tinged with nimble-footedness" . . . And when it was time to register all the players for the upcoming international cup competitions, the nation was reminded that our Malawian recruit and myself were players 'seen as pivotal to the winning strategy if the Weslians are to retain their lost spark'.

I felt good about the way the team was improving, and about my own role as its lone left winger. Together with the coach, we worked on a strategy to use the left wing to maximum effect. The friendly games started to follow each other fast and furious, and the team started to gel well as a unit. We all took turns scoring and providing goals, and nobody shied away from the defensive work that is so hard for strikers to perform. Soon the newspaper articles became even more glowing in their praise, calling me 'lethal' and 'deceptively creative'. Just before another friendly match against Sihlangu, the national team of Swaziland, the nation was told to come and watch this European player "whose ball handling is so deceptively casual that it belies the lethalness behind his accurate shots and crosses". What I also learned from this particular match was that at the Somhlolo National Stadium, a pass played along the sideline would never go out. The chalk lines on this particular field had been piled up over the years, and the lines were now about 5 centimetres higher than the rest of the field. So we soon learned to use these lines as some kind of a wall, and played passes that would have gone out of play on any other field. Of course, we had to be careful not to trip over the lines while crossing them in full sprint! Our hurdling skills improved drastically every time we played at this stadium . . .

In all fairness though, the Somhlolo National Stadium was the only football ground worthy of the name. Down in Mhlume, in the northeastern corner of the country and in the middle of the endless sugar cane fields, we also found a decent grassy field that allowed us to put a couple of passes together without anyone twisting their ankles. However, when the field was not being used for a football match, it was occupied by the resident cow family.

SIX

SWAZILAND IS THE KIND OF country in which every town, every village and every homestead has a church and a football field. Well, maybe there are some villages that don't have a church yet. But any open space is used as a football ground by the young and the old alike. There isn't a moment during the day that the dust isn't being kicked up by a bunch of eager children who run after a ball made of plastic bags. They play barefoot, their goals consist of no more than two rocks or two car tires, and they play from sunrise to sunset. Football is not only the most popular pastime here. For most people, it's also the only one.

The second city of Swaziland, Manzini, had just the one decent ground where the Trade Fairs, the night tournaments and the occasional music concerts were held. This is where I played in that very first game against Mozambique's Ferroviario FC, and to this day I have not yet figured out the architectural lay-out of the ground. The field was mostly rectangular, with some slight bends near the corner flags. On the one side of the field there was a large fence that kept the fans off the field, or the players off the stands. The various sections of the main stand however seemed to have been put together by a small boy who had just had a violent fight with his Lego collection and thrown all the pieces around. In one corner of the field, the sidelines actually had to bend inwards in order to avoid that part of the stand. The distance from this corner flag to the goal must have been at least eight meters shorter than the distance on the other side. Good news for those of us who easily mastered throw-ins of thirty metres.

Playing in Swaziland allowed me to learn a lot about the way football is played, run and organized in this part of the world. There were numerous interesting experiences and eye openers for me. In a way, football in Africa allowed me to have a special and often privileged look at the local society and its dynamics. It certainly broadened my horizons and facilitated my understanding of the new society of which I had just become a small part. It was a privilege that not too many people had, and I took full advantage of the learning opportunities that presented themselves.

Football tactics in Swaziland were based on the 'numbers system' where a player occupies 'the number two position' or where he plays 'number nine'. This was a concept foreign to me, but at least I could bring the flavor of the good old European winger system. I remember the times when our coach would stand on the sideline, gesturing number four or number six with his fingers. That was the sign for me to put the boot, accidentally of course, in the corresponding player on the other team. To be totally honest, I did not always need these reminders, as I liked to let defenders know from the start of the match that they were going to have a rather busy hour and a half. What these defenders simply could not cope with was the fact that very often, I positioned myself between the two centre-backs, or between the right back and the centre-backs, or between the right-back and the right midfielder. Now, who was going to mark me? Most of the time, neither. When the right-back made a move to come and mark me, I would move closer to the centre-back, and vice versa. I can still see the confused look on their faces. Evidently, they had been told by their coach to mark 'number nine' or 'number eleven' . . . Unfortunately, this number eleven didn't do what the opposition's coach had told his defenders he would do. I often found myself with much more freedom than I had experienced on Belgian fields, and this of course allowed me to deliver those lethal and pin-point crosses that the journalists were raving about so much. At the start of my career in Swaziland there was quite a stir about this 'umlungu' who kept on dashing up and down the left wing and crossing the ball to the central strikers.

In Swaziland most footballers have a nickname, and it didn't take long before I was given the name of "Kapsie Dans". I asked the reporter who first came up with this name what it meant, and he told me that there was a player in South Africa who had the same nickname. In Afrikaans the name means "the dance of the Cape", and apparently this South-African player had the same style of playing football as I did : deceptive football with a lot of pin-point crosses from the wings. It didn't take me long either to be called "the best crosser of the ball with either foot in the country" in the local newspapers. I realized then that those hundreds, and probably thousands of hours kicking footballs at the crossbar in the Belgian mud were paying off. Bruce Lee had been right.

The nickname stuck, and up to this day my Swazi friends use this name when we meet or call each other. The range of nicknames that players were given was mindboggling, and I was glad that I had not been given names such as "Roadblock", "Never Say Never", "Bushknife", "Electric Man" or "Ayashisa'mateki" (the latter meaning something akin to "blazing-hot football boots") . . . On the other hand, I had never thought that I would play against "Pelé", "Maradona", "Barnes" or "Schuster" on the fields in Southern Africa—but I did!

The local newspapers of course had a field day. My daily activities became a matter of national interest. At least, that was the impression that the journalists gave me. It had been about ten years since the last 'umlungu' had played in the national First Division, so here was an opportunity for them. All sorts of superlatives were used when a match report came out. Some examples, of which I kept copies, are "his accurate crosses never fail to threaten the opposition's defence when they connect with the itchy feet of the

Dlamini brothers" and "this Belgian winger is a calculating striker with pin-point accuracy". Does one need more to have their self-confidence boosted? Of course there were days on which our performance wasn't too good, and on such occasions it was better not to read the next morning's papers. As flattering as they can be one day, journalists are also out to destroy you as soon as things start to go wrong or when the goals dry up. That's all part and parcel of the game though, and I was ready for the occasional criticism.

In those days I became aware that in this part of the world one has to be very careful with the media. It happened quite regularly that what appeared in the papers did not correspond at all with what I had actually told the reporter, and soon I became much more mindful when doing interviews and making comments. This is a very serious piece of advice that I want to offer to all the players of today, and especially the young ones : stay away from the reporters, let your coaches or managers do the talking. A player's business is on the field. And often it would also be wise for players not to pay too much attention to what the papers say about them. I have over the past few years had many players come to me and ask "Coach, why did you say this or that about me?" or "You know, coach, the papers say this and that". More often than not, the reports are untrue, but it is not always easy for a player to believe or accept that.

The start of the new Premier League season was not far off, and the club elders thought that it was time for my introduction into the realities of Swazi football. The trainings were all good and well, but in Swaziland there is much more to match preparation than sprints, drills and tactical discussions. An equally important, and sometimes even more important aspect of match preparation, are the rituals of superstition and animism. In my early days with Manzini Wanderers, my presence in this top football club opened up a whole new world in the sense that I became exposed to the local belief in witchcraft, or *muti* as it is called in Southern Africa. Nobody should ever underestimate the power of the *muti*, neither for the physical impact it can have on those who choose to use it, nor for what it does to the psyche. I soon realised that the animistic beliefs and the powers of the famed witchdoctors occupy an important place in the football scene. However, I have always appreciated the fact that my Swazi hosts did not insist too much that I subject myself to the use of the different forms of witchcraft. I became well aware that this *muti* could encourage players to perform better, and in this sense there was absolutely nothing wrong with it.

Everybody believes in certain rituals or procedures that improve one's performance, and what is called *muti* in the south is called 'superstition' or 'good luck charms' in Europe. Many professional players in Europe, and not just footballers, have some sort of a ritual that they go through before starting a game. It may be that they will first step on the field with the left foot, or that only their wife is allowed to wash their shirt. Pelé used to lie on his back in the dressing room before a match, close his eyes and think of the most beautiful actions of his career. During the game, he would then try to do even better. Manchester United's Mexican forward Chicharito kneels down on the kick-off spot before the start of the match, raises his hands towards the heavens, and says a rather public prayer. If in some parts of the world the pre-match build-up consists of having a meal together or of praying in a specific way, then that can only improve the team spirit and therefore it should be encouraged. The team huddle is famously executed around the world, and the New Zealand rugby teams have even turned their famed *hakka* into a pre-match spectacle that supporters eagerly look forward to.

However, some of the rituals that we were asked to perform were a bit more dubious to me. I still need to be convinced that it is wise for a whole team to run up a steep hill in the middle of the night, a few hours before a Premier League match, to then bathe together in the ice cold stream near the top, and to then run down the hill, get into a small hut, put a blanket over their heads and inhale handy-gas for half an hour, all in the presence of a witchdoctor who utters unintelligible but certainly very useful war cries and who threatens the next day's opposition with complete and total destruction. Similarly, I appreciate a pep-talk and a good song in the dressing room, but I have not yet understood the benefits of players urinating inside the opposition's goal, or of team leaders burying the heart of a deer or a lion under the penalty spot inside the National Stadium. I've seen it happen, but I decided not to ask questions.

For a white man in Swaziland though, there was a dilemma. There were certain rituals in which I did not want to participate, and this refusal could have two possible effects on the comments after the match. Throughout my time in African football, I steadfastly refused to eat or drink any substance that was unknown to me. At best, some of the potions I saw would have given me a severely upset stomach, and at worst . . . well, I don't really know what could have happened. And I wasn't going to find out. Similarly, there were rituals where the *inyanga*, or witch doctor, inflicted small cuts with a razor blade on the arms of the players. That, for me, was an absolute no-no. But as said before, this created a dilemma. The technical team and my fellow players never criticized me for not engaging in some of this witchcraft activity, but I knew that I was between a rock and a hard place. One has to understand that *muti* has such a strong reputation, and that the services of the *inyanga* are so expensive, that if a team wins, the victory is usually attributed to the positive effects of the *muti*. The inyanga has done his job, and the money was well spent. The amount of training that had gone on during the previous week was not really important. However, if we lost, then it was because the *umlungu* hadn't taken the *muti* and hadn't participated in the real preparations for the match. This of course put me in a no-win situation, but that was all part of the deal, and I dealt with it. Fortunately for me, we won most of our matches, and I was happy to let the *inyanga* take his weekly allowance home.

I had now settled in well in the team and in my new job, and I decided to buy a car. I thanked the King's father-in-law for his dedication and his goodwill, and I started to make the daily journey from Mbabane to Manzini and back myself. I always had with me a couple of teammates who also lived and worked in Mbabane, and we enjoyed the 42-km drives along some of the most beautiful landscapes one can find anywhere on the planet. Just outside Mbabane, we headed down into the Ezulwini Valley, or the Valley of Heaven, and passed a curious rock formation called "Sheba's Breasts". I will leave it to the reader's imagination to decide what this particular geological phenomenon looks like. We then crossed the Lobamba Valley where all the major royal sites were, and once we had passed the Royal Palace and the Matsapha International Airport and industrial sites, we arrived in the town of Manzini, formerly called Bremersdorp. Along the way back to Mbabane, we sometimes stopped at the local Hot Springs Spa resort, and soaked for an hour or so in the swimming pool or the jacuzzi there. Or we'd take a break at a local restaurant, high up on a cliff overlooking half the country, and enjoyed a meal of porridge and tough meat presented to us as beef. Even though football in Swaziland was run as an amateur activity, I must credit the club elders with the fact that they helped me with expenses for fuel and the car's wear and tear. They offered me a weekly allowance equivalent to what they saved in bus fares for the other players, and I thought this was a nice gesture. More often than not, I used this allowance to buy a small meal for my fellow commuters, and we became very good friends.

The league season went well for us. We accumulated the victories and had a couple of defeats. We did particularly well in the night-time tournaments that were scattered around the league calendar. Whenever a company wanted to get some exposure and do some advertising, they would approach the National Football Association, which would quickly put together a tournament consisting of the country's four biggest clubs, and lots and lots of revenue was generated . . . and tucked away in private pockets. The night-time matches in the poorly lit stadiums were great fun though, and the fact that before, during and after the matches there was musical entertainment by some of South Africa's biggest artists, all added to the wonderful atmosphere. As players we mingled freely with the spectators, we shook hands and we danced together, but now that I come to think of it, I never signed a single autograph. Just not part of the culture over there . . .

The African tradition of taking players to a 'camp' the day before a match was something that I was not used to. When the team had a Sunday afternoon league match, anywhere in the country, we were all required to gather around Saturday lunchtime, and spend the afternoon, evening and night together, officially so that we could prepare for the match far from the media, the interference from the most critical fans, and of course, from the damage that our opponents' *muti* could do to us. Later on though, I was told that many of our own players needed to be kept in such a camp, so that they would not go out partying all night long, and show up for the game in an advanced stage of drunkenness or with a giant hangover. It must be said that, with Swaziland being such a small country, as players we could never go very far without being recognized, stopped or invited to some function. I fully understood the importance of keeping the team under wraps before the matches, and never objected. For our home matches, we used to gather at the home of one of the club elders, and after a meal of porridge and the toughest meat you can imagine, sometimes bordering on a strain of leather, all eighteen of us slept on four or five mattresses on the floor in one of the rooms of this home. As explained before, the club's budget for accommodation and players' matters was not all that big.

However, for away matches in different parts of the country, we occasionally stayed overnight in a luxury hotel or a resort. Our stay was paid for by the local 'big shot', usually a business tycoon who owned the land, the supermarkets and the petrol stations in that particular town or area. As you can imagine, we loved to feast on the buffet lunch and dinner that awaited us, and we spent time around the pool or going for a walk in the local game reserve. The local tycoon also paid for our *inyanga* and *muti*, but enough said about that. These camps gave me a great taste of the various parts of the country, and I was glad to have these opportunities for discovery. All the while, I continued to try and learn some more of the siSwati language, with clicks and everything!

During one of our camps, I suddenly found out that our goalkeeper, Charlie, was not only an accomplished shot-stopper, but also Swaziland's national disco dance champion! I pretended to be very skeptical of our teammates' claims and challenged him to prove his skills. Someone went to take my CDs of Vanilla Ice, Culture Beat and Ace of Base from my car, we cleared the mattresses off the floor, and Charlie took centre stage. I could not believe my eyes. I had heard of contortionists and snakemen, but this guy was in a league of his own. He moved body parts that I didn't even realize we had, and he entertained us for most of the evening. He slid up and down the premises, moonwalking from left to right and back to the left, and it seemed as if his feet never touched the floor. Now I understood where the agility that he usually showed between the goalposts came from. I learned that Charlie regularly participated in dance contests, and a week or two earlier he had earned a handsome sum of money in a competition in South Africa. He called his prize money his *'lobola'*.

Lobola means dowry. In Swazi custom, when a couple decides to get married, the family of the groom and the family of the bride each choose a representative who will negotiate the dowry, or the amount of cows that the groom will pay to the bride's family. Such negotiations can take several weeks, and eventually a number of cows is decided upon. The number of cattle depends largely on whether the bride is a first-born, on whether her family is of a certain social standing, and on her age. A typical dowry ranges from fifteen to twenty-five cows, which of course represents a significant amount of money to any family in the villages as well as in the cities. In modern times, the custom of offering cattle has largely been replaced with financial payments, but in the rural areas and in many parts of Southern Africa, the bride's value continues to be calculated in heads of cattle. Charlie did not yet have a girlfriend, but he knew that one day he would have to offer *lobola* to his future family-in-law, and I admired him for planning so far in advance.

SEVEN

The Swaziland Premier League seems to have a different number of clubs every year. While the title race is usually a pretty straight-forward affair between the big clubs of Mbabane and Manzini, the smaller clubs at the foot of the table contest a much hotter battle. Relegation from the Premier League has dire consequences for any team, and I would not be surprised if every year in Swaziland there are more Court cases about the relegation and promotion of football teams than about business fraud or defaulted payments. In a year when sixteen teams have contested the Premier League, it is not exceptional that two of the three relegated teams file all sorts of complaints and appeals about 'ineligible' players in other teams. There are often 'defaulters', players whose registration was not completed, or who were not registered at all. At the end of each season, the Premier League Management Committee or the National Football Association would have to decide on such cases, and more often than not, the 'relegated teams' are told that they can stay in the Premier League for another year, while two teams also get promoted from the Second Division. Well, let's just play with eighteen teams then. As for the members of the Premier League's Arbitration Committee who received 'sitting allowances' every time they met to discuss these cases? Well, let's just say that they were not hungry around Christmas time . . .

Being the royal club that we were, we sometimes had the honor of receiving a visit from His Majesty, King Mswati III. In between his state duties, he took a keen interest in the progress and the performances of the team, and he regularly came to give us words of encouragement. At times we were also invited to a private audience at the Royal Palace in Lozitha, where we would all sit on Persian carpets whilst the King sat in his gold-plated armchair. More than once did he invite me to sit in the armchair next to his—a special treat of course! We could hardly receive a stronger nod of approval than having His Majesty gracing our matches with his presence.

Swaziland's national stadium, Somhlolo, is a stone's throw from the Royal Palace, and is a place of national interest. Of course it serves as the main stadium for Premier League matches, African Cup matches and national team matches, but it is also where King Mswati III was crowned King in 1986, and where Swaziland's independence from

Great Britain was declared in 1968. National and traditional ceremonies are regularly held here, and whilst it may not be the most technologically advanced stadium in the world, it certainly has atmosphere and character. The crowds are compact, the noise can be deafening, and from the field of play it is impossible not to be either encouraged or intimidated—depending on what the crowds are shouting! It happened a few times that ten or fifteen minutes into our match the referee would suddenly blow his whistle, even though no foul had been committed. No, instead, the referee had just been informed that His Majesty's convoy had arrived outside the stadium, and everyone should salute him when he entered the stadium. We stopped playing and stood, together with the thousands in the stands. The gates opened, and a modest convoy of fifteen to twenty shiny black convertible Mercedes cars appeared on the running track that surrounded the football field. His Majesty always sat in the back of the second car, an open-top limousine, and waved at his subjects as he took a drive around the track. During this lap of honorary entrance, we would simply wait on the field until the protocol and the ceremonies were over. When the King's car reached the centre of the main stand, four or five minutes after he first made his entrance, he got out of the car, waved a few more times, and took his seat in the VIP section of the tribune. As players, we then all gathered just inside the sideline and saluted the King together. When the formalities were over, we sprinted back to where we found ourselves when the whistle went, and the game continued. On a lucky day, the King would even offer a goat or a cow to the victorious team . . . provided it was Manzini Wanderers! Only in Swaziland . . .

Once a year, in early September, the whole team and the officials were invited to attend the Umhlanga Reed Dance ceremony in Lobamba, in the central part of Swaziland. In this annual ceremony, which lasts for three consecutive days, thousands of maidens from all around the country bring reeds to the Royal Kraal, and offer them to the Royal family, so that their many homes and huts can be re-thatched. As part of the celebrations, these maidens, all of whom are dressed in traditional costumes, dance for hours and hours in front of the King and the Queen Mother. The highlight of the ceremony arrives on the third day when the King and his mother join the masses and dance with them. During the third day, there are also thousands of men warriors who join the ranks of the dancers, and I enjoyed watching them shuffle by in their traditional regalia. The symbolism behind the ceremony is that the whole nation participates in the construction of the Royal family's homes, and thus ensures the wellbeing of all the people in this peaceful and beautiful nation. This is of course a very colorful affair, with plenty of great Kodak moments, and part of its unique nature is that one can be as close to the King as one wants. Since the King was also a patron of my place of employment, we met quite regularly, talked a lot about football, and struck up a friendship that continues to this day.

Towards the end of the season however, the strain of combining the daily trainings down in Manzini with my full-time job in Mbabane started to show. Not only did I teach all day long. As I was working in a boarding school, we also had duties during the evenings and during the weekends. In order to lessen the load, I decided that I would try and join one of the Mbabane-based clubs instead. As luck had it, during the course of the league season I had scored against all the leading clubs, and when their officials found out that the *'umlungu'* was looking for a new club in town, it was soon up to me to simply pick the club that offered me the best terms. Of course, I wanted to do things the professional way, and asked one of my colleagues at work to be my agent. He kindly agreed, and contacted the leaders of four clubs. I will never know what he told them, but within the next two weeks we had four wonderful dinners, each one with the leadership of a different club. We had frogs' legs, we had duck, we had onion rings and we had ribs, each meal better than the last. The newspapers were of course eagerly following all our movements, and just before the registration and transfer deadlines expired, I signed for my new club, Mbabane Highlanders.

Even though football in Swaziland still operated on an amateur level, the leaders of the clubs clearly knew when an opportunity to make some money availed itself. As soon as my new club confirmed in the newspapers that they had reached an agreement with me, the Secretary General of Manzini Wanderers called me up. "You better tell the Highlanders Executive that we will ask for a large transfer sum!". I asked him why he would want money, as they had signed me for nothing a year earlier. "Well", he said, "we made you famous in Swaziland, you were an unknown when you arrived here and now everybody knows you . . . We want to be compensated for that". Stories about transfer fees often do the rounds in the Swazi newspapers, but in reality they never materialize. Clubs simply don't have the money to pay for the clearance of a new player, and as soon as a player decides to leave his club, there isn't much they can do about it. After all, it's hard to select a player who has clearly stated that he does not want to play for the team anymore. I informed the Secretary General that I would inform the leadership of Mbabane Highlanders, knowing very well that they would laugh it off. The story soon took on a life of its own, and was played out in several newspapers.

When it looked like the two clubs were deadlocked and my transfer might be in jeopardy because of the looming registration deadline, I decided to approach the Football Association's Management Committee myself, and asked them to issue me with my clearance. This rather unorthodox approach had its desired outcome, and I left the two clubs to fight it out amongst themselves about who was right and who was wrong. And the Chief Editors of the newspapers, they laughed all the way to the bank with the footballing soap opera that was being played out. Investigative journalism in Swaziland was still in its infancy, and the Times of Swaziland, the country's leading newspaper, loved to bring hot and sometimes controversial news to its thousands of readers. Newspaper dramas like these were not unheard of:

How did Mulder register?

BY
SPORTS REPORTER

Former Manzini Wanderers winger, Peter "Kapsie Dans" Mulder, has been registered by Mbabane Highlanders.

This was confirmed yesterday by Management Committee Secretary, Michael Mabuza, who said Mulder was registered before the deadline on Wednesday last week.

However, Wanderers have said that it issued Highlanders with a clearance on Thursday, a day after the deadline for registration had closed.

According to the Manzini team's General Secretary, Sipho "Shushu" Mkhwanazi, Highlanders' Manager Nqabeni Dladla approached Wanderers for the clearance of the Belgian international on Thursday and said that when asked about the urgency after the expiry of registration, Dladla had just insisted on the clearance.

"Since we had no reason to hold back the player's clearance, we gave it to Highlanders without any further delay", Mkhwanazi said.

Mulder resigned from Wanderers last week Tuesday and according to Mkhwanazi, he refused to change his mind when he was asked to by the club and stated that he just wanted to move to Highlanders and train in Mbabane.

Mulder, continued Mkhwanazi, even went to the extent of offering to pay for the clearance from his own pocket if money was the issue.

Until last week Wednesday—the day of the deadline— Wanderers had still not been approached or received any indication that Highlanders were interested in the player's clearance.

Michael Mabuza of the Management Committee yesterday tried to shed some light on the matter when approached to explain how Mulder was registered after the deadline when Wanderers only issued his clearance a day after when they were apparently approached by Highlanders for the first time.

Mabuza said that Mulder wrote a letter to his committee asking for its assistance in having him cleared and registered with Highlanders.

In response, Mabuza said that the Management Committee issued the Belgian international with a provisional clearance to enable him to beat the deadline, while Highlanders concluded negotiations with his former club.

Mabuza made example of their actions and said that what they did was similar to the decisions that were reached which involved four teams which were locked in disputes over players and said that some of those teams only concluded their negotiations after the deadline passed.

He said that even then all the players in question managed to register before midnight on Wednesday.

When asked if the Manzini team was aware of the provisional clearance that was issued to Mulder and his subsequent registration by the Management Committee, Mabuza said that his committee had agreed to send a letter to Wanderers inviting them to a meeting this week where they would be formally informed of the actions they took.

"However, that decision too was dropped after we learned that Highlanders and Wanderers had reached an agreement last Thursday", Mabuza said.

Answering another question on the provisional clearance that was issued, Mabuza said : "Under good reasons or explanations, a provisional clearance can be withdrawn and our decision when issuing this one was based on the interests of the player."

Thank you, Management Committee.

That same afternoon, this story also appeared in the local siSwati newspaper, Tikhatsi TemaSwati, a sister paper of the Times of Swaziland. Under the title "Mulder wabhaliswa kuNkunzi angenamvumo?", the same quotes and reasons were shared with the siSwati-speaking part of the nation. Nobody had to miss any part of the saga.

Even though the issue seemed to have been resolved, the newspapers were having none of it and continued to probe and solicit comments from anyone who had some kind of an opinion. Two days later, the following story was printed:

Wanderers query registration

BY
SPORTS REPORTER

Manzini Wanderers have accused the Premier League Management Committee of having violated the constitution of the Football Association by registering a player after the registration had been constitutionally closed.

Wanderers' statement follows the registration of the team's former Belgian international Peter "Kapsie Dans" Mulder with Mbabane Highlanders. Mulder is also said to have been registered a day after the registration period had closed.

Wanderers' General Secretary, Sipho "Shushu" Mkhwanazi, said in a statement yesterday that his team was still shocked at the way the registration of Mulder was effected.

"We are shocked by what the Management Committee has done to Wanderers over this issue. Our team will never stand in the way of any player who wants

to leave the club. Because of this policy, the club has lost many good players to other teams.

"I want to put it on record that Wanderers issued the player's clearance at 11.30 pm on Thursday to Highlanders and that was because that was the first time that we were officially contacted by the club for Mulder's clearance, Mkhwanazi added.

According to Mkhwanazi, the player did approach him on Monday for his clearance to join Highlanders. But he said that he told the player about the procedure to be followed by Highlanders if they were interested in his services. Mkhwanazi said Wanderers cannot understand how the Management Committee then decided to register Mulder without a proper clearance from Wanderers.

He said his team's constitution stipulates that if a player wants to leave the club, he has to resign before any team interested in his services comes

forward for negotiations for his clearance. But in this case, Mkhwanazi said, Highlanders never approached them.

Mkhwanazi went on to support his claims with clauses taken from the constitution of the Football Association which states under "The Status and Registration of Players and Referees" that "transfers of amateur and non-amateur players shall be subject to agreement between the interested clubs provided that such transfers shall be accompanied by a Clearance Certificate, and provided further that the prescribed transfer fees have been paid".

Mkhwanazi said that they should not therefore be held responsible for the late decision by the player to ask for his clearance. "Accordingly, we are going to follow this up with the Management Committee for an explanation on the matter that Highlanders seems to have known before us", Mkhwanazi said.

What I thought would be a straight-forward move from one club to another was clearly becoming a bit of a dramatic story. A lot of words were exchanged between the clubs and towards the Management Committee of the Football Association, but it was also clear that some of the discussion started to move towards the main bone of contention : the transfer fee. Let's hear what the Chief Editor of the Times of Swaziland himself had to say in his weekly column.

The Premier League Management Committee comes under the spotlight again. Again, they have willfully or otherwise misinterpreted the rules and regulations of the Swaziland National Football Association (SNFA). How the Management Committee can explain Peter Mulder's registration without a clearance from Manzini Wanderers after the deadline is a mystery.

The Management Committee claims that Mulder was given a provisional clearance pending the acquisition of one from Wanderers. Now, the understanding or lack of it in this matter arises from the fact that Mbabane Highlanders, to whom he was cleared, had not even approached Wanderers despite the player's indication that he intended joining them in his resignation letter to his former team.

According to article 22 (a), if a player changes his club he shall have a "Clearance of Transfer" Certificate entitling him to transfer his registration to a new club. The Regional or Women's League Committee or Management Committee of the Premier League shall not register such a player for one of its clubs before being in possession of the Clearance Certificate", reads the article.

The Management Committee kingpin, Secretary Michael Mabuza, said that Mulder wrote to them asking for their assistance in being cleared from Wanderers. Highlanders did not write a letter supporting this request. Without the knowledge of Wanderers, he was issued with a provisional clearance and Wanderers were to be informed this week about the developments regarding their player.

Nowhere in the rules and regulations do we see such provisions.

After registering Mulder, the Management Committee heard that Highlanders and Wanderers had met and resolved this matter. But significantly, Mulder had been cleared without prior knowledge of his team, which was well within reach for the Management Committee to consult. It is also peculiar that Mulder wrote to the Management Committee instead of the team interested in him. Mabuza said that this was done in the interest of the player. However, he seems oblivious to the interests of Wanderers.

In fact, Highlanders approached Wanderers for a clearance on Thursday evening after the Wednesday deadline. The FIFA statutes which talk about the provisional clearance are not in the constitution of the FA. And the Management Committee couldn't have possibly revoked this clause as this is the exclusive preserve of the Executive Committee of the Football Association.

We take this time to remind the Management Committee that it is the custodian of the running of soccer in the country at Premier League level. Its actions must be exemplary of good administration.

As leaders they are expected to adhere to the highest traditions of this job, which first and foremost, demands loyalty to and for the clubs.

The incongruous manner in which this registration was done raises the question of the Management Committee's credibility one again.

The other clubs which the Management Committee has touched on are in a class and category alien to this one. They were bickering over players but Wanderers knew nothing of Highlanders' interest in the player as they had not been approached.

It wasn't long before one of these investigative reporters asked me for my side of the story. I was not going to get drawn into the squabble between the two clubs, but did want to put the record straight. Quite a bit of misinformation had already been spread, and it was only fair that the correct sequence of events was published. Thus, the next day I got to have my say in the matter.

Mulder blames Wanderers for registration confusion

**BY
SPORTS REPORTER**

Former Manzini Wanderers' Belgian international, Peter "Kapsie Dans" Mulder, has attacked his former team of playing dirty tactics with an aim to delay his registration with Mbabane Highlanders before the deadline last Wednesday.

Mulder said Wanderers deliberately tried to hold back his clearance until the Wednesday deadline had passed.

Mulder yesterday showed this reporter two letters he had written to the Management Committee, seeking their help in the matter. Both letters were addressed to Manzini Wanderers and the Swaziland National Football Association.

The letter dated November 26th, which he claims to have personally handed to Wanderers' General Secretary, Sipho "Shushu" Mkhwanazi, reads :

"As a follow-up to my resignation letter dated November 25th and handed over the Mr Dumisani Mthethwa, the Manager of Manzini Wanderers, I would like to inform you that I have been talking to officials of Mbabane Highlanders FC. I resigned from Manzini Wanderers for personal reasons, the main one being the impossibility to combine my work in Mbabane with the daily evening training sessions in Manzini.

That is why I have approached a Mbabane-based team now and I sincerely hope you will provide Mbabane Highlanders FC with my clearance very soon. I thank you for your kind cooperation."

In his letter to the SNFA dated November 28th, Mulder complained that he was not getting any cooperation from Manzini Wanderers officials.

He made the example of the way the team's General Secretary and the club President behaved on the day of the deadline. He claims to have been told by General Secretary Mkhwanazi that the team would only meet him that evening to discuss the issue. Mulder said he tried to contact the club President to urge him to issue the clearance before it was too late, but the President refused to speak to him saying he was too busy.

In part he says in the letter to the Football Association : "This is why I want to ask you to provide me with a provisional clearance to join Mbabane Highlanders, so that we can overcome the registration deadline which Wanderers will surely try to reach without clearing me".

Mulder was registered with Mbabane Highlanders on Wednesday by the Management Committee to beat the deadline by a few hours . . .

EIGHT

Mʙᴀʙᴀɴᴇ Hɪɢʜʟᴀɴᴅᴇʀs, ɴɪᴄᴋɴᴀᴍᴇᴅ "Tʜᴇ Bᴜʟʟ", was Swaziland's biggest and most successful club, and the only Swazi team to have ever made it to the final stages of a continental cup tournament. It was an honor to join them, but more importantly, their training sessions were held on a field just an eight minutes' drive away from my home. Much easier to combine with the job of course. The coach of Highlanders, a former Zambian international goalkeeper, knew all about the exploits of my left foot, and quickly understood where best to deploy my strengths. Again, we played many a friendly match, and my integration into the team went impeccably. Despite one or two injuries that season, I managed to pick up a winner's medal for both the Premier League and the national cup tournament, sponsored by a famous British petroleum company. We qualified for two continental tournaments, and of course we preferred to join the African Champions' Cup, where we could test ourselves against the strongest teams in the region. Traditionally, the Swazi teams that qualified for the African Cup tournaments first had to play a preliminary match against their counterparts from Lesotho, Botswana, Zambia or Mozambique. During my years in Swaziland, the regional minnows were teams like Botswana Defence Force, Gaborone Black Peril, Township Rollers FC, Kabwe Warriors, Green Mamba and Eleven Men in Flight.

Once that preliminary hurdle had been cleared, the champion or cup winner of South Africa awaited us. And just as traditionally, that was where our interest in international football ended for that season. It was never a question of whether we would win or lose against Jomo Cosmos, Mamelodi Sundowns, Kaizer Chiefs or Orlando Pirates. It was just a question of how many goals they would score against us, and whether we would manage to get at least one corner kick ourselves. When we did get a corner kick, or even a throw-in, we celebrated as if we had won the World Cup no less! The gulf between South African football and that of its immediate neighbors was gargantuan, and remains so to this day. Feel free to compare our matches with a titanic clash between Welsh club Cwmbran Celtic and London's Chelsea FC.

As luck had it, even this Zambian coach was a fervent supporter of physical torture. His favorite exercise was a medieval torture method that we called 'rowing in the air'. We would all sit down in the grass, lift our knees and feet, keep our back straight up, and then simultaneously stretch our legs forwards (without touching the ground!) and our arms backwards (as if we were rowing). Please don't ask your children to do this . . . The *muti* at this club was just as important as at Manzini Wanderers, and I started to wonder whether *muti* cancels itself out when applied by both teams playing each other . . .

We had a great season, and I had a good time. This club had one private sponsor, who provided all of us with a pair of soccer boots. It may not sound like a lot, but in the context of Swazi soccer in that era, it was huge. At least all the players had proper boots, and we proudly wore the sponsor's logo, an image of a large wild cat, on our black and white team uniform and tracksuits. The training sessions were intense, and the competition between the players was sometimes brutal. Every player on the team was either a current national team player, or had been one not so long ago. This was a team of egos, with a few international stars thrown in for good measure. We played every training match as if it was our last chance to ever play football again, and the majority of the injuries that our squad had to deal with were self-inflicted. On some occasions, some players overstepped the mark to such an extent that fists started flying, and more than one training session ended earlier than expected because some players had started throwing punches at each other . . .

Through these experiences I learned quickly that tempers in Swaziland are sometimes very short, not just in football, but in all kinds of situations. And when a very nasty tackle had caused yet another teammate to hobble off the field in agony, the offending player simply offered a 'sorry', and expected that to be sufficient. When one day some of us queried the mental state of one of these serial assassins, a teammate stood up for him and said : "Well, he said 'sorry', what more do you want?"

Towards the end of the season, I joined the long list of casualties. During a tightly contested league match, I picked up an injury that ended up nastier than it initially looked. As I was about to play one of those famed crosses with my left foot, an opposing defender decided that going for the ball was pointless, and instead targeted my left foot. As I swung it towards the ball, he came in studs-first, and planted the sole of his boot right on top of my swinging foot. It felt as if I had kicked a wall, a rock or a lamp post. At first, I thought that I could 'run off" the pain, and I completed the match. However, the next morning the instep bone had become severely bruised, and there was considerable swelling at the top of my foot. I decided to have some X-rays, and even though there was no fracture, I was told that it would take 'a couple of weeks' before the swelling and the pain would be gone. A couple of weeks soon turned into a couple of months, and before I knew it, I had missed more than half of the following year's league season.

As we all know, time waits for nobody, and by the time I was ready to start training again, all the registration deadlines for the league and for the international tournaments had passed. I found myself without a club and realized that loyalty had not yet been invented in Swazi soccer. When I reported back for duty, some of the team leaders shunned me, as they were not able to face me and explain that they had decided to sign other players instead. I soon realized that it would be a pointless waste of time trying to convince them otherwise, although I also felt that given the team's league position, they could have used my services . . .

Rather than fighting a lost cause, I spoke with some of my closest friends who played for other clubs around the country. Soon I got invited to join my third Premier League club. Bhunya Black Aces was a small club from the west of the country, and was hovering in the lower half of the league table. Every year, this team managed to pick up just enough points to survive and live another day in the Premier League. You may call it the Wigan Athletic of Swaziland. The town of Bhunya had seen much better days a long time ago, and was now little more than a ghost town. The constant foul smell that hung around the area served as a reminder that the local pulp mill was still semi-functional, but the population had gone to look for better opportunities elsewhere. The Bhunya area is very scenic though, as it is right in the middle of an enormous artificial plantation of pine trees—one of the largest man-made forests in southern Africa.

My transfer met with the usual delays and debates, and someone at Mbabane Highlanders was intent on making some money from my move, thus delaying the issuing of the clearance by a number of weeks. However, in the end everything was sorted out, and I was now the first ever white "Black Ace" . . .

Some of the players worked in the pulp mill, and combined a long, hard shift on the machines with their evening training sessions and weekend matches. Together with four friends from Mbabane, we started to commute daily to Bhunya and back—a half hour drive through the forests and with the cool, fresh air gushing in through the car windows. These were the days when artists such as Black Box, Milli Vanilli and MC Hammer were all over the airwaves, and we were still young enough to blast the music and scream along with whatever it was these pop stars were singing. The lyrics weren't deep and didn't matter much. What mattered was that we had fun. Our desire to simply enjoy ourselves translated easily in the way we trained and played our football. Since we were a rather small team that every other team expected to beat, we felt no pressure, and we simply played the way we liked. Most of my teammates had been rejected by bigger clubs, some were journeymen who joined a new club every year so they could collect the signing-on fee, but this was possibly the most homogeneous team in the league. There was huge camaraderie, we all had a good laugh when one of us made a huge blunder during a match, and arguments were unheard of. However, since we were completely carefree during the matches, we often pulled off great results against the so-called big teams. We were never in contention for the title, but we certainly influenced the title race by taking points off those that were battling it out at the top. At the end of the season, more than one rival team looked back at their league position and reflected on what might have been if only they had beaten Bhunya Black Aces . . . twice.

Our coach was a Ghanaian globetrotter, and none of us knew whether he had any qualifications to coach. We seriously doubted any credentials that he may have shared with the club leadership on the day of his interview though. He might have been a Physical Education teacher back in Accra, but as the season progressed, we became more and more convinced that he had never been a coach before and that he had never really played football himself. There was very little that he could teach us. However, when we had a Saturday morning practice and got into a team huddle, he certainly showed us what an *umqombothi* hangover smelled like. *Umqombothi* is a local and traditional beer made from maize, malt, yeast and water. Depending on the level of skill of the brewer and the availability of ingredients, it may also contain battery acid and it has been linked to high incidences of oesophageal cancer. Not something that we players were interested in, but our coach certainly got his daily dose and had a hard time shaking off the effects.

The training sessions consisted of two distinct parts : running for about an hour, and then a practice match for the remainder of the time. We ran distances that Kenyan and Ethiopian marathon runners would have been proud of. Most of the time it was endless laps around the field, the purpose of which was lost to us. The monotony in running thirty or forty laps in one hour was exacerbated by the fact that we had so little to think of that the smell of the nearby pulp mill became even more offensive. Our coach was not aware that football fitness is quite different from second-gear endurance running, and soon we decided to introduce interval training and short sprints in these laps.

One of the training exercises that I vividly remember saw us running up and down the field for one hour, from penalty box to penalty box. On a good day, we had three footballs to share amongst the whole team, so while the lucky three had a ball in their feet, the rest of us simply jogged behind them to the opposing penalty area. When those who had a ball reached the 18-yards line, they had to take a shot on the unguarded goal. We all waited then until they had retrieved their ball, either—and rarely—from inside the net, or—and more commonly—from the marshy area down the slope behind the goal. Once the three balls were back, the next three lucky players got to dribble their ball across the field, and the rest of us . . . you guessed it. No passing, no turning, just pushing the ball forward—if you had one!—and taking a shot on goal at the end of another 60 metre jog. It happened regularly that we could not retrieve one of the footballs from that muddy marshland that bordered the football field, and when there were no young children around that we could send into the forbidden zone at the risk of getting caught by a crocodile or a snake, we had to continue our precious little exercise with just two footballs . . . This drill just went on, and on, and on . . . and I don't miss it now. Maybe our coach felt that at least one of us had the potential of imitating Diego Maradona's unstoppable run right through the English midfield and defence, but the pattern that we trained so hard to master never materialized in any of our matches . . .

After a while, some of the players couldn't bear it any longer, and stopped attending training. This is when I found out that we had some prima donnas in the team. Some of these absent players were never seen again, whilst others, those who had been playing for the club for a number of years, simply showed up for the camps on Saturday, and were in the starting eleven on Sunday. These 'untouchables' had their personal following, a group of people who would shout their nickname every time they were in possession of the ball during our matches, but in all fairness, they were also the better players on the team. They obviously knew that they could take a leaf out of Diego Armando Maradona's book—train or not, which coach would be bold enough to leave him out of the team? Was he not the player that Argentina coach Carlos Bilardo referred to when he replied to the question which players he would take to the 1990 FIFA World Cup? "Diego Armando Maradona . . . and ten others." Our Diego was a thirty-something year old nicknamed "Shoes". One of our star defenders was a young man with protruding eyes—when I first met him, he was introduced to me as Tuesday (yes, you guessed it, he was named after the day that he was born on), but just like everyone else, I was free to call him "Roll-On". I am sure that this allows the reader to better visualize what he looked like. And the captain of the team was Thamsanqa Nxumalo—with a loud click for the 'q' and a softer one for the 'x'!

Like any self-respecting coach, ours also had his own technical team. He had brought with him a friend from West-Africa, possibly from Ghana, possibly from a neighboring country with an equally impressive reputation for producing outstanding coaches and trainers. This friend, whom we shall call Anthony in order to protect the guilty, functioned as our team doctor. To be honest, any twelve year old child in Bhunya probably knew more about medicine and injuries than Anthony did. But like a loyal sergeant, he sat on our bench, next to his friend our coach, every Saturday and every Sunday. His medical equipment consisted of a small bucket of ice-cold water and a cloth. During the week this cloth probably doubled up as a car-washing tool. If we dared to be injured and Anthony applied his cloth, we would bear the grease marks for a week or so. Anthony's knowledge of medicine was even more limited than his equipment. When a teammate went down after another potentially career-ending tackle, Anthony would jump up from his small wooden bench, grab his bucket and cloth, and sprint onto the field to go and help the fallen. He would get down on his knees, apply the greasy sponge to some part of the player's leg, and tell him : "Sukuma!" "Get up!" It did not matter what the extent of the injury was, Anthony would simply tell the poor fellow to sukuma. A severely twisted ankle, a knock on the kneecap, a brutal tackle on the Achilles tendon . . . the treatment was always the same. A bit of water, a smudge of grease, and "Sukuma!". Anthony stayed in the job just as long as the coach did . . .

NINE

BEING INVOLVED IN SWAZI FOOTBALL was fun, and allowed me to discover a culture from a perspective that very few foreigners ever enjoyed. I took all the cultural differences in my stride, kept my eyes and ears wide open, and decided to embrace the Swazi culture as much as possible. Very few foreigners will ever have the privilege of being adopted as an international football star, of becoming a close personal friend of a King, and of course, of being driven around by his Majesty's father-in-law!

During my time in Swaziland, I also started to develop my coaching career. Not in the clubs, where I only spoke with the coaches when I was asked to do so. It happened from time to time that my head coach at Manzini Wanderers or at Mbabane Highlanders sought my opinion on technical matters, and I happily contributed. I preferred not to speak up in public though, as I did not want to undermine the coach's authority. Of course I was happy that my experience from Belgium was being recognized, and I know that some of my suggestions did make a difference in our games.

My first steps in football coaching in Africa were taken at the school where I worked. I took charge of the school's football team and immediately applied my learnings about the strengths and the skills of my young African players. Of course my students knew that I was playing for some of the biggest clubs in the country, and their interest in my career translated into enthusiasm and a belief that they too could one day play for those teams. Besides the many African players, there were also some great talents from South America and Europe, and we soon built a pretty solid team. I decided to build a strong central axis with a fearless Pakistani wicket-keeper ... sorry, goalkeeper, a seventy-kilo South-African central defender, a hugely talented Colombian midfielder nicknamed "Valderrama", who never seemed to run out of tricks and energy, and a tall, fast South-African striker who firmly believed that one day he would be playing for Manchester United. If connections could get players in Sir Alex Ferguson's good books, then he would certainly have made it : he was the grandson of Nelson Mandela. With this axis established, I then covered the more peripheral positions with those that were best suited. I never found a left-footer, and had to instruct those playing on the left to simply give the ball to those in the middle, and to otherwise stay out of the way. The improvising left-wingers were happy to be in the team, and were wise enough to oblige. Next to our South-African sweeper, I planted the heaviest student that I could find. He knew that he was significantly heavier and much slower than the rest, but in order to give him self-confidence we kept on reminding him that he had now reached his target weight. A pity then that he hadn't reached his target height yet . . . His job was to block the oncoming opposition strikers, and he actually became quite adept at putting up an insurmountable human wall.

On one of my trips to Johannesburg I picked up a basic football coaching manual, had a quick look at it, shortlisted the exercises and tactical points that I felt could serve us, and off we went practicing. In those pre-Internet days, of course we had to rely on our personal experience, and try to blend that with the fascinating skills of these young African and Latin-American boys. We started by practising three times per week, but soon the players asked whether we could train in the early mornings also. Since we were all living in a boarding school, this was no problem. So we got up at 5.30 in the morning, met on the field, and trained in the purest air and under the most beautiful morning skies one can imagine. More often that not, we could see the morning clouds rise up from down below, and by the time we went for breakfast, we had already had a good work-out and a sporty start to the day. The team quickly improved, and since there was a dearth of interschool competitions, most of our matches were friendlies against company teams or league teams. One of our most frequent opponents was the team from the Swazi Central Bank, which comprised of about three quarters of the Swaziland National Team. Professional football was non-existent in Swaziland, but it is fair to say that those who played for the bigger clubs often got a job with either the government or one of the major banks. In recent years, this trend has been switched—nowadays the only clubs that can offer employment to their players are those that belong to the Police force, the Prisons Department and the Army. In fact, in order to play for one of these teams, one has to be employed by their institution.

We fought many a heroic battle against the bank team and other visitors, and in matches where I knew that the boys would struggle a bit, I joined them as a central defender. I found this way of supporting and guiding them extremely useful, as I was not just shouting from the sidelines, but instead, directing and teaching from within. And of course, this tactic provided me with a few extra matches against some of my teammates from Sunday afternoons, as well as regular opponents from the Premier League. There was a good sense of camaraderie, and more often than not our school team made the big boys work hard for their draw . . .

It was a real challenge to combine rigorous European tactics with the African skill, exuberance and spontaneity, but the team responded very well, and it was clear that there are a set of 'universal' basics and tactics that one can apply anywhere in the world. Mandla Mandela, Nelson Mandela's grandson, was one of the players who each time rose to the occasion. He was very lanky and casual, and very difficult to mark. Some of the Premier League defenders dreaded playing against him, as he was an amazing and tireless runner, a pretty good header of the ball, and someone who simply didn't know the meaning of 'pain'. When he got kicked or fell down heavily, he would simply get up, wipe the dirt of his arms or shirt, and get on with it. His drive was a great strength, and it didn't come as a surprise when we saw a few years later on that he had become a prominent Chief and speaker who often represents his famous but ailing grandfather at overseas functions.

After a couple of years as a boys' team coach, I also created a girls' team at the same school. This team, called the *Bantfwana Bantfwana* ('the babes'), soon became very popular in the country. South Africa had recently come out of its many years of isolation after the abolishment of Apartheid, and there was a general wave of optimism going around the region. Sporting success was immediate, with South Africa's triumph in the 1995 Rugby World Cup and in the 1996 football African Cup of Nations. The 'Bafana Bafana', or 'boys', became a concept in Southern Africa, and the standard that all other teams measured themselves against. So we called our girls' team the 'Bantfwana Bantfwana', and embarked on a path of endless victories. We played friendly matches, we organized and won tournaments, and after a short while we received invitations from the National Football Association to play a number of curtain raisers for First Division matches. Our prominence in the press created a buzz, and suddenly a number of other ladies' teams started to emerge. A Ladies' football league was formed in 1994, and it continues to this day to enthrall the masses. I am proud to say that I was one of the forces behind the creation of this league.

At one stage the Swaziland national ladies team was invited to play against the South African selection, and I was asked to coach and manage the team. It was a great experience for all of us, and this acknowledgement gave great impetus to ladies' football in Swaziland. As for the game itself, we put up a brave performance against the much stronger South African ladies. Unfortunately I cannot remember the score in that match . . .

Most of my time was still taken up by playing football rather than coaching it, but I did become more and more involved in the technical aspects of the sport. I had the opportunity to attend several coaching courses organised by the Swaziland Football Association and taught by local and foreign coaches and instructors. The main focus for me was finding the right way to wisely channel the inimitable skills and the limitless supply of energy of the young African players. I have never forgotten my learnings from those early coaching days, and soon enough they were going to come in very handy.

After a few years in Swaziland, the travel bug started to play up again, and even though I continued to enjoy every moment of my time in this amazing country, I felt that it was time for another change. I was not prepared to leave Africa, but wanted to find a new environment in which to further develop my understanding and appreciation of the world's cultures. After six wonderful years in the beautiful Kingdom of Swaziland, I packed up my belongings, said goodbye to my many friends, and boarded a flight to the great unknown. From the plane I looked down over the endless land, the winding rivers, the forested mountains and the scattered towns and villages. Three and a half hours after take-off, I landed in my new home. I was ready to start a new life in Dar Es Salaam, Tanzania.

TEN

Dar Es Salaam, on the African east coast.

THE EAST AFRICAN COUNTRY OF Tanzania is an absolute gem. Rich in culture and history, its location on the shores of the Indian Ocean have given it a front-row seat in history. Tanzania has some of the most thriving cultures anywhere in Africa, it is one of the few countries to have been united through its language, and the rocks and hills could tell us thousands of fascinating stories from the past. Tanzania is also a country that is looking forward and heading towards ever-increasing prosperity. Within the confines of Mount Kilimanjaro, Lake Victoria, Lake Tanganyika, the Indian Ocean coast and the mysterious islands of Zanzibar lies a world that many have visited but few have ever really understood or gotten to know. And while the natural features of the endless Serengeti plains and the incredibly scenic Ngorongoro Crater are major selling points in overseas travel agencies, it is really the people of Tanzania that make the country what it is. Having visited the country before, I knew exactly how I wanted to get closer to its people, and very soon the opportunity availed itself.

As soon as I had landed at the Dar Es Salaam International Airport and settled in at my new place of employment, my feet (and especially the left one!) started to itch. I needed to get onto a football field as soon as possible. I didn't know the local football scene too well, so I thought that my best option was to ask one of my new Tanzanian colleagues which club I could join. During the first week in my new job, I met Zachariah, the storekeeper, and at that point we had no idea yet that he would be the person who would help me find a new footballing challenge. Zachariah was well in his fifties and had been working in my new school for over twenty years. He was a fountain of knowledge on many topics, and his whitened hair gave him a professor-like look. He was very soft-spoken, but his voice exuded a certain level of authority and wisdom.

After our initial introductions, we soon started to talk about football and found that we shared a common interest. Whilst sharing a cup of Chai Bora, Tanzania's most famous and most succulent type of tea, Zachariah showed that he was very much aware of local and overseas football. I knew then that Zachariah and I would get along very well indeed. Even though he had never played football of any significant level himself, he clearly knew his way around the local clubs. As a newcomer in Tanzania, I didn't have any particular preference for a team, and told him that I just wanted to play football at the highest possible level that I was fit for. After all, I was still young!

I explained to Zachariah what I had achieved in football so far and asked him if he could help me find a club. He replied:

"Don't worry, Peter. I will talk to some of my friends in the city, and I will get back to you tomorrow or the day after. I am sure there will be some interested clubs!"

Zachariah immediately started looking for a phone that worked. As soon as he had found a ringing tone, he started calling a couple of friends. I was starting to get rather excited myself, and hoped that the next day would bring good news.

When I arrived at work the following morning, Zachariah came running to me, his cup of Chai Bora in his hand, and told me that he had something exciting to share with me. He said:

"After work today, at 2.30 pm, we are going to town together to meet somebody."
"Somebody like who?" I asked.
"One of the leaders of Safari Sports Club."

I had only vaguely heard about Safari Sports Club, but from the tone and excitement in his voice I understood that they were a rather big deal here in Tanzania. I asked him:

"Can you tell me a bit more about this club?"
"Of course, my friend. Safari Sports Club is, together with Ndovu Football Club, the biggest club in the country. They have a huge following, not just in Dar Es Salaam but right across the country and even in neighboring countries. They have over the past few years been the outstanding club in Tanzania and East Africa. Actually, a few years ago they even went all the way to the final of the African Confederations Cup. Many of the club's players are also on the Tanzanian national team. So you can see that this is a big club we are talking about."
"Great! I look forward to meeting their leaders. Who exactly are we going to see this afternoon?"
"We are going to meet the Chairman of the Club, Mr Simkola. He has been leading the club since 1992. He is very serious about ensuring that his club signs the best players for the coming season, and you will like him. He is expecting us early this afternoon, so come and meet me here as soon as you finish your classes and we will go together."
"OK, great! *Asante sana rafiki!*" (Thank you very much, my friend)

During the course of the morning I talked with a few more Tanzanian colleagues about football in their country, and one thing became very clear. Not only was Safari Sports Club the most successful and biggest club in the country, much of its status and success was measured against that of the local rival, Ndovu Football Club. One of my colleagues even told me that the city of Dar Es Salaam is pretty much split along the lines of the two clubs. People identified with one of the two clubs, and were therefore either 'red and white' (Safari) or 'green and yellow' (Ndovu). There was no other option, and the rivalry sometimes even cut right through a family!

"Well", I thought, "that should make for some very interesting matches to look forward to?"

That morning I taught my classes with one eye on the students and the other eye on the clock. Whoever told us that time is relative was absolutely right. We had very productive classes that day, the students easily fed off the excitement that pervaded the classroom, but it definitely felt like each hour lasted as long as five hours!

Early that afternoon, Zachariah and I took the short drive to the Safari Sports Club house located in Kariakoo, one of the city's many districts.

Kariakoo, a small part of Ilala District just to the west of the Dar Es Salaam city centre, is a feast for the senses. It's the kind of place that never sleeps. No matter at what time of day or night you pass through, there is always something to see and do. The name 'Kariakoo' derives from the English "Carrier Corps", which was a British military organization based in Dar Es Salaam that provided support to the UK forces against Germany during World War I. Soon after the end of the war, this area became the main settlement for the local people. About a century ago, the population of Dar Es Salaam was around 25,000, and it has since grown to well over three million. While development and modernization have certainly left their mark on the more coastal parts of the city, Kariakoo has steadfastly maintained its East African flavor and atmosphere, and it should be one of the first ports of call on any visitor's itinerary. On any given day of the week, there are thousands of traders walking down the streets, selling everything that the human mind can imagine. There is a constant buzz, constant noise from the traffic and the music stalls, a terrible smell from the exhausts and the garbage that lies around the place, and there is a constant coming and going of thousands of people. The main minibus station of Dar Es Salaam is also located here, and literally thousands of 'daladalas', or small combis, come and go all day long and all night long, transporting the masses to the various areas of this vast city. For a mere 200 Tanzanian Shillings, or 20 cents of a US Dollar, anyone can have the pleasure of being squeezed like sardines in one of these brightly colored and comically named vehicles and travel to any part of Tanzania's biggest city. Residents of the city can actually keep informed on the latest gossip stories, scandals or manhunts just by reading the names of the *daladalas*. I have travelled more than once in combis named 'Monica Lewinsky', 'Osama Bin Laden' or 'Saddam Hussein'. Often the minibuses are so tightly packed that the driver himself has half his body hanging outside his window. Because of the slow-moving traffic that this mass of *daladalas* causes, traffic accidents are almost unheard of in Dar Es Salaam. Kariakoo market covers a massive area, part of it in the open air and some parts of it covered. It is certainly one of the most interesting places for visitors to see, and it is definitely one of my favorite places in Tanzania. I hope that the place will remain unchanged for a long time to come, so that it can preserve its unique character.

Before arriving at our meeting venue, I asked Zachariah for a few Swahili greetings and phrases, so that I could address Mr Simkola in his own language—at least for the introductions!

Inside the Safari Sports Club house, located right in the heart of the busiest part of Kariakoo, Zachariah and I were greeted by a lady who, upon seeing a white man walk in the door, knew who I was and welcomed us. She asked us to walk straight through and into a room where she said Mr Simkola was waiting. I had expected a meeting with one person, but when we opened the office door we found about fifteen seriously-looking club officials gathered around two large plastic tables. The set-up certainly looked like a boardroom, but the furniture did not do justice to the importance of this particular meeting. Apparently the whole Executive Committee, as well as some other elderly club officials, had been invited to meet 'the white man'!

Zachariah and I were offered a cup of Chai Bora, and we eagerly accepted. We all introduced ourselves. Zachariah let the whole meeting know that he was now my agent, he then winked at me, and we started to talk about football. The Chairman briefly told me the history of Safari Sports Club, and he explained why he and his colleagues were very interested in signing an overseas player for his team. He elaborated that the club had reached the top in Tanzania and that they now wanted to try and make an impact on the continental competitions. The team was about to play in the East and Central African Championships, as well as in the Africa Cup tournament. The Committee felt—and rightly so—that my experience, my semi-professional footballing background, my upbringing in the European coaching schools and my left foot could help the club a lot in its tough upcoming assignments. I couldn't have agreed more. When he mentioned my particular skills as a player, I was a little bit surprised at his rather detailed knowledge—he certainly had not learned this through the Internet (which made its appearance in Tanzania three or four years after this meeting). Apparently the accuracy in my left foot had been the topic of extensive discussions amongst the club leaders, even before they had met me! Later on I found out that some people had watched me play for a competitive expatriate team at a well-known local sports club near State House, and they had already reported me to the club's leadership! I was happy though to stick with my newly-acquired and self-proclaimed agent.

I was very impressed with the tone of the Chairman. I could hear that I was dealing with people who had ambition, who wanted to look ahead and most importantly, who had a common vision and strategy that each member believed in and that were in the interest of the club. There was talk of moving forward, of taking that next step after having dominated the national football scene for a number of years, and of introducing more scientific and professional methods into the running of the club and the team.

I was asked to shed some more light on my background in football and on the reasons why I wanted to join Safari Sports Club. I explained that I was very keen on getting involved with a top level Tanzanian club, and that I wanted to offer my experience so that the team could excel in the new season. In a way, I paraphrased what they had just told me, and lo and behold, they liked what I told them . . . It was clear that we all shared the same ambition, and soon Mr Simkola invited me to the team's next practice session at the Karume Memorial Stadium in Ilala. There I would meet the team's coaches and the other players. To be honest, I couldn't wait to get started!

The meeting took about three quarters of an hour and three refills of Chai Bora, and we managed to clear all the hurdles. I needed to explain that I might not be able to play in all our games, because I had important commitments at my place of employment. At times it would be impossible for me to travel up-country with the team, or to travel to international assignments. Except during the school holidays, of course, or with the permission of my employer.

The leadership assured me that they perfectly understood my position, but this was not going to be an obstacle to my involvement with the club. We agreed to meet the next day at the practice ground. Meanwhile, I decided to apply for my International Clearance Certificate from the Swaziland Football Association, so that I could register with Safari Sports Club.

ELEVEN

THE NEXT DAY I WENT to the Karume Memorial Stadium in Ilala for my first practice session with Safari Sports Club. I hadn't been reading the local papers, and I was unaware that they had published my arrival in the team. I was completely surprised when I arrived at the practice ground and found that there were at least three thousand spectators there. Most of them seemed to have been waiting for the white man, and when I entered the ground a loud cheer went up. Realising that it was for me, I duly replied by waving at my new fans . . .

"*Karibu mzungu*!" (Welcome, white man/foreigner!), people shouted from everywhere.

This was certainly one of the best welcomes that I have ever experienced. Many of the Safari Sports Club fans came up to me to shake my hand and to extend their *Karibu sana*, while the young boys all gathered around me and observed my every move with their big, curious eyes. I had a good feeling about joining this club. I was introduced to the coaches and the players, and again, the welcome was very big. I also noticed a couple of cameras in the melee, and clearly the local press boys were out to get some details about Safari Sports Club's new overseas signing.

I completed my first training session with my new team mates, and drove back home with a cluster of little boys running behind the car, cheering and waving and shouting "Mzungu!". I already knew : this was going to be fun . . .

The next morning, my colleague and agent brought me a copy of one of the local daily newspapers.

"Have you seen this?", he asked, and showed me an article about the '*mzungu*'.

I replied in the negative, and looked at a story in Swahili.

"Well, what does it say?, I asked him."

And so he told me.

Foreigner to play for Safari Sports Club

BY OUR REPORTER

Peter Mulder, a player from Belgium, has joined Safari Sports Club for the upcoming Premier League season. Talking to Majira newspaper yesterday after the club's practice session, Mulder said that he has decided to join the club after meeting with the Executive Committee.

The player, who is left-footed, was accompanied by the club Chairman, Mr Simkola. Before arriving in Tanzania, Mulder played for Mbabane Highlanders in Swaziland. He also played for Manzini Wanderers in the same country, and won several national championships and cups. This Belgian player arrived in Tanzania in August of this year, and is working at an international school in the city.

"I have decided to join Safari Sports Club because I know of the club's status and achievements. I was introduced to the club by one of my colleagues, and I have had very productive talks with the club's leadership. I can't wait to get started and to help my new club reach greater heights!", an obviously excited Mulder told our reporter.

My first few practices immediately taught me a couple of natural and cultural aspects of life in Tanzania.

It was hot here! Afternoon temperatures at this time of year were well in the thirties, and with the coastal humidity thrown into the mix, I needed a bit of time to get used to this new environment. My teammates ran for hours on end, and even though I pushed myself as much as I could, I needed quite a few more water breaks than they did. I told myself I'd get over it though. One of the best remedies for overheating, I soon found out, was another cup of Chai Bora. The hotter the tea, the quicker the body cooled down. A pot of Chai Bora soon became an integral part of my evening routine.

Secondly, I became determined to learn Kiswahili as soon as possible. The entire training sessions were conducted in Kiswahili, and I didn't like the fact that the instructions needed to be translated into English just for me. Many of my teammates were less than proficient in English, but they certainly tried to make me understand what they wanted me to know. Fortunately, in those early days, both our coaches mastered the English language quite well, and we were able to communicate at a reasonable level. I had found the motivation to learn the local language and I knew that speaking Kiswahili would not only allow me to understand the instructions or add my comments, but that it would also accelerate my integration in the team and into the culture.

It wasn't very hard picking up the basic football vocabulary in Kiswahili, as it got repeated a lot during the sessions : *kimbia, ruka, piga, kitchwa, nenda, panda, rudi, kaba, mpira, angalia, mbele* and *nyuma* are very common words on a football ground in Tanzania. And so are *pembeni, ndani, kati* and *bao*. I soon learned to do a particular exercise *mara kumi* (*ten times*) or for *dakika tano* (*three minutes),* and I also learned what it means when *kesho mazoezi yataanza saa tisa na nusu.* Literally translated, this means that 'tomorrow training starts at nine thirty'. However, in the Swahili culture, the counting of the hours starts at sunrise, which is six o'clock in the morning. This is why, in Kiswahili, nine o'clock really means three o'clock—you always have to take away six hours from the time given. I soon stopped arriving at the ground at nine thirty in the morning or evening, when in fact trainings started at three thirty in the afternoon!

More often than not, punctuality was not really important, and slowly I discovered the difference between *mzungu* time (shown on a watch or clock) and Swahili time (not shown anywhere, and to be determined by he or she who is late). To be honest, it is harder to get used to the latter than to the former! The difference between the two is a couple of hours at the best of times, and when making a plan to meet up sometime later in the day, it was essential to add whether the 'three o'clock' was according to *mzungu* time or Swahili time! I should add though that even when all the parties concerned agreed to meet at seven thirty mzungu time, there were always a few people who would show up at least an hour late. As a foreigner, that was one of the most difficult cultural aspects to adapt to, or to even learn to tolerate. Eventually it ended up being one of these things that one tries to live with when moving into a new culture . . .

It was important to accept, from the start, that the concept of time in the East African culture is very different from anywhere else. Many people may casually joke about 'African time', but it is a real fact of life. Getting upset or annoyed over someone's tardiness does not make things any better, so I soon learned that I should always have a good book with me when I expected to meet someone at a specific time. In a culture where the position of the sun still determines the time of day and where many people don't have watches, one has to understand that the concept of "two o'clock" or "five o'clock" is often subordinate to the concept of 'early afternoon' and 'late afternoon'. And of course, those condemned to waiting for the others could always order a cup of Chai Bora.

From my first few practice sessions I also realized that the coaches of Safari Sports Club were rather competent people. They had a good grip on the players and they commanded enough respect to get the national team stars to work together. Their level of tactical knowledge was also good, and both were very much able to explain why certain exercises and drills were important. I learned that both coaches had been top-level players in Tanzania, and one of them, Mr Kimora, had guided the club to the final of the African Cup Winners' Cup a few years earlier. So he was a local legend, and could hardly put a foot wrong. However, having been a decent player does not automatically mean that you are going to be a top-level coach as well. Playing the game is one thing, teaching the game is a different proposition altogether. There are many examples of former top players from all over the world who have tried to coach at the top level and who have either failed or found it extremely hard to live up to the expectations, or simply to get their players to play in the way they played themselves. Diego Armando Maradona is still searching for that magic coaching formula, and former stars like Glen Hoddle, Mark Hughes, Brian Robson and Roy Keane have so far been unable to achieve the same level of success in coaching as they had when they were players. Of course there are former top players who have proven to be excellent coaches as well : Johan Cruyff, Franz Beckenbauer, Daniel Passarella, Michel Platini and more recently Josep Guardiola are just a few examples.

Have you ever wondered why former greats like Pelé, Garrincha, Socrates, Puskas, Eusebio or Di Stefano have never tried their hand at coaching? Probably for exactly that reason : their play was mainly driven by their instinct, their natural skill and their immense talent, and not so much by their tactical awareness or rational thinking. Everybody remembers the great Brazil teams of the fifties, the sixties and the seventies, whose only tactical plan was to score at least one more goal than the opposition . . . It is quite impossible to teach instinctive football to your students . . .

Anyway, to come back to the coaches of Safari Sports Club, they seemed to know quite a bit about conditioning, team play, group dynamics and motivation. What I also liked about their position was the fact that the players didn't call them 'coach' or 'trainer', but rather 'teacher' or *mwalimu*. I was told that a football coach in this part of the world is called a teacher, and I liked that analogy. Because they are teachers. They are the people who educate footballers about the game, its physical requirements, its tactical foundations, and the importance of team spirit and a feeling of belonging. They are educators and that role needs to be taken very seriously. Teaching is a skill which is partly acquired and partly inborn. Many aspiring or self-proclaimed coaches are not skilled teachers, and they cannot be successful in this profession.

The Safari Sports Club players, including the national team stars and the senior players who had played in the CAF Cup Final, all respected the coaches. There was a very good spirit of cooperation, which was also extended to me. Despite their poor command of the English language, and well aware that my knowledge of Kiswahili was in its baby stages, several of the players immediately came forward and wanted to know more about me. From day one I felt that I was now a part of this team. I was looking forward to being successful with Safari Sports Club and to making my contribution towards the development of my new club.

Even though I had started training with my new teammates, I was not yet eligible to play for the club in a competitive match. For that I would have to wait until the East and Central African Championship at the end of December . . .

The first time that I saw my new teammates in a competitive match was in a local derby against Ndovu Football Club. The occasion was the President's Cup, a match traditionally contested between the national champions and the cup winner. Tanzania's equivalent of the Charity Shield, so to speak. Since that season Safari Sports Club had won both competitions, it was decided that the local rival would be invited to contest this match. A bonus to this was of course that this was the only fixture that would guarantee a packed stadium—where a few happy officials would carry plastic bags with the gate collection home in the evening. It was a very colourful and an extremely noisy occasion at the National Stadium, and I knew then that I would love being a part of the Tanzanian football scene. The stadium had a capacity of about 40,000, but it felt as if at least twice that number had managed to force their way into the stands. And those who had been unable to get their hands on a ticket, mostly because of economic reasons, had climbed into the trees and up the electricity poles just outside the stadium. This was not just a football match, this was a celebration, a duel, a coming-together of the city, and a chance for half the city to hold the bragging rights until the next derby match.

The National Stadium itself was not a very attractive structure. It had clearly seen much better days, and it was in need of some major renovation, or maybe of a complete make-over. When I enquired about its poor condition, I was told though that the National Stadium was a historical monument. It was the place where Tanzania declared its independence on December 9th, 1961. It was also the place where Mwalimu Julius Kambarage Nyerere addressed his compatriots and set them on the path of socialism. Because of its status as a historical monument, it was completely out of the question that any kind of alteration could be made. And there was certainly no way that it could ever be taken down and replaced with a more modern structure.

The fans at the stadium were all joyful, very positive about the occasion, and although the game produced a winner and a loser, there was never any violence, neither verbal nor physical. Quite different from most European grounds! The earlier comment that Dar Es Salaam was split along club lines was clearly visible here. Literally half that stadium was dressed in red and white, waving flags and playing trumpets for well over two hours, while the other half stood out in yellow and green, and spent the afternoon chanting "CCM". The *"Chama Cha Mapinduzi"*, or 'Party of the Revolution', has for decades been the ruling party in Tanzania and Zanzibar, and Ndovu Football Club has always associated itself with this party. All of Tanzania's presidents, from "Father of the Nation" Julius Kambarage Nyerere to current incumbent Jakaya Mrisho Kikwete, have hailed from this party. In sharp contrast, Safari Sports Club has always had strong links to the more democratic but less influential parties.

TWELVE

THE SIGHT OF A FOREIGNER in the stands at the Dar Es Salaam National Stadium was rare. The sight of a foreigner being guided right to the bench of one of these two superclubs was as unlikely as a tsunami in Nepal. It simply doesn't happen—until it happens. As I was being led through the hordes of photographers, journalists and self-proclaimed team officials, I could feel that thousands of eyes were gazing at me. Who was this *mzungu* who walked onto the running track and made his way towards the Safari Sports Club team bench? And then of course reality dawned upon the fans. "This must be the new signing, the Belgian teacher!" A loud roar went up from the red and white half of the stadium, and I duly waved at those who were waving back. Almost simultaneously, a loud chorus of whistles rose from the other end of the stands. I glanced across and saw a lot of commotion in the yellow and green part—and waved at them too! And to myself I thought : "Just wait and see, one of these days I hope to let my feet do the talking and I'll settle this little score right there and then!".

Safari Sports Club's 2-1 victory in that derby was rewarded with the President's Cup, and ended a glorious season during which we qualified for the next season's African Champions' League. A few days later all the players and officials of Safari Sports Club were invited to the State House, the presidential residence where we received the trophy from the then President of the Republic, His Excellency Ali Hassan Mwinyi. During his short speech, he wished the team well in its upcoming assignments, and he extended a particular 'karibu' to the new foreign player.

A few days after this titanic clash of the country's two power houses, a feature article appeared in one of the English-language newspapers.

Belgian teacher aims to be in top form with Safari Sports Club

BY
OUR REPORTER

Former Royal Antwerp FC player, Belgian Peter Mulder, who has a two-year teaching contract with a local international school, is booked to play for Safari Sports Club in next season's mainland league and international assignments.

Peter says that he is ready to play in any position but would prefer to be on the left side.

"I can play on either side but my whole career has been on the left", he says, adding that he is a versatile player equally happy in defense, midfield or attack.

He says that he likes Tanzania because of its stimulating football climate and the local population's mass support. "I came to realize that Tanzanians like soccer as much as my countrymen when I watched the Safari—Ndovu match on November 4th at Dar Es Salaam's National Stadium", he said.

He says Tanzanian teams play a similar style to Belgian sides.

"Soccer is the national sport in Belgium. Belgium has a good football reputation, we were number four in the 1986 FIFA World Cup".

Peter says his first visit to Africa was in 1973 when he spent half a year as a child in Zaire, now the Democratic Republic of Congo. This was when he started to develop a rapport with Africa and he knew he would be back.

His first trip to Tanzania was in January this year when he came as a tourist and visited Mount Kilimanjaro, various safari parks, the Ngorongoro Crater, the Serengeti National Park and finally Zanzibar. Peter had been a teacher and football player in Swaziland since the late eighties.

He says that he has the highest regard for Brazil's Pelé, for Holland's Johan Cruyff and for Germany's Franz Beckenbauer. "These players always showed high levels of tactical and pro-fessional discipline, and this is one of the main requirements to become a good footballer."

When soccer fans saw Peter for the first time with some of the Safari Sports Club coaches and players last Saturday, they responded very enthusiastically.

Peter teaches French, Spanish, German and English at his international school, and he is keen to learn Kiswahili as soon as possible.

"I want to immerse myself in the Swahili culture and get to know my team mates and the club's fans as well as possible. This can only be done if I learn Kiswahili, and I have already started studying the key words!", a clearly enthusiastic Peter added.

He will be just the fourth European to play for a Tanzanian team. The first was a Yugoslav with Ndovu Football Club, and the other two were Bulgarians who played for Zanzibar's Malindi FC.

The training sessions went very well, they were varied and interesting, and they soon made me realise how much technical skill the Tanzanian players have. Many of my teammates could do almost anything they wanted with a football, and it was often a joy to just watch my friends make their feet talk. As a white player who grew up in an environment where the emphasis is more on fitness, strength and tactics rather than on technique and natural skill, I felt that there was a lot that I could learn from my teammates, and on most days I spent at least half an hour after the end of the day's practice trying to imitate the skills of my friends. At times, I even found myself admiring their technique in the middle of a practice match. I also continued my daily shooting practices, as I still believed that hard and accurate shooting is one of the most powerful weapons in football. Remember, no goals, no victory! When I first asked one of our international goalkeepers to stay behind after training so I could have some shooting practice, he was rather puzzled. But once we got going he became just as enthusiastic as myself at the extra training, and soon enough all three goalkeepers volunteered to add thirty minutes to their daily training sessions. The fans also realized that we were working hard, and they enthusiastically cheered every goal and every great save. Clearly, things were shaping up nicely at this club.

The major problem that I encountered during the practices was not the language barrier, the culture or the different footballing backgrounds, but simply the summer heat and humidity in Dar Es Salaam. The afternoon weather in the latter months of the year is quite brutal on the African East coast, and I literally drank hundreds of liters of water, both during practices and during games. At least, I did so until the day that the holy month of Ramadhan started. From now on most of my teammates were fasting during the daylight hours, and I didn't think that it was appropriate for me to start drinking water in front of them halfway through the practice session. Surely they were as thirsty as I was, but they weren't allowed to drink until later that evening. So I tried to ignore my thirst, which was impossible to do, and carried on with the practice. However, as soon as the training session ended I would hide in between the seats of my car and drink at least a liter of water! It was a sacrifice that I felt I had to make in order to show my cultural sensitivity, but believe me, it wasn't easy!

My contributions to the system of play at Safari Sports Club included a more specific use of wingers and the introduction of first and second post crosses, the increased mobility of the front players, turning defense into attack, and variations on set pieces like throw-ins, corner kicks and free kicks.

All the teams in Tanzania played the same 4-3-3 formation, and with a little bit of creativity and tweaking in how we set ourselves up, it was rather easy to dominate matches and create more chances than the opposition. Similar to what I had already done in Swaziland, I introduced the concept of a striker causing positional confusion amongst the opposing defenders. In the good old traditional way of defending, one of the two central defenders was a man-marker, while the other was a sweeper. I showed my teammates how easy it is to turn these two defenders into all kinds of knots by operating as a striker right in between them. When I first demonstrated this in our own practices, the two central defenders ended up shouting at each other whenever neither was in my vicinity, and I still smile at the confused looks on their faces. So soon enough we moved

63

from man-marking to zonal defense, while our own central strikers quickly mastered the art of confusion. Slowly but surely a system was developed in which the skills of each player complemented the others.

As we started to play so-called friendly matches, which I prefer to call practice matches or pre-season matches, the team started to grow, and it was clear that we had the potential to do well.

The strength of the team became most apparent at the end of December and in early January, when we won the East and Central African Championship on our home turf in Dar Es Salaam. It was a joyous occasion, a nail-biter until the final minute of extra time, when we managed to score the only goal of the final. First tournament, first title. My career in Tanzanian football could hardly have started any better!

After this major tournament we played a high number of games, both in Dar Es Salaam and in Dodoma, and most games were rather easily won. In my second game of the new year, I reached a milestone when I scored my first competitive goal for Safari Sports Club in a 3-1 victory over UEB—the Uganda Electricity Board team—which was also preparing for one of the African Cup tournaments. You won't be surprised to read that I scored that goal through a 25 metre left-footed shot which was at first blocked by the goalkeeper, and which I managed to put into the net at the second attempt. You will however be shocked to read that on the rebound I actually kicked the ball and scored with my right foot! Up to today, it is one of the very few right-footed goals that I remember myself scoring in any sort of competitive football match!

My teammates and I celebrated that goal with a Bebeto-like dance right in front of the main stand, which had the fans cheering on their feet! This same celebration was shown on the local TV news throughout the week, but it was too early for me to understand the accompanying comments in Kiswahili.

The media reports about this *mzungu* were usually quite positive. I had by now been given the nickname "Mark Fish of Safari Sports Club" after the South-African defender who had made a big impression during the African Nations' Cup Finals which South Africa—with Mark Fish—won in front of their own fans at the start of 1996. Mark Fish was one of only two white players on the South African national team, the *Bafana Bafana*. Because of the fact that he had performed so well for his team, I assumed that—by being compared with him—the Tanzanian reporters quite liked what I did in the field of play. In one of the Kiswahili papers, a special feature appeared in which my new nickname was officially launched.

STAR OF THE WEEK : Peter Mulder— Safari Sports Club's own "Mark Fish"

BY

OUR REPORTER

It was obvious during the recently held African Nations Cup that Mark Fish was the delight of South-Africa's football lovers and the star amongst the twenty-two squad members. The images on our local TV channel, ITV, clearly showed how the fans cheered vigorously whenever he touched the ball, and chants of "Fiiiish" were all over the airwaves. Mark Fish also displayed amazing silky skills that delighted the millions of fans in the stadiums and around the football-mad country.

As it sometimes happens in football, one player in the team can stand out and enthrall the fans with his style of play and his skills. In Belgium's Peter Mulder, Safari Sports Club seems to have found its own Mark Fish.

Peter has great experience and tremendous talent and will be a great asset to his new team. If guided by a good coach, he could well turn out for his national team also.

His talents were on display during a recent match between Safari Sports Club and Uganda's Electricity Board team at the Dar Es Salaam National Stadium.

Whenever he received a pass from one of his teammates, he took a very short time to control the ball and play the next pass. He never delayed as if he wanted to smoke a cigarette before deciding what to do next. He played the passes at the right time and into the correct spaces for his teammates to receive the ball.

When he was not in possession, he made intelligent runs and moved into positions that allowed him to receive the ball, as modern football dictates. A complete innovation in our football is that after his passes, he offers himself for a return pass in order to maintain possession of the ball within the team.

Peter also showed goal-scoring perfection as he was lethal in one-against-one situations as well as at the end of a great team combination. However, these were not the only characteristics that endeared him to the fans.

They liked the way in which he teamed up with the other players, and the respect he showed to the players and the fans around the stadium. Several times during the match the fans shouted "Mzungu, mzungu", and each time he acknowledged their support. The fans also cheered wildly when he displayed some skills usually reserved for African players, such as passing the ball with his heel, or playing it between his opponent's legs.

A few minutes before the end of the game, and when it was clear that Peter had used up all of his stamina, his coaches wanted to bring on a replacement. As soon as the fans noticed this, they started to shout at the bench, and another player was substituted instead.

It is certain that amongst the 480 players that have been registered by the various clubs for the upcoming Premier League, Peter "Mark Fish" Mulder will stand out throughout the season. All the Premier League teams around the country are certainly starting to shiver, but they will find at least some consolation in the fact that Mulder may not be able to play in some of his club's away games.

I hoped to live up to the pressure of being the local Mark Fish, and I worked hard in order not to disappoint the thousands of fans who followed our progress day in, day out, and who attended our training sessions and matches.

We were preparing ourselves intensively for our first African Champions League assignment, a clash with Primeiro de Agosto, the strongest club in Angola. We felt confident that we could beat this team, and we all worked hard towards achieving victory against the Angolans.

Fast forward to a more recent past.

THIRTEEN

Ilala District, Dar Es Salaam, a few days later

"John Fashanu is in town. He's coming to watch our game this afternoon!"

My teammates were quite excited. Most of them dreamt about one day playing professional football in Europe, and they believed that the visit of John Fashanu, the former England and Wimbledon striker, would help their cause. In fact, John was here as a UNESCO Ambassador, which meant that he was certainly not here to try and spot footballing talent. But anyway, he was going to be the guest of honor at our practice match against Kipanga of Zanzibar at the Karume Memorial Stadium in the city.

We got changed at the Safari Sports Club house in Kariakoo, sorted out the team's line-up, and then took the short drive to the stadium. There we warmed up for a couple of minutes, and then we all lined up in order to be introduced to the guest of honor. Our team captain, Athumani Abdallah, walked the line with John Fashanu while introducing each player. When they reached me, Athumani, whose English was not too good, said:

"This P-Peter, from B-Bulgaria."
"Make that Belgium, John. Pleased to meet you", I said.
"Pleased to meet you too, big man", John replied.

John walked on, and neither of us knew that an hour or so later fate would strike a cruel and fatal blow to someone's football career.

The game started well for us, and by half-time we were leading 2-0. The fans were delirious, we were toying with our opponents from the Spice Islands, and most of the tactical plays that we had been practicing started to materialize on the field. During the second half we went 3-0 up, and a few minutes later I suddenly met the end of my career as a top-level football player.

One of my teammates played a through-ball, and I ran at full speed in order to try and reach the ball before Kipanga's central defender and right back. They came from two different directions, and after I narrowly beat them to the ball, they both 'sandwiched' me, meaning that they both made contact with my right leg from two different angles.

For a brief moment everything in my head went dark, and the first thing I remember after landing on the gravel was the excruciating pain in my right knee. I have never been someone who fakes pain or injury, but that time I could do nothing but stay down on the ground. I tried to get up, but realised that my right knee had completely pulled up and that my right leg was bent backwards as far as it possibly could. I was totally unable to even slightly stretch my leg. It is a very discomforting experience when your brain tells your body to do something and your body can't carry out the task. Paralysis must be an extremely frustrating and hard-to-accept condition, if my experience from that day in April was anything to go by.

Upon seeing that I didn't get up, the team's head coach and doctor came running onto the field to check the extent of the damage. I was grateful that the doctor did not simply apply a greasy sponge and told me to 'get up'. He took his time to assess the damage, and the look in his eyes didn't bode too well.

Very slowly we managed to stretch the leg. It took about three full minutes to do so, but once the leg was stretched again I felt a little bit better. I managed to get up and took a few steps to check if my leg could support me. Most of the pain had now gone, and when the coach said:

"Come off the field, we will substitute you so than you can rest",

I replied:

"No, it's OK, I think I can continue."

There were only a few minutes of the game left, and I managed to play out the match. However, something in my right knee told me that some internal damage had been done. There was some sort of a burning feeling inside my knee, and after the game I walked to my car to go and get changed again.

About fifteen minutes after the accident I noticed that my knee had started to swell, and I started to get worried.

It is a well-known fact that knees are very susceptible to football injuries, and I also knew that knee problems often mean a long injury lay-off for football players. In the days before non-invasive surgery and arthroscopy, many a player had seen his mobility seriously affected by knee injuries, and there were even worse scenarios.

Surprisingly, before I left the stadium for home, none of the Safari Sports Club officials came to see me or asked me how I was. Was this a sign of things to come?

I drove home and cleaned out my knee, which had sustained an open wound when I fell on the gravel of the football ground. Later that evening I was resting in front of the television with my swelling knee in an ice-pack, and I saw on one of the local TV stations a report on John Fashanu's visit and his presence at our game. And there it was, a shot of the Zanzibari tackle, followed by a close-up of the *mzungu* lying on the ground with the coach and the doctor around him. I managed to record the report on video, and now I can watch the final minute of my competitive football career as often as I want. It doesn't make happy viewing, I can tell you that!

The next day, the nurse at my place of employment saw me walk with difficulty and asked me what had happened. I told her about the events from the previous day, and she advised me to go see a specialist at the Muhimbili Orthopaedic Institute. I visited the hospital that same afternoon, and I was told by the resident German doctor that I had most probably damaged my meniscus. We took some X-rays in a machine that might have been retrieved from a U-boot just after the Second World War, but these X-rays didn't show anything special. I was given a splint, some anti-inflammatory tablets and a week's rest. Now that I reflect back on this episode, the rather arrogant and very unfriendly German doctor didn't do much more for me than apply a greasy sponge and tell me to 'get up'—just like my long-lost Ghanaian friend in Swaziland used to do a few years earlier.

After a week the swelling had gone down a bit, and I started to do some physiotherapy at the hospital in order to try and regain full flexibility in my knee. The German doctor, who may well have been an exile from the former East-Germany and who had serious people-management problems, simply could not correctly diagnose the problem. She had a look at the knee and referred me to a local physiotherapist, a Tanzanian doctor that she had trained, and who turned out to know as much about physiotherapy as the mechanic who looked after the hospital's decrepit ambulance . . .

During one of our first sessions, he asked me to sit on the edge of a table and shuffle my legs forwards and backwards as fast as I could. When I told him that this was rather painful and that there was a high level of discomfort in the knee, he replied that he was "just trying something out". The few pseudo-physiotherapy sessions that I underwent had very little effect, but as with all injuries, after a while the body has its own way of getting a bit better. The progress was slow, but after about two months I could start swimming again. Slowly but surely I got back into cycling and walking, then running as well. At first it appeared that the injury had healed, but when I started to play social football again, my knee would often make all sorts of abnormal clicking noises like bones cracking all the time, and at times it even felt like the knee dislocated. One thing was for sure : the problem with my knee had not been solved.

I continued to play social football, simply because I could not tell myself that I shouldn't play football anymore. However, after every game my knee would swell up again, and there was always pain. Eventually I decided that I would ask a more qualified specialist to look at my knee, and one summer I took advantage of the fact that I was in London for some courses to go and see one of England's most reputable knee surgeons.

This doctor asked me to lie down on a bed, he put his hands under my right knee, and he told me after five seconds:

"There is nothing wrong with your meniscus. The problem is that your ACL is gone."

"My what?"

"Your anterior cruciate ligament. The one that goes right through your knee."

"Are you sure?" I asked.

"Well, pretty sure. That's certainly what it looks like. We'll get the confirmation from a scan."

Two days later I underwent an MRI scan, and the doctor's diagnosis was confirmed. The ligament in my right knee had snapped when I was fouled during that fateful game against Kipanga, and since that day, more than a year before my trip to London, both ends of the ligament had started to disintegrate. The scan showed that there was hardly any ligament matter left in my knee.

I went back to the doctor with the results of the scan, and he said:

"You have two options. Either you have an ACL reconstruction operation soon, or you continue like this and risk getting arthritis at a later stage. If you have an operation, you will be unable to play football for about one year. In the longer term however, the operation is the better option. If all goes well, then your knee will be back to about 90 to 95% of its capacity."

The doctor had easily convinced me that an operation was the better option, and we agreed that I would go back to London the next summer in order to have the operation.

When I returned to Tanzania, I continued to play social football, through the pain and the little noises. I simply couldn't say goodbye to the game that had dominated my life up to that point, and playing with pain was still better than not playing at all. In the knowledge that the following summer I would have the ACL reconstruction, I didn't think that I could be doing a lot of permanent damage to the knee by playing social football three times per week.

At this point it is important to inform the reader that during all this time, since the day on which I sustained the knee injury, not one single official or player of Safari Sports Club ever bothered to come and see me or call me to ask how I was. I had been completely abandoned by the club, and very disappointingly so. Again, this could have been an indication of things to come . . .

The next summer I went back to London as planned, and I had my ligament reconstruction. The operation took about two hours, and I spent one full week in hospital. On my crutches and with my right knee in a brace, I hobbled to Heathrow Airport and boarded the flight back to Tanzania. A friendly flight attendant took pity on me and realized that I could not bend my knee enough to sit in an economy class seat, so she duly upgraded me to business class! I flirted with the idea of using that brace on many more flights for years to come, but have never actually put that brilliant thought into practice. Ten hours after leaving London, I landed back in Dar Es Salaam, and wondered what the next few months would bring. I certainly wasn't capable of playing top-level football with Safari Sports Club anymore, and I wasn't particularly looking forward to the many hours of physiotherapy that awaited me either.

FOURTEEN

National Stadium, Dar Es Salaam, several months later

"Perdone, Señor Fullone, ¿ tendría Usted algunos minutos esta tarde para hablar conmigo?"
"Sí, claro."
"¿ Dónde podemos vernos?"
"Venga al Hotel Kilimanjaro esta noche a las ocho."
"Muy bien. Gracias, y hasta luego."

("Excuse me, Mr Fullone, would you have a few minutes to talk with me?
Yes, of course.
Where can we meet?
Come to the Kilimanjaro Hotel tonight at eight.
OK. Thank you, and see you later.")

OSCAR FULLONE, THE ARGENTINIAN COACH of the Ivory Coast's ASEC Abidjan, was in town when his team came to play against Ndovu Football Club in an African Champions' League match. During the long road to recovery from my knee injury and surgery, I had started thinking about how I could get myself involved in football coaching in one of the local clubs. I realised fully well that my playing days at the highest level were over, but I could not say goodbye to the game that I loved so much. I wanted to keep the adrenaline flowing, and I felt that I could contribute my experience and my understanding of the local culture to help in the development of Tanzanian football. One starting point was to find out which steps I could take in order to become a qualified coach in Africa. Surely Oscar Fullone would be able to provide me with a lot of valuable information, as he had already been a coach in Africa for many years. He also understood my European background, as he had been a player and then a coach and manager in England, before trying his luck with some of the biggest and most successful clubs in Africa.

That evening I went to see Mr Fullone at his hotel, and this meeting can be considered the moment when I embarked on my new life as a senior football coach.

"Look, Mr Fullone, I know that you have achieved a lot as a foreign coach in Africa. I have played football for many years on this continent, and I have now come to the point where I want to instil my knowledge and my experience into the younger generation. I am driven by ambition and passion, and of course I want to go the same way as you. So what would you advise me to do in order to get started? There is no point in me waiting for a FIFA coaching course to be held here, because that could take several years. And besides, I feel that my footballing experience is extensive, and that I can put it to good use for any club that is interested. I have had excellent coaches myself, and since I also am a professional teacher, I believe that I have the skills to teach football to young and upcoming players."

"You are absolutely right. There is no coaching school in the world where they teach you what you have learned as a player and from the coaches that you have had. Coaching courses are very good to give you ideas and to show you how to structure your season and your planning, but each team and every player is different, so as a coach you are dealing with individuals rather than with 'the average player'. The cultural context that you work in is also very important, and you need to work with the strengths of the individuals and the culture, while trying to develop and minimize the weaknesses."

So what do you suggest I do, as I will still be in Tanzania for at least a couple of years?"

"Do you have any contacts with local clubs?"

"Yes, I have played for a Tanzanian Premier League club for several years, until I injured my knee and had to stop playing."

"Well, with your experience and enthusiasm, the best thing to do would be to throw yourself in a club, and to take it from there. Obviously people are not going to come and ask you to coach their club, as they do not know your coaching skills and abilities. But you can go forward, become involved in your old club again, and show them what you can do."

"Do you think that might work? You know, clubs here are often poorly run, and I may be a bit too demanding in terms of material support and care for the players. Often there are also money problems, power struggles and so on."

"It can work. Show them that you have ideas and initiative, and don't let anyone stop you in your ambition. This is a hard world, but if you can make it clear that you are working for the benefit of the club and in the interest of the players and the fans, then even the leaders of the club will realise that good things are happening and that your contributions are valuable. And between you and me, when the leaders of the clubs in this part of the world realise that there is a quick buck to be made, you will probably receive all the support you ask for . . . Don't ask me for details, but just know that I speak from personal experience."

"Well, I expect that there will be a lot of resistance at first, but I also know that I can make a contribution, and I think that I'll give it a try."

Later on in our meeting, Mr Fullone showed me some of the achievements at ASEC that he had been involved in and that he was proud of. They included a club newspaper which sells 25,000 copies every week, the construction of a sports complex on the outskirts of the city of Abidjan (ASEC now has its own stadium, which receives about 50,000 spectators for every match the team plays!), and others. This is also the same club that has produced top class footballers such as Kolo and Yaya Touré, Salomon Kalou and Didier Zokora. Mr Fullone certainly knew what he was talking about. And if it could work for him, then why wouldn't it work for me? If it could work in the Ivory Coast, then why not in Tanzania?

Mr Fullone and I said our goodbyes, I wished him well with the rest of the competition (which his club eventually won), and he wished me well with my coaching career. We promised each other that one day we would meet again in the field of play, hopefully casting our respective teams against each other in international competition.

After this meeting I started to think about where my opportunity to start coaching would be. I was in a foreign land and had never really been involved in a small club. Not only would it have been difficult to find a small club that would be interested in my services, it would also have been very hard to implement any kind of developmental plan and get any kind of substantial support in an obscure club that nobody had ever heard of. I toyed with the idea of starting my own club, but that would have meant working our way up from the lowest league divisions. I didn't have the time for this. I wanted to make an impact right at the top levels of the game, right there where it mattered, and right there where people would notice. In order to be heard and in order to ensure that I would give myself the best possible chance at success, I had to aim for the biggest clubs in the city, not the smallest.

Dar Es Salaam is a vast city with huge potential for promoting and merchandising a football club. Every inhabitant favours either Safari Sports Club or Ndovu Football Club. However, throughout their existence and despite some small successes, neither club had ever seriously tried to get their fans involved in the running of the club. Merchandising was virtually unknown. Across the city, one could spot hundreds, if not thousands, of football fans wearing soccer jerseys—but none of Safari Sports Club or Ndovu Football Club. The most popular jerseys for sale and worn in the streets were those of AC Milan's George Weah, England's David Beckham and Brazil's Ronaldinho. I am sure that nowadays Lionel Messi's jersey, be it from Barcelona or from Argentina, is a much-coveted possession. Pretty much every Barclays Premier League team and every Serie A team, as well as the traditional powerhouses from Madrid, Barcelona, Milan and Munich, sell thousands of replica outfits in the streets of Dar Es Salaam. Whether these clubs know this is anyone's guess, and whether they benefit from these shirts sales at all is extremely doubtful. But what was very clear was that there was a huge market for merchandising a Tanzanian club. I knew that if I wanted to be accepted as a coach by one of the local clubs, I would have to do more than simply show players how to master the *tikatika* of Barcelona in the field of play. By improving the training and health conditions of the players, I knew that increased performance would logically follow. I wanted to present my club with a strategic plan to help them develop and 'take that next step'. Providing a club with the chance to sustain itself financially, without having to depend on gate collections or small contributions from a couple of half-interested individuals, would undoubtedly lead to greater success and a better vision for the future. I needed to find a club that gave me optimal access to the wallets of its fans in this city of a few million people.

The next day I tried to make concrete plans to throw myself into a coaching career. It was inconceivable to me that I would not succeed in some way. After all, once I set my mind to something, then I am determined to achieve my goals, whatever it takes. I've said it before, failure was never an option.

So I started to look at the opportunities available to me. In a sense it was a blessing in disguise that my former club, Safari Sports Club, was in a lot of internal turmoil. There were a number of 'committees' which all claimed to be the one in charge, and at the end of the day nobody was really taking care of the club anymore. The days of our Chairman, Mr Simkola, had since ended. Some of the members of his Executive Committee, one that had been democratically and legally elected, had either passed away or resigned 'for personal reasons'. Two members, the former Treasurer and his Assistant, had been sacked from their posts when it was found that they had been funnelling substantial amounts of club funds into their own pockets. Both these officials were now involved in a number of court cases to try and get reinstated—or avoid going to jail. In a nutshell, there was no Executive Committee, and the running of the club was mainly in the hands of the Council of Elders (*Baraza la Wazee*).

During my enforced absence from the club, I had been following these political and structural developments from a distance. Even though none of the club officials ever bothered to enquire about my health or about the progress during the recovery period, I did maintain an interest in how my teammates were doing, both on the field and in their personal lives.

I met up with some of them during the course of the year, and tried my best to get one or two of them to go for trials in Belgium. I had maintained good contacts with my former club, the Royal Antwerp Football Club, and there was a genuine interest to have some of my Tanzanian teammates go to Europe to try and obtain a professional contract. I had always been convinced that some of them were good enough to make it as a professional, it was just a matter of ensuring that they were in the right frame of mind to live and work in Belgium, and that they could show the required amount of self-discipline. Some of them gave me videotapes showing matches of the national team that they had played in, but despite my best efforts, the Tanzanian market somehow did not appeal enough to my contacts in Belgium. In order for a greater interest to be created, the country and its national team would have to do a bit more in the world of continental football. So this gave me an extra incentive to help my adopted home country in its quest for better football recognition.

My attention turned back towards Safari Sports Club. Another season had ended, the prizes had been handed out, and the annual round of political wrangling in the clubs had resumed. Safari Sports Club had once again won the Nyerere Cup and had consequently qualified for the African Cup Winners' Cup. Not all was gloom and doom at the club, but there were serious issues that needed fixing. In the Premier League the team had finished a distant fifth, and that was simply unacceptable for a club of its stature. The Cup win was a mere consolation prize, and all in all the season had been a poor one. At the end of the season, everyone started to blame everyone else, and the reporters had a field day. The coaches had left the club in search of greener pastures, and there was talk of some of the senior players leaving also. When there were no matches to report on, the press boys either found or created stories about various factions of the leadership, about those who were in power and those who wanted to be in power, and about how the players were used as pawns in these political games. I was about to learn a whole lot more about the intricacies of football leadership in Tanzania!

FIFTEEN

THROUGH THE MEDIA I FOUND out that there was going to be a members' meeting during the first week of December. The Council of Elders had called this meeting in order to discuss the plans for the upcoming season with all the club members who were up to date with their payments. The Club claimed to have a membership of well over 25,000 supporters, but when the time came to pay the yearly subscription, the number of fans seemed to be significantly lower than that. Cash was a rare commodity in Tanzania, and when faced with the choice between paying for their club membership or buying a couple of cans of beer, the overwhelming minority typically chose to renew their allegiance to Safari Sports Club.

The meeting promised to be a momentous occasion. Never before had the Council of Elders been tasked with running a members' meeting. This was normally the prerogative of the Executive Committee, comprising the Chairman, the Vice-Chairman, the Secretary General, the Assistant Secretary General, the Public Relations Officer, the Treasurer and the Assistant Treasurer. As explained earlier, not all of them were with us any longer, and some were fighting allegations of embezzlement and corruption. They understandably preferred not to show themselves in front of those whose money was now nowhere to be found. The Council of Elders, or in Kiswahili the 'Baraza la Wazee', was there to try and defuse the tension that had been brewing for a couple of months. Little did I realise that this was only the start of my involvement in club politics.

When I saw the newspaper report announcing the members' meeting, I soon realised that this was my opportunity to introduce myself to the Elders and to offer my services to the club. I also thought that meeting with a large group of members would bring a certain level of enthusiasm and support from those who, at the end of the day, are rather powerful when it comes to the running of the club. So that's what I did.

The meeting was due to start at 10 am on the next Sunday morning, and I went to the club house at around 9.45 am to find . . . nobody. After my long absence, I failed to remember what 10 am means in the Tanzanian football world . . .

Anyway, I waited for a while and at around 10.45 two members of the Council of Elders arrived. They were involved in a very intense conversation, and went straight into their office without noticing me there. I hadn't been seen at the club for about a year, and wasn't really surprised that they did not immediately recognise me . . . The Elders always preferred to remain in the background, and most of them hardly ever attended games anymore.

I didn't know them either, so when they entered one of the offices I asked one of the ladies who were roaming around the building who they were. I was told that they were Mr Malazi, the Chairman of the Elders' Council, and Mr Aly, the Vice Chairman. Exactly the people I wanted to see!

I followed the *Wazee* and knocked on the door through which they had just walked. A friendly *Karibu*! sounded through the door. I entered and asked if I could have a few minutes of their precious time.

"*Karibu sana*. How can we help you?"

"*Ahsante*. I don't know if you remember me, but I am a former player of Safari Sports Club. I played for the team until last year, and had to quit because of an injury."

"Peter!"

"Yes, that's me."

"Yes, I remember you. I still remember you scoring that wonderful goal against a Ugandan team at the National Stadium. How have you been?"

"Well, working hard and playing a lot of social football."

"And how is your leg now?"

"Much better, thank you. But I won't be able to play again—too risky after the operation."

"*Pole sana*! (Very sorry) So, what can we do for you?"

"Well, lately I have been watching the developments at the club, and I must admit that it pains me to see my former team doing so badly. It looks like there is a lot of work to be done, and I am here today to offer my services. In the absence of an elected leadership, I think that I can assist the club both on and off the field. I bring with me a lot of footballing experience, I know quite a bit about Tanzanian football, and at the same time I have quite a number of ideas as to how this club can be developed and turned into a more professional outfit."

"This sounds very interesting. It is true that the club is now under the supervision of the Council of Elders, but we don't really want to involve ourselves too much with the daily running of the club. We are awaiting elections which should take place in the not too distant future, but with the ongoing court case we don't really know. This case, in which the club's Treasurer and Assistant Treasurer are contesting their sacking, has been going on for a very long time now, and it is impossible to predict when it will be over. However, we believe that elections are on the way, and therefore we have agreed to run the club in the meantime."

Well, I am prepared to help you if you so wish. Have you contacted any coaches so far?"

"Yes, we have been in touch with Mr Kimora. Do you remember him?"

"Of course! He was my coach here. We had a very good relationship, and it would be great to work with him. When will he start working?"

"We are still discussing some issues with him. He is currently employed by Kahawa United, so we are trying to find a way to bring him back to Safari Sports Club. We are hopeful that he will come, but we don't know yet when exactly he will arrive back in Dar Es Salaam."

"And how about players? Do we have any for the coming season?"

"No, we don't have any. We need to go through a screening exercise, and recruit a complete new squad. We have a couple of players on our list from last year, but we can't be sure that they will be with us next season . . . You know, during the off-season, they sometimes disappear, or they go and talk with other clubs. We will have to wait and see who shows up when pre-season training starts. In the meantime, we need to start recruiting some young and promising players."

"Right, so when is this recruitment drive going to start?"

"It should start soon, but we don't have anyone to do it."

"I am offering to do it for you."

"*Ahsante sana*! But what's the deal?"

"No no, there is no deal. I don't ask for anything from the club or from the leadership, only that you allow me to do the recruitment and training sessions, and that you let me devise ways as to how to develop the club. I ask you that you give me the freedom to bring a slightly more professional flavour to the club, and that I select players who respond well to the levels of responsibility and commitment that I will be demanding."

The Chairman had a quick discussion in Kiswahili with his companion, who nodded in agreement. At this moment, the tea lady entered the room and offered the three of us a nice cup of hot Chai Bora.

"*Ahsante*. One sugar please."

"Peter, your offer is perfectly acceptable to us."

It's important to inform the reader here that my ambition was to help the club and at the same time to develop my coaching and management skills. There was never a financial aspect to our deal, and there has never been talk about any other type of remuneration. I was happy to be able to test my expertise and my coaching ability, and the club's Elders were happy that someone was prepared to help when the club, and especially its finances, were at an all-time low. So we all felt that we should at least give it a try.

"I will tell the members in today's meeting that you have come forward to offer your services to the club. I am sure that they will all be thrilled."

"Fine. And please give me a chance to also explain how the members can help the club recapture its lost glory."

"*Hakuna matata*! No problem. Let's go upstairs, so that we can start the meeting."

It was by now close to 12 o'clock, and some 350 members had gathered on the top floor of the club house. When the *Wazee* and I walked in, quite a few members seemed to recognise me, and the *karibus* went up from all corners. The meeting room was hot. Very hot. There were no windows where the windows should have been, and because the electricity bill hadn't been paid in months, the standing fans stood silently in the corners, unable to at least get some air circulation going. Standing against the wall I also recognised a few reporters and two cameramen. This was indeed going to be an important meeting for everyone involved and interested in the welfare of Safari Sports Club, and we could not have picked a better moment to launch my coaching career.

Mr Malazi went through the agenda of the meeting, which was dominated by the court cases and the dangerous split that had occurred along political lines. A number of fans were loyal to the suspended leadership, presumably because they also benefitted financially in some way. The majority of the members though rejoiced at the forced removal of the suspended leadership, and were looking forward to better times. So the Chairman went on to talk about the plans for the coming season. The whole meeting was conducted in Kiswahili, but I understood every word when he started to explain my presence at the meeting. When Mr Malazi announced that the *mzungu* had come back to help his former club, the hall went into delirium as the members all stood up and wildly cheered my return. I knew from that moment that I could count on the members' cooperation. I decided to seize the opportunity to explain that I was not going to be able to overhaul the club by myself, and that everybody's support was needed. I stood up and explained, half in Kiswahili and half in English.

"Dear friends, our club is not in a good state. It hurts me to see the depth to which this once proud club has fallen. I have decided to try and contribute my bit, rather than watching Safari Sports Club waste another year because of internal problems. I have a pretty good idea as to how we can improve the club's condition, but I need your help. You have to assist me in my work, you have to ensure that there is unity amongst us, you must cease the fighting, the conflicts and the political mess that is currently reigning here. There are a lot of issues that need to be resolved, and there are a lot of problems that need to be fixed. Each and every one of you has a role to play, so please do not simply stand by and watch others do all the work. I will give my all to the club in order to help us forward, but we all need to pitch in and contribute. I can not be everything to everyone. The only way forward is the way of unity and cooperation. Only then can we restore the lost pride of Safari Sports Club as the number one club in East Africa! *Safari juu*! (Safari up!)"

"Safari juu!", shouted the members.

The room was clearly getting hotter, and I decided to seize the moment.

"We must let the courts decide what needs to happen with the outgoing leadership, and not interfere with their work. Let us look forward rather than backwards. Let us move on from past mistakes, and make this club great again. Safari Sports Club is the only club in Tanzania that has the potential and the support to be an international ambassador for Tanzanian football. Individually, we can dream. Together, we can turn these dreams into reality. *Safari juu*!"

"Safari juu! Safari juu!"

"Our first task is to create a strong team for the coming season. Please come and watch us during the recruitment period. Come and talk with us, and if you know any promising players who may be able to strengthen the team, let us know. With your help, we can build the strongest possible team, and we will dominate every tournament that we compete in next year! *Safari juu*!"

"Safari juu! Safari juu!"

"To those of you who work for the media. Please help us by focusing on the development of the club and the team, and please stop creating or propagating stories about our problems and challenges. With your positive coverage, more and more fans will support us, and we can turn Safari Sports Club into a truly professional club. *Safari juu*?"

"Safari juu! Safari juu! Safari juu!"

Loud cheers, of course. The members were by now out of their chairs and punching their fists in the air. They liked the language they were hearing, and the meeting ended in very good spirits. Numerous members came up to me and shook my hand, thanking me and showing me the thumbs up.

"Ahsante rafiki, ahsante sana!" (Thank you, my friend, thank you very much)

After the meeting I asked Mr Malazi and Mr Aly when I could start work, and they told me that they'd let me know as soon as possible. The recruitment drive was about to begin, and I'd be partly responsible for it.

The next morning, the newspapers showed that they shared in the excitement. The Daily News of that day reported on the members' support for the decisions made by the Elders' Committee, as well as my introduction as the new club coach.

Safari members back up elders

BY CORRESPONDENT

Dar Es Salaam's Safari Sports Club members have unanimously supported the club's Elders Council's efforts to register players for the forthcoming league season. The 248-plus members who attended the meeting at the club house along Msimbazi Road in the city yesterday roared in unison 'yes!' when the Council's Chairman, Mr Malazi, asked them if they supported the agenda and the plans of the Council or not.

The meeting had been called by the Elders' Council to clarify various matters pertaining to the club's development and iron out some issues raised by a few members who were not happy with the club's state of affairs.

Earlier, Mr Malazi told the fully packed club hall that the club was facing a trying time and that only solidarity and strong unity by members will save it from collapse. He urged members to support the Council as that was the sole body that can get the club out of its crisis, at least for now.

Meanwhile, former Safari Sports Club international player, Peter Mulder, a Belgian, will be part of the club's panel of coaches to recruit new players for Safari Sports Club at a stadium yet to be identified in a few days to come.

Mulder, who is also a teacher at a local international school, attended yesterday's club meeting and was introduced to the cheering crowd by Mr Malazi who informed them that Mulder will perform the job to show solidarity with his former team.

Speaking to the members, Mulder said he felt pity that Safari Sports Club was locked by a serious crisis and requested members' support in their bid to recruit players for the next season.

A few days later my phone rang, and Mr Malazi told me that the first practice session would take place at the Tanzania Cigarette Company (TCC) ground in Chang'ombe, on the outskirts of Dar Es Salaam, the next afternoon.

"I'll be there! How is the recruitment exercise being set up?"

"You will meet with Mr Kimora, who has now arrived back in the city, and who has agreed to help us out on a voluntary basis, at least until we find a sponsor to help us cover expenses. You can discuss the recruitment procedures with Mr Kimora, and some of our members have already brought some players from upcountry to come and show what they can do. You will probably find about 15 players from outside Dar Es Salaam at the stadium tomorrow."

"Sounds good!"

"We will also announce in the local press that players who want to be considered for Safari Sports Club must report at the TCC ground tomorrow afternoon by 3.30 pm . . ."

"*Mzungu* time?"

"Yes, *mzungu* time."

"Fine, I will be there."

"We will also try to be there, if we can find transport."

"I look forward to seeing Mr Kimora again. Oh, and could I ask you to please confirm my appointment in writing? I will then share your letter with my employer, who has already told me that he is very supportive of my intention to help out the team, and who has just become a Safari Sports Club fan himself!"

"*Hakuna matata*. We will send you a letter of appointment shortly."

"*Ahsante sana*, and see you soon again."

Now I was even more convinced that things were going to work out. I knew that Mr Kimora would be a great colleague and his experience in Tanzanian football, both as a player and as a top-level coach, would provide me with a free apprenticeship. I could not ask for more, and got ready for the first selection session.

The next day I would have my first session as a coach of Safari Sports Club. Mr Fullone's advice, to throw myself into a top club and get involved, had worked out extremely quickly . . . I could hardly wait to get started.

SIXTEEN

TCC grounds, Chang'ombe, the next day

I HAD NO IDEA WHAT WAS in store for me over the next few months and years, but one thing was for sure : I was going to try and help Safari Sports Club with all the means at my disposal : creative ideas, experience, through studying other clubs, and by talking to insiders. It was clear that the situation at the club could not get any worse, and I also liked the fact that we could select players and build a team from scratch.

When a coach or manager walks into a new job, he usually finds a squad already selected by his predecessors, and he has to make do with that squad. He is not usually able to overhaul his complete squad, and has to wait until the end of the season to make some changes. Mr Kimora and I were in a privileged position : the Chairman told us that we only had about 8 players that remained from the previous season, and even some of those were rumoured to be leaving. Each year during the off-season, a large percentage of the players who had played at least one season in the Premier League marketed themselves to a number of clubs. Since there were no professional contracts to be gotten, all these players tried to get signing-on fees from new clubs. Some of our own national team players would approach rival clubs and ask if they could sign for them. Of course, they would not do so for free. They asked, at times, hefty signing-on fees, not unlike transfer fees, but in this case all the money would remain with the players. Some players went as far as signing registration forms with three or four different teams, and collecting their signing-on fees from all three or four clubs. This inevitably led to all sorts of conflicts on the day that the clubs were required to submit their squad lists to the National Football Association.

There were, with monotonous frequency, players who appeared on the squad lists of several clubs at the same time. On rare occasions, the clubs themselves managed to sort out the conflicts amongst themselves, usually involving some transfer fees to help support the Chairman's family. But at times, the double or triple registration of a player also led to never-ending court cases, and in the end it was the player himself who missed out on his share of the gate collection from the matches. Some players were effectively out of the game for a full season, and with their reputation in tatters, few clubs jumped up and down in order to sign them the next year.

The big winners in this annual chaos were of course the officials of the Football Association. For every registration case that they needed to decide on, they received a substantial sitting allowance as well as a couple of plastic bags from the interested parties. And in the cases where a player was eventually registered with one team rather than with the other, I am sure that the size of the plastic bag was the main deciding factor.

Mr Kimora and I would have to wait and see which ones of our senior players, many of whom I had of course played with myself, would return for pre-season training. We agreed that we would choose about 20 to 25 new players, and then merge the most needed ones with the returning players. We put all the pressure of finding the right players on ourselves, so no excuses then for getting it wrong . . . or so we thought.

I arrived at the TCC grounds at about 3 pm, and a few minutes later Mr Kimora also arrived. He had been told by the Chairman that I would be joining him, and he extended a very warm *karibu* to me. I was equally happy to see him again, and we set out to start our job as 'recruiters'. We briefly discussed our plan for the day, and we called the players. At first glance it looked like there were around fifty interested young men. However, once all the players had gathered around and come out of the club house and from behind the trees, there must have been close to a hundred pairs of eyes staring at us. Clearly, my appeal in the Members' meeting, for members to encourage some young talents to show up for trials, had had its desired effect. Surely we were going to find some promising players in this group.

They were all wearing very different and mismatched football outfits. A red jersey of Manchester United combined with the sky-blue shorts of Lazio SC, or a claret and blue Barcelona FC shirt combined with the bright yellow away shorts of Chelsea FC. Some of the players were wearing socks, mostly with gigantic holes in them, and a few of them even had football boots. Most though were wearing tattered running shoes that had probably covered the length of the Equator twice, with the soles hanging loose, or with the big toe poking through, or without laces, or simply four or five sizes too big. I also noticed a number of players who were not wearing any kind of footwear at all. We clearly had our work cut out here, and I realised that if we were going to achieve any kind of success with this club, we would have to start from scratch. This thought filled me with excitement, as Mr Kimora and I would be able to start developing the team in accordance with our own beliefs and strategies.

Mr Kimora started by introducing himself and his assistant, and he then explained the process that would be applied during the next few days. There were going to be daily training sessions during which each player would have plenty of opportunities to show his skills, his intelligence, his attitude and his hunger for the game. We were going to monitor each player individually, but we were also going to tell a player when it was obvious that he didn't meet the required standards. No need to waste time and energy on those who weren't going to make the mark. We knew that we would have to disappoint the vast majority of this huge group, but that just came with the territory.

When Mr Kimora ended his talk, I asked for two minutes as well.

"I extend to you all a very warm welcome, and I applaud you for having chosen to try out for Safari Sports Club. You are going to try your best over the next few days, but you must be prepared for failure. I don't care who you are or who you know, and I certainly don't care how good a football player you think you are. What I want is that you show us what you can do in the field of play, and what sort of contribution you can make to this club. This goes beyond playing football. We believe in the strength of a team, not in individual players. Prove to us that you are a team player, that you believe that the team is more important than the individual, and that you have a winner's mentality. Only then will you be successful. We will be very frank with you, so if you do not give 100% every day, we will thank you for having shown an interest and ask you not to come back the next day. Show us how badly you want to be a part of this club!"

I looked around a bit, and saw that none of the previous year's players were there. They could have been forgiven as these were only try-outs, but I knew that if I had been a returning player myself, I would have shown up for these sessions, even if it was just to get myself back into shape after the summer break. In a way, and based on the stories that I had heard about senior players, I was not really surprised at their absence though.

The practice started with an intelligence test, in which the players needed to show whether they mastered some abstract thinking. A watch can be regarded as having three, six, nine and twelve o'clock on it, or as indicating right, back, left or straight ahead. Simply say "9 o'clock" when you want the players to turn to their left, and confusion will reign! To make the switch from directions to times is not as simple as it seems, and shows you to some extent how fast a player can switch his way of thinking. After this quick mental test, which very few candidates actually passed (results were getting better after fifty or sixty trials), we divided the group into teams of eleven, which played each other in twenty minute games.

Most of the players threw themselves in these matches with full enthusiasm and with bundles of energy. They ran, and ran, and then ran some more. Some showed more skill than others, some showed more leadership qualities than others, and some showed a poorer attitude than others. It was quite easy to downsize from a hundred candidates to about fifty.

Our selection exercise continued over the next few days, and at times Mr Kimora or I spotted a player with some promise, and we then called this player to ask for his name and particulars. This exercise revealed that players from other top Tanzanian clubs were also showing an interest in joining Safari Sports Club. The same exercise also showed that some players were trying to impress us more through their lies than through their footballing ability.

"Number 9, can you come over here please."
"Yes teacher."

"Tell me a bit about yourself."
"I am 24 years old, and I am a striker."
"Good. Where have you played before?"

(This player must have remembered that I once played in Swaziland.)

"I have played in Tabora and in Swaziland."
"Oh really? *Kunjani*? ('How are you?' in the siSwati language)"
"*Kunjani*". (He was supposed to say *Ngikhona*, meaning 'I am fine')
"And where in Swaziland have you played, in Mbabane or in Manzini?"
"Yes, I played in Mbabanemanzini."
"???"

Needless to say that this player did not make it onto our final list . . . In fact, he didn't even make it to the next day's trials . . .

Neither did the one with whom I had the following conversation:

"Hello, what's your name?"
"Yes, I am Ismail."
"And where are you from, Ismail?"
"Yes, I am from Jangwani, not too far from here."
"How old are you?"
"Yes, I am nineteen."
"And which position do you normally play?"
"Yes, I play right midfield. Number seven, teacher. Yes."
"I noticed that you did quite well this afternoon. I would like to see you again tomorrow."
"Yes. Thank you, teacher."

Nothing wrong with this conversation of course. Until Ismail started to walk towards his backpack, and two small boys ran up to him. They must have been five and three, or four and two . . . Suddenly the elder boy said:

"Baba, twende nyumbani! Nina njaa!" (Daddy, let's go home. I am hungry.)

As soon as I heard this, I called Ismail back.

"Yes teacher."
"Ismail, are these your children?"
"Yes teacher. They are my sons. They also like to play football."

87

(pointing at the elder of the two boys)

"And is this your first born?"

"No teacher. I have a daughter who is eleven."

"I see. And you are still eighteen years old?"

"No teacher. I lied to you."

"Ismail, thank you for trying, but you don't need to come back tomorrow."

"Yes teacher."

The day after our first selection session, the newspapers yet again fulfilled their responsibility to keep the nation informed on the latest developments in the beautiful game.

Kimora and Mulder to coach Safari Sports Club for free

City giants broke, looking for volunteers

BY
OUR REPORTER

Hassan Kimora and Peter Mulder yesterday started the recruitment of new players at Dar Es Salaam's Safari Sports Club. Because of the ongoing wrangles within the club leadership, both coaches have been asked to volunteer as the club currently has no money to pay them.

Safari Sports Club's Abdulbakar Malazi, the Chairman of the Elders' Council, earlier told a members' meeting at the team's headquarters that Kimora and Mulder had agreed in principle to take up the jobs. He said the club was currently facing a debilitating cash crisis and players who wished to sign for the team for the new season should not expect cash incentives from the club.

He told the members who attended the brief meeting that the coaches would start getting paid once the new leadership had been elected.

Mr Malazi confirmed that the recruitment exercise was ongoing, and asked the club's members to be supportive of the coaches' efforts.

Every day new candidates showed up, and since it was impossible for me to recognise and remember them all, I am quite sure that some of the rejects reappeared a couple of days after having been told not to bother again. A simple change of shirt or a slightly different hairstyle would have been enough to fool me. By the end of the first week of trials we found ourselves again with close to a hundred applicants. Many had been told to try their luck somewhere else, but many new ones also kept on showing up. Mr Kimora and I continued to inform some of the players that they were not up to standard and should continue to work hard on their game elsewhere. The same of course applied to those players who had tried to mislead us about their past footballing experiences.

One day a rather large player showed up, and I called him over. He must have been at least 20 kilos overweight, and the toll on his knees showed when he came walking towards me.

"Have you been playing any football lately?"

"Yes teacher, I play for three or four hours every day. I have been invited by several Premier League teams for trials, but Safari Sports Club is my favourite team. That's why I decided to come here."

"You look completely out of shape."

"No teacher, I am in shape. You may not like my shape, but I am in shape . . ."

Well, from a semantic point of view, it was hard to argue against that. After all, we're all in some sort of shape, aren't we? When he took almost four minutes to jog one lap around the field with a ball, I called him over again, I thanked him for his enthusiasm, I wished him well with his trials at the other clubs, and I asked him to keep jogging all the way to the exit gate. Suffice it to say that I never saw him on the opposite team during the league season . . .

One or two days later, another new hopeful showed up for trials. As soon as he walked onto the field I could see that he was not quite sober. He also looked very, very sleepy. I walked up to him and asked him whether he'd just woken up.

"Yes teacher, I slept late last night and didn't get enough sleep."

"What time did you go to bed?"

"At around eight o'clock this morning, teacher."

"Why? Do you work the night shift?"

"No teacher, I was out with my friends and some girls. We only got home this morning."

"But it's Wednesday today. You went out all night long on a Tuesday night?"

"Yes teacher. My friends and I, we go out every night."

"Every night?"

"Yes teacher."

"Well, that's not really what I would expect from a serious football player. And if you want to have any chance of playing for my team, you will have to drastically change your ways. You won't be going out anymore."

"Teacher, in my private life I do what I like. The night is my friend. If I don't go out, I don't score, it's as simple as that."

"Thank you for telling me this. I guess you won't be scoring for us then. See ya!"

SEVENTEEN

WHAT AMAZED ME FROM THE very beginning was that after each practice session, Mr Kimora had to give several players some bus fare to get home, and to come back the next day. Mr Kimora understood the financial needs of the players, and decided who did and who did not need this bus fare. Of course, there were lots of applicants, and the process of handing out the three hundred Shillings (about a third of a US$) took almost an hour every day. This got me thinking about organisational matters in the club. It could not be a good thing to keep players and coaches waiting for up to an hour after the end of a practice. Everyone was feeling hot and tired, dusty and sweaty, so the best thing would have been to go home, wash and rest. I did not know where the money came from at this stage, but fans who came to observe the practice paid a 200 Shillings entrance fee, and there were a great number of fans there every day, so I guess that the players' fare came from the daily gate collection. I never asked Mr Kimora . . .

A lot of time was also spent on listening to the views of the fans after each practice. Everybody was keen to provide information on almost every single player, and a lot of little notes exchanged hands. In Africa, it is no exaggeration to say that every person is a football coach . . . or at least claims to be one. In a stadium of ten thousand people, there are ten thousand coaches . . . Before practice started, it happened quite regularly that a fan came to me with a note and a player, and told me that this player was starting trials today and that he was a must for the team. Some sounded as if they had played in the World Cup, that's how good they were said to be! However, our selections were based purely on the achievements of the players during the practices and the trial matches which followed soon. Late in the afternoon, when all the players had finally left, Mr Kimora and I sat down at a table in the club house, and over a cup of Chai Bora we shared our opinions and impressions about the most promising players.

While these trials were going on, I also started to pay a little bit more attention to the politics within the club. If I was going to have an impact on how the club was run and on how it could be developed, I needed to create a deeper understanding of the inside story—and a story it certainly was! I tried to figure out why this club was being run by a committee of "Elders", and thankfully, the newspapers came to my rescue as a source of detailed information.

Safari Sports Club conflicts continue

BY
MAIL REPORTER

Safari Sports Club Elder, Mr Malazi confirmed in an interview yesterday that the club is facing some difficulties.

Safari Sports Club has of late been engulfed in an internal leadership wrangle following a decision by the club's former Treasurer to file an appeal against the ousting of the elected leadership. The Elders Committee was put in charge during an explosive members' meeting three months ago. A Court Magistrate upheld the members' meeting decision after the Treasurer and his Assistant filed a case to have the decision reversed. The former Treasurer had filed a case when Safari Sports Club were planning to hold elections. Following the filing of the case, the elections were scrapped.

Currently the club is under the leadership of the Elders' Committee, after the suggestion of having an Interim Committee was dismissed by Mr Malazi.

It was clear that there was no harmony within the leadership of the club, and I felt that I needed to lay down some early markers for the leadership and everyone involved in the club. While this strategy had its risks, I did not want to become involved in the politics of one group or the other. Surely the club was struggling because there had been a strategy of 'divide and conquer'. It was clear that the two major factions within the members' base simply supported their own leaders, and the reasons for this became evident very quickly. As a coach, it did not matter to me who would eventually run the club. What mattered was that there was a structure and a set of goals to work towards, and in the technical area, I felt that it was up to me and Mr Kimora to decide what was best for the club's future. Having my say in the future direction of the club, and possibly antagonising a couple of people with a different agenda in the process, was a risk that I was prepared to take.

In Tanzania, the only way to reach out to the masses and to get a message across without it being distorted too much is to go through the media. As the reader will remember, I had a good number of friends in the local printed, televised and audio media industry, and several of them showed up at our daily recruitment sessions. I made it a point to always give them something to write about or report on, and they duly obliged. They were my voice to the public, and I took full advantage of this bridge between the technical bench and those who would certainly support us once we started winning our matches. Since my command of the Kiswahili language was also improving at supersonic speed, I could be heard more and more often on the evening sports shows on the local radio stations. I felt that being able to speak 'live' on the radio offered the least chance to the reporters of misquoting or misinterpreting my words.

I was determined to show my far-reaching ambition from the very beginning, and one morning one of the local papers printed the following story:

Safari coach wants club to turn pro

**BY
OUR REPORTER**

Safari Sports Club's Belgian coach, Peter Mulder, wants the club to turn professional effective this Premier League season.

Speaking exclusively to this newspaper in Dar Es Salaam yesterday, Mulder offered his full-time services to the club without pay from the team.

He called for the fans and members to come out in support of the team and the coaches' program. He said that he was working out strategies to make sure the players received all the necessary services related to professional sports, such as salaries, medical support, training equipment and other basic team needs. "To allow players to fully demonstrate their talent and their potential, we have to provide them with their basic needs. It does not make sense to expect a high level of performance from a person who hasn't had a decent meal for several days."

He added that the team would soon start playing some friendly matches to assess the quality of the players that have so far been shortlisted, and to expose these players to a competitive environment. However, he also called upon the team's senior players to resume training and to assist in building the team.

Mulder appealed to the club fans, members and sponsors to help the team with financial, material or moral support, and he assured transparency and accountability to the donors. "Nowadays sponsors are an integral part of top sports. Without financial backing, no club can achieve anything. As coaches we are ready to share our expertise with the players. Sponsors and responsible leaders now need to come in and meet all the other needs. We ask for potential sponsors to come forward, and we will develop a financial strategy together so as to ensure that all the funds are spent in a justifiable manner."

He also called on some members and the club authorities to stop trading accusations and instead concentrate on building a winning team, as division amongst the leaders will harm the club's progress. "You know, when club members are divided, then the club automatically becomes weak, and the players and coaches can find themselves trapped between the warring factions. This will demoralize them, and these conflicts will definitely affect the performance of the team as a whole. We must all remember that a club is only as strong as its weakest link."

Mulder said that he was ready to chair a conciliatory meeting between the club's former Treasurer and the members of the Elders' Council, so as to resolve the existing hostilities.

This reporter feels that the will demonstrated by Mulder is worth mentioning, but the Tanzanian clubs will take time to realize what people like him are planning, due to problems such as greed and personal clashes between club leaders, as well as a lack of unity amongst the members.

We played maybe five or six practice games at the Karume Memorial Stadium and at the National Stadium, and while for us coaches these games were nothing more than trials for our candidate players, the fans already expected results and showed their discontent when we lost. At that stage I could not care less about the score. I was only interested in seeing the players at work in a competitive context, which taught me a lot about their team play, their tactical awareness, their stamina and their strength. We didn't give these players any detailed instructions, so it was all down to their own tactical awareness.

Slowly but surely some of the stronger candidates for a place in the squad started to emerge. By now we had probably seen about two hundred hopefuls, but Mr Kimora and I agreed that only a few of these could eventually join the club. Of course one can not fault any of these players for their lack of tactical awareness or understanding of the game, but the reality was that we were going to play in the Premier League, and we needed to have a firm base. We could not afford to become a football academy—we simply did not have the luxury of time on our hands. We had to get a competitive team together within a couple of weeks, but we also agreed that we would look into the issue of youth development once the senior team was up and running.

The Tanzanian Premier League takes up eleven months of the year and follows a tiered structure. For most of the year, there are two parallel leagues going on, one on the Mainland (formerly called Tanganyika) and another on the islands of Zanzibar and Pemba. At the end of the season, the top three clubs of each league come together and compete for the title of 'champions of Tanzania' in what is called the "Tatu Bora" or 'best three' finals. Safari Sports Club was also going to compete in the Nyerere Cup tournament, the equivalent of the FA Cup, and in the African Cup Winners' Cup tournament. Having won the Nyerere Cup three months earlier, the club had earned itself the chance to compete with the continent's superpowers. We were going to need a reliable and strong squad in order to compete on all three fronts, and Mr Kimora and myself spent a lot of time analysing and evaluating the many hopefuls that showed up for trials. Always over a few cups of Chai Bora, of course.

After three weeks of daily selection sessions, Mr Kimora and I differed on the number of successful trialists that we would invite to join the club. I had found about ten players for whom I had realistic hopes, whilst recognising that there was a lot of work that needed to be done. But the teacher in me was ready to help them develop and to bring them up to speed. Mr Kimora had spotted just one player whom he deemed fit to play in the Premier League. He was indeed looking for the finished product rather than for a player with the potential to do well within three months, and this helped me determine our respective duties and responsibilities. I was very interested in further developing our younger players and those who had come from backgrounds without any coaching to speak of, and Mr Kimora would focus almost exclusively on the preparations for the matches. He had a lot more experience with everything surrounding the Tanzanian game, and I was keen to observe him and learn.

It was obvious that we needed to get our senior players to report for practice as soon as possible. We sent out messages through the fans and through the media, and one by one our last year's players started to report for duty. First one, then two, then four, five, and a few more. Within the next week, we were able to start putting together a team comprised of new recruits and senior players.

Some of the senior players though excelled in their refusal to return, and I thought that a little bit of scare tactics might do the job. After all, most of these players were unemployed, so the small allowances that they would receive after the football matches were their only guaranteed source of income. After consultation with Mr. Kimora, I asked some journalists to inform these players, through the newspapers and the radio bulletins, that anyone who did not report for duty within the next three days would be suspended indefinitely by the Elders' Council.

We soon had another two or three players turn up, but some remained conspicuous by their absence. We heard that some might have left for South Africa in search of a semi-professional club there, and apparently one of our former stars had even made the journey to Indonesia to go and make a small living playing football in that beautiful island nation. We did not know at first whether these reports were true. What we did know though was that, just like every other year, we had a couple of players who had already signed for two or three different clubs. This was going to cause some problems at registration time, so we decided not to pursue these players. Of course the players' intention was to eventually play for the highest bidder, but I was not prepared to go along with this tactic. Either you sign for my team only, or you don't sign at all. I knew that I'd only have to go through this once, and all the other players who were thinking about doing the same thing would quickly change their mind.

Another week went by, and we still had at least six or seven players missing. So I decided to forfeit the threats and to offer an incentive. I could not realistically expect all these uneducated young men to suddenly understand the full extent of what I said, and I decided to give them some leeway.

I went back to the newspapers to inform them of the introduction of an 'earn as you train' scheme. I decided to offer a cash incentive and to pay every player a small amount of money from my own pocket at the end of each week. This amount of money was in direct proportion with the number of training sessions they had attended, and with the amount of effort put into the practices. I was not going to be satisfied with a player simply showing up at 4 pm in order to collect his bus fare and a little bit extra. No, he would have to show significant effort and a willingness to work hard and learn.

Bingo! A masterstroke, even if I say to myself. Within the next two days, almost all the missing players had shown up, and the scheme took off. Why hadn't I thought of this cash incentive earlier? Apparently money moves mountains in this part of the world!

The journalists also liked this personal sacrifice, which had never been seen before. They reported to the nation that

> "the allowances to be given to the players would from now on depend on how often they attended training and their effort in the drills. Cash—strapped Safari Sports Club have in recent months been unable to pay the players their allowances, and Mulder has on several occasions been forced to dig deep into his own pockets to provide the players with at least their bus fare back home after training".

One day, a search akin to a manhunt started in Dar Es Salaam. Mr Kimora had mentioned that two international players from our city rival, Ndovu Football Club, had decided to sign for Safari Sports Club. Ndovu apparently mobilised all its officials and members to go and look for the two players, and to force them to sign the registration papers for Ndovu Football Club. At first the players could not be found, as both had travelled abroad to play in some short-term tournaments in the Middle East and earn a few dollars. But as soon as they returned to Tanzania, they were forced to sign for Ndovu Football Club. A pity, because they were really good . . .

By the end of the year Mr Kimora and I were asked by the Council of Elders to present our list of 30 players, so that registration could begin, and so that transfers could be sorted out where needed. Some of our players were still registered with Zanzibari clubs, and Mr Kimora must have made at least five ferry trips to Zanzibar in ten days in order to sort out some of these transfers.

Three of our own main players still had not returned for duty. We eventually learned through the newspapers that we should not expect two of them back.

Safari Sports Club name final squad

BY OUR REPORTER

Safari Sports Club have dropped two players from their provisional 31-man squad for this season's Premier League.

According to Mr Malazi these players have been replaced by two new ace strikers. The Elders' Committee Chairman said that Safari Sports Club were forced to drop the two players after learning that one of them had left for South Africa in search of greener pastures, while the other was dropped following a Committee member's recommendation that he was not fit to feature for the club.

The third player, who happened to be Tanzania's most capped goalkeeper, had become a pawn in the political battles amongst the suspended leadership and the Elders' Council. The suspended leadership, now effectively down to the Treasurer and his Assistant, stopped him from attending training, and would only allow him to join us if they were reinstated by the Court. Since the registration deadline was approaching fast, there suddenly was a flurry of activity in the Courts. Motions were being filed, cross-motions were being prepared, and it was rather impossible to figure out who would come out tops at the end of the process. What was certain was that unity and harmony were still a long way off.

I did not want to find myself in a situation where we did not have the three required goalkeepers, and through the media I invited all interested goalkeepers to come for trials. Only goalkeepers please. As you can probably imagine, out of the seventy-seven young men who showed up, only a handful had ever experienced being a goalkeeper. So it was quite easy to shortlist those that had at least a hint of a glimmer of a shadow of goalkeeping potential. When we were down to the last four or five, one of the hopefuls came to me at the start of one of the training sessions and told me that his knee was hurting.

"How come? What happened? Did you fall badly?"
"No teacher."
"Did you knock your knee against something?"
"No teacher."
"Then what happened?"
"Well, teacher, you see, I haven't had sex in three weeks now, and if I don't have sex for such a long time, my knee always starts to hurt . . ."

I wasn't quite sure what to advise him. But the next day I saw him jumping and diving like a spring chicken and I could only assume that he had gotten lucky the night before. When I asked him if his knee was feeling better, he flashed a boyish smile and he winked at me. My assumption had been correct.

Mr Kimora and I drafted our list of 30 players, which included ten players who were retained from the previous season. I presented the list to Mr Malazi, and he approved of it in its entirety. He then organised a press conference during which he revealed the names of the squad members for the upcoming league season. It seemed like our recruitment drive had come to a successful end. It was time to take a short Christmas break, and after the holiday we would start preparing the team for the upcoming Premier League.

I encouraged all the players to travel to their homes and to spend Christmas with their parents and families, because the next year promised to be a busy one. We wanted them to be happy and to feel that they were now part of a real club. Mr Kimora was going to spend the break in his hometown of Lindi, and I decided to use the holiday to discover the breath-taking natural beauty of the East African coast, southern Kenya and northern Tanzania for two weeks . . .

EIGHTEEN

Upon my return from Kenya, I crossed the Tanzanian border in Namanga and checked the Kiswahili newspapers in order to see if anything new had happened at my club. I was rather surprised to read that suddenly the court case involving the suspended leadership had been resolved, and that the former Treasurer had been reinstated. He had obviously done his cash-counting job well enough, and found sufficient support in the court and in his plastic bags to return him to office. This was an unexpected outcome, as it had become very clear in the weeks leading up to the court hearing that this man had been treating the club's resources as his own. During the daytime, the Treasurer could usually be found in the city centre, where he ran a tiny stationary shop that earned him, at best, the equivalent of five US dollars per day. However, in the evenings and on the weekends, you could find him burning up the rubber up and down the city's major roads in a shiny and very expensive four-wheel drive vehicle. He would have had to sell millions of pencils and notebooks to the local schoolchildren in order to afford such a car. But within one and a half year of becoming the Treasurer at Safari Sports Club, he had managed to get himself this vehicle, the envy of the city. I was keen to find out more once I returned to Dar Es Salaam.

The court order had made the provision for new elections to be held within one month. This was a very positive development, because for the first time, I would have the opportunity to somehow influence these elections myself. During my short break I had devised a strategic plan for the development of all the aspects of the club, and I was going to share it with everyone, and most of all the voting members of the club. Interested candidates would have to take notice of the plan, and somehow figure out how they would contribute to its implementation. In order to get the attention of the members, the main focus of the development plan was income. Money talks in Tanzania, and a discussion on cash always finds an interested audience. I did not come up with any earth-shattering plans, but instead focused on simple ideas that could easily be implemented and that were guaranteed to be successful. All I needed was the support of the leadership.

When I arrived back in the city, I informed all the players that pre-season practice would start very soon. The league season was just around the corner, and we now also knew that we would play against Zimbabwe's Chapungu FC in the first round of the African Cup Winners' Cup. All the players were to report at our usual training ground, and I called Mr Kimora to ask him if we could start by having a meeting with the players. I wanted to lay down the law in terms of expected discipline, attendance and punctuality. In order to grow as a team and reach our stated goals, it was absolutely necessary to speak directly with the players and to get them to hear the same message, from the same source, at the same time. When Mr Kimora answered the phone, he startled me with the news that he was not returning to Safari Sports Club. During his Christmas break he had been approached by the leadership of his hometown club, Zindi FC, and even though they only had a tiny following compared with that of Safari Sports Club, they promised him regular payment. Mr Kimora had a responsibility to provide for his family, and I completely understood his decision. But I didn't like it, and I told myself that in my first meeting with the new leadership, I would ask them whether they were prepared to see more people leave because of the poor state of our finances. I made it clear to all the voters that such scenarios were detrimental to the club, and many agreed. I asked the Elders' Committee what they intended to do about the fact that our most experienced coach had left, and they told me that they were looking for someone else. The prospect of coming to coach a club that had no money can not have been too attractive, but a few days later Mr Malazi called to inform me that they had appointed two new coaches, Mr Mahmoud and Mr Mwengo. They had also confirmed my own appointment as coach, and decided to let me continue with my work within the club. I was glad to be given the chance to work on my ideas for the development of Safari Sports Club.

Mr Mahmoud had been recruited from an up-country club, Police Force FC, which had clinched the Mainland League title the previous season. He had obviously performed a very good job, and was eager to shift to Dar Es Salaam and coach Safari Sports Club. Mr Mwengo, his assistant, was a very educated man who had a lot of experience with youth coaching in Dar, and whose ideas on football coaching impressed me from the first day. All three of us received our long-awaited letters of appointment for the coming season. When the envelope arrived in the mail, I took out the club letterhead paper and read:

Appointment as coach of Safari Sports Club

To our coaches:

Mr H. Mahmoud

Mr A. Mwenga

Mr P. Mulder

I hereby have the pleasure to inform you that the Elders' Council and the Executive Committee of Safari Sports Club have appointed you as Coach.

We are all very grateful that you have shown your interest in serving our great club during the upcoming season. We hope to work closely with you, and we offer our heart and energy to work with you on the progress and the development of the club.

We look forward to a positive cooperation and to the success of Safari Sports Club.

The letter was signed by Mr Malazi, Chairman of the Elders' Council. This gave us the reassurance that his Elders' Council was still in charge. I had no idea which 'Executive Committee' he was referring to, but I guessed that he wanted to remind us that soon there would be one, and that we would report to them from that moment onwards. With the upcoming elections, the last thing I needed was a letter of appointment signed by an official who three weeks later would be in court, defending himself against all sorts of allegations about embezzlement . . . I felt proud to have finally received my first letter of appointment as a football coach. Mr Fullone, thank you once more.

The next Monday we started our pre-season training, and I went to the TCC grounds to meet my new colleagues. We got along extremely well from the start. I felt that we could do good work together, and that same evening we went out for a drink and discussed how we were going to shape our team and develop our club. By the time we ended our meeting and had agreed on a way forward, each of us had downed at least four cups of Chai Bora . . .

Mr Mahmoud and Mr Mwengo shared with me their ideas on the pre-season programme, of which I also received a detailed copy. They had already developed a plan for the next six weeks building up to the start of the Mainland Premier League competition. This was very impressive indeed, and it told me that my two colleagues were very serious about their work and about the responsibility that they had accepted.

I presented my list of ideas that could help the club become semi-professional, and most of these ideas will be described later on. I was happy for my two colleagues to focus almost exclusively on preparing the team—I was mostly interested in setting up some structures and routines that would help the club move forward as a whole, and that would provide us with some much-needed income. But I spent every minute of every training session on the field, keen to impart my knowledge and my experience, and clearly showing the players that they would have to play according to instructions from the coaching panel. The days of playing football without a plan had gone; time now to build a team and have a strategy.

NINETEEN

MONEY. WE NEEDED SOME. AND soon. Before the Christmas period, I had been giving the players bus fare from my own pocket, but this practice simply could not continue. Players also had medical expenses, they needed to eat, they needed to buy proper equipment, and they needed to be compensated for their time and for their dedication to training. So I devised a plan to make money off the many fans that we had and that attended our daily training sessions. We had a Treasurer who had just been reinstated by the Court. Nobody ever saw him anywhere near the training ground, and he stayed well clear of players who needed a little bit of cash to feed themselves. He was probably too busy selling his pencils.

Our training ground at the Tanzania Cigarette Company was a private ground, and we were required to pay a daily fee of 20,000 Tanzanian Shillings, roughly the equivalent of twenty US dollars. Not a big amount, you might think, but in Tanzania, this represents a huge sum, more or less equivalent to a monthly salary. Furthermore, as a daily fee, this quickly added up to a handsome amount for the TCC company. Besides receiving this daily fee, the TCC also had their own people manning the gates and charging every fan who came to watch our practices a 200 Shillings entrance fee. When I looked at how much money we could generate through the practice sessions, I started to think about the best way to ensure that the money would benefit Safari Sports Club and nobody else. I wrote a proposal to the TCC club in order to come to a compromise and give both them and ourselves the best possible deal, but I never received a reaction from them. They were quite happy to charge us 20,000 Shillings per day and then, from one day to the next, see us disappear and receive nothing at all. Their greed was exemplary, and eventually it cost them everything they could benefit from us. On an average day there were at least 400 fans who came to watch our trainings. We coaches advised the Council of Elders that we move away from the TCC grounds and find an alternative venue for our training sessions. The venue had to be cheaper, and the owners had to allow us to collect all the entrance fees ourselves. With the promise of a 10,000 Shillings daily fee to the owners of a football ground that, right now, was making no money at all, we found such a venue in no time, and moved to the Bandari College grounds in Temeke. I recruited some volunteers to help us collect the entrance fees at the gates to the stadium, and we immediately started to collect enough money to at least pay the players' bus fare and cater for some medical expenses. But it still wasn't enough. We had to pay some transfer fees for players that we had recruited from other clubs, we had to buy training gear and materials, we needed money to finance a trip for trial matches in the inland town of Morogoro, and there were numerous other expenses. On some days there wasn't even enough money to pay each player his bus fare, and on countless occasions did I pay from my own pocket, so that my players could at least get home, have a decent meal and have their injuries or illnesses treated. I spent thousands and thousands of Shillings, and decided to figure out why it was that the gate collections were usually quite low despite the fact that there were a large number of spectators.

One afternoon I called Murtaza, who was in charge of the gate collection, and asked him:

"Why is it that there are over five hundred spectators here and you tell me that today's collection is only twenty-five thousand Shillings. If my calculations are right, then we should have collected a hundred thousand."

"I don't know what happened. I don't think we can trust the people at the gate."

"But you are in charge of supervising these people. Does it mean that I can't trust you?"

"No, it doesn't mean that."

"Then what does it mean?"

"It means that we can't trust the people at the gate."

"Oh, I see. But I can trust you, right?"

"Yes teacher, you can trust me. And maybe some spectators come in without paying."

"And who is in charge of that?"

"I am, teacher."

"So?"

"I don't know. Maybe the *askaris* (guards) aren't doing their job properly."

"And who supervises the *askaris*?"

"I do."

"So?"

"I need to check everything more closely."

"Right. Tomorrow I want a bigger gate collection."

"No problem!"

The next day the gate collection that was handed to me was hardly more than the amount of the day before . . . This couldn't continue. The culture of giving favours to one's friends was clearly present here, and if we were going to make this exercise successful, I had to come up with a better plan. To simply allow Murtaza and his team to decide who had to pay and who didn't was not getting us the income we needed. It was clear that a lot of money was not being accounted for, and if there was one thing that we needed more than anything else at this point in time, it was money. I needed to find a system that would ensure that every Shilling that came into the club was accounted for.

I developed an initiative in which we held a simple raffle at the end of our daily training session. Every person who entered our practice ground was encouraged to buy a ticket of 200 Shillings, which would enter him or her in the raffle. The prizes in the raffle were very attractive, ranging from foodstuffs to clothes. Having this raffle ensured that every spectator would insist on getting his ticket, and I made sure that I had a counter copy of each ticket sold. So if on a particular day we sold 650 tickets at 200 Shillings each, then I knew that our gatemen had collected 130,000 Shillings on that day. There simply was no way for them to do any "creative accounting" here . . .

I decided to inform the fans through the media that this system would be used from now onwards, and the response was tremendous. The journalists themselves absolutely loved this inventive idea, and realised straight away that it would work. They enthusiastically informed their readership.

Fans must now pay to see Safari Sports Club train

BY OUR REPORTER

Safari Sports Club will charge fans coming to see the team train in order to enable the cash-strapped club to pay allowances to their players.

The decision was made yesterday when the club's Elders' Council approved a proposal by their coach, Peter Mulder.

It was agreed that during every training session, one member of the Elders' Council and two volunteer officials would man the gates wherever the team trains, with a view to maximizing receipts.

"This will enable the club to at least provide the players with their bus fare back home after training", Mulder explained.

He added that he had already printed tickets which will be sold at TSh 200 each to those willing to watch the team train ahead of their campaign in the Premier League.

He said that the club was supposed to pay every player TSh 1,000 per day after training, but that it had failed to do so in recent weeks owing to the debilitating cash crisis the team were going through.

Mulder has been paying each player TSh 200 from his own pocket every day for bus fare after training at the TCC grounds.

This initiative has certainly encouraged the players to work harder. Goalkeeper Athumani Wamala said that the financial doldrums that the club was going through was no excuse for players to show a lack of discipline and commitment, and he added that the care shown by their coach meant a great deal to the players.

After a few days the raffle became one of the main parts of the practice session, and every day a number of spectators went home with food or clothes that were worth much more than what they had paid for their entrance ticket. Every evening, there were some happy men walking home with two kilograms of rice, or a bag full of sugar or beans, and the main prize every day was a beautiful kanga—a cloth worn and highly appreciated by the ladies. By giving the men the chance to make their wives or girlfriends happy with a new kanga, I was sure that the wives would allow them to return every afternoon to our training session—and everyone was a winner! On average once a week I offered a grand prize, in order to keep the interest going. The fans did not know on which day of the week this grand prize would be issued, so they had to attend every session. This prize could be two kilograms of meat, or a small radio, or a new white shirt, or a six-pack of beers—there were plenty of options to make our staunchest supporters happy.

The system worked wonders. The gate collections that reached me increased by the day, and soon we were collecting over 200,000 Shillings per day. This money was used for all our regular expenses like training allowances, the use of the ground, security, football boots, medication, players' house rent, transfer fees, transport expenses etc. I don't believe that the fans started to spend more money on the team. I do believe however that this watertight system ensured that the money that the fans spent all ended up contributing towards the club's and the team's development. And this was what we set out to do from the start. There must have been a few disgruntled people who were no longer able to pocket the fans' money, but I couldn't care less about that. I was helping my club and my players, not some unscrupulous thieves.

The players also started to react to the changes. They realised that they were being taken care of, and they responded by becoming more conscientious in their behaviour and more hard-working during the training sessions. There was a general air of optimism and good spirit, and even the journalists started to come to the Bandari College ground to confirm that Safari Sports Club was on the road to success.

One problem that we were still facing was the fact that one or two of the senior players, the ones who had been retained from the previous season, were still not reporting for practice. This made me decide to draft a code of conduct and an allowance system, which my fellow coaches endorsed and which had an immediate effect on players' attendance.

The code of conduct included the clause that a player would be financially penalised if he didn't attend practice sessions without a valid reason. Basically a player would receive 2,000 Shillings per training session that he attended, but he would lose half his allowance if he arrived late for training, and he would lose a full allowance if he missed a day's practice without a valid reason. The allowance system was firm and tough, and in the beginning some of the players struggled with it. Players were supposed to be on the practice field at 4.30 pm, and not a minute later.

"Rajabu, what's the time?"

"It's half past four, teacher."

"*Kweli*? (really?) Look at the watch."

"OK, it's five past half past four."

"What does that mean?"

"That means that I am late. But teacher, I stay far and I didn't have transport."

"Oh, so today there are no *daladalas* in Dar Es Salaam?"

"There are, but I stay far."

"And what did I tell you the other day?"

"I don't remember, teacher."

"I told all of you that you need to leave your home on time, so that you arrive here by 4 pm. Do you remember now?"

"Yes teacher, I remember."

"So what will you do tomorrow?"

"I will leave home on time."

"And will there be *daladalas* tomorrow?"

"Yes teacher."

"Fine. Get ready for practice now. Mohamed!"

"Yes teacher."

"What's the time?"

"It is half past four, teacher."

"Are you sure?"

"Yes. Hey, Salum, what's the time?"

"Twenty to five!"

"Oh. It is twenty to five . . ."

"What does that mean?"

"But teacher, my sister is sick."

"And is your sister going to get better by you being late?"

"No, teacher. But I was also in town looking for money."

"Listen, I told all of you last week that football is your job now, so this is where you get your money. Have you forgotten?"

"No, teacher."

"Now you will lose half of today's allowance. Is that going to help you?"

"No, teacher, I will be on time tomorrow."

"That's what I want to hear. Get ready now."

In the beginning it wasn't always easy to have to cut a player's allowance, especially when they said that they had a sick parent or a sick sibling, but it was impossible to know whether these explanations were true or not. I felt that it was better to be tough in the beginning, and very soon the system worked. Almost all the players adapted to the code of conduct, and late-comers soon became a minority. But the odd incident would still happen.

105

"OK guys, practice is over. Come and collect your allowances for today. Athumani, can you write down the names of the players and how much they are getting today?"

"OK, teacher."

"Right, Jonah, you were late today, so you are getting one thousand only."

"Teacher, don't insult me now."

"Listen Jonah, even though you are one of the most senior players on this team, I don't make any exceptions. You were late, so your allowance is cut. Here is your money."

At that moment Jonah took his money, looked at it for two seconds, and then threw it at me.

"I don't come here for the money. If you can't give me my full allowance, then I don't want any money!"

"Take your one thousand Shillings or nothing."

"I don't need this money. I'm going!"

"Fine. See you tomorrow at half past four."

"Grrmmppff . . ."

In a way I was grateful that this conversation took place, because all the other players heard it and realised that we were making no exceptions. My words from a few weeks before, that I didn't care how good or how important my players might think that they were, were being put into practice here. It settled the allowance issue once and for all . . . I kept a tight record of the attendance, the lates and the absences, as well as the reasons given. As soon as I found out that a particular player told me for the second time in two weeks that his absence was due to his father passing away 'last night', I knew how to deal with the situation. I had only been in Tanzania for a couple of years, but I knew full well that even in East Africa, you only die once . . .

All but one of the senior players now also showed up for practice, clearly enticed by the handsome daily allowance. I have never blamed these young people for trying to make a buck here or there. Most of the players were from poor backgrounds, and until the day that we could offer them a decent income, it was hard to expect them to commit all their time and energy to what was, after all, just a pastime for them. Some would shine shoes or sell newspapers in the city in the mornings, one or two had a small job in a factory, and there were those who had no other option but to go and visit the members and the fans of our club and to ask them for small hand-outs. But at least we were trying to improve their conditions, and they responded very well indeed. I sent out a few more warnings to the missing player, our goalkeeper, through the media, and told him that he should report for training or be excluded from the final squad list. He had been used as a negotiation tool by the warring Treasurer, but now that the Treasurer had been reinstated by the court, I felt that the goalkeeper should end his stand-off and join us for training. No reaction came, so we dropped him and prepared to sign another keeper. I was determined to avoid signing the one who was liable to have painful knees on match days though . . .

Discipline, or *nidhamu* as it is called in Kiswahili, has always been one of the main priorities for me. Without discipline and commitment, we were never going to achieve what we had set out to do. And I let the players know at every possible opportunity.

One evening, just after we had finished that day's training session, one of the candidates for the right wing position took the plastic bag that contained his sandals and some water, and took out a baseball cap. Such caps, and mainly those with the emblems of American teams, were very popular in Tanzania at that time. Almost everyone wore one, ladies included, and I had absolutely no problem with my players wearing them. However, when Abdi put on his cap, I suddenly realised that it wasn't facing forwards and it wasn't facing backwards either. The visor was pointing towards three o'clock. I wouldn't call myself a fashion expert, but surely this couldn't be right. The way that the players presented themselves and represented the club during their free time needed to be worked at. So I called him over.

"Abdi, can you come over here?"

"Yes teacher."

"Can you turn your cap to the front?"

"No teacher. This is how I wear my cap."

"Can you turn your cap to the front?"

"Teacher, this is my style. I wear my cap like this. It's cool."

"Abdi, listen to me. Turn your cap to the front, or I will turn your head to the side."

Abdi duly turned his cap to the front.

It was time for a little team talk, and for clarifying to the players what their responsibilities were. So I called the whole group together, and made a short but strong point:

"As far as I am concerned, you should consider yourselves a privileged group of young people. There is a lot of hardship in Tanzania, and a lot of young men your age face a daily struggle to make ends meet. Everywhere you go you see boys selling cashew nuts or car jacks, pushing hundreds of kilos of merchandise through the streets, or even begging. All these boys were given talents, but they don't have the chance to develop these talents. For you the situation is different. You were given a talent, which is to play football. And you are also given the chance to use your talent, and to even make some money by doing so. For the coming year at least, you will be taken good care of. You will have food, clothes, medicine and cash. But you also have a responsibility towards your club. You will show discipline and work hard. If you fail to meet the standards that we coaches set for you, then we will tell you to go find a living elsewhere, and maybe you will then have to go and join the cashew nuts sellers . . . Do I make myself clear?"

"We understand, teacher. Thank you."

A couple of days later, and completely out of the blue, the Treasurer surfaced and made some comments in the newspapers. Claiming that he was now the only elected member of the Executive Committee still in power, he wanted to take full control of all matters pertaining to the club, and make wholesale changes to the squad list. He wanted to register his own players, including of course that poor goalkeeper. If allowed to go ahead, this man could have undone everything that we had managed to rectify and improve over the past few months. He instructed the Elders' Council to back off from the team's affairs, and he called a meeting for his own supporters. The Chairman of the Elders' Council reacted by going back to the Court and got the Treasurer's meeting called off. A tug-of-war ensued, and fortunately the Court had the bright idea to call for fresh elections within the next fourteen days. As you can imagine, I had my own say and reminded the Treasurer that the club belonged to its members, not its Executive Committee. For a number of days, the Treasurer threatened to de-register about half the squad and to install his own favorites. He even produced a list of players to the Court, and asked for an order to be issued that he be allowed to register these players. Where he got the technical knowledge to decide which players were up to the task of playing in the Premier League, I don't know. The Court saw the futility in his actions, and declined his request. Eventually he had to roll over and accept the fact that new elections were coming. The positive outcome from this episode though was that our goalkeeper had now returned to the squad, and we were ready to get started on our pre-season friendly matches.

During the days that followed, I tried to remind all the candidates for the upcoming elections that they should put the well-being of the club and the players first. Anyone who had the intention to simply come and enrich themselves at the expense of the club should think again and maybe try elsewhere. This was a time for change, an opportunity to steer the club in a new and better direction, and I made as much noise as I could. I dared the candidates to contribute their funds to the team so that we could purchase some training equipment. Instead, many of them chose to use their cash to buy votes from the members, who of course also had families to feed, or a thirst to quench.

We would find out very soon what the winds of change in the leadership would bring . . .

TWENTY

THE INCOME FROM THE RAFFLE ticket sales was helpful, but no club worthy of its name can solely depend on what is, after all, a very unpredictable source of revenue. We could not train during a rainstorm or a tropical downpour, and on such a day there would be no income at all. I needed to start looking at more permanent financial support, and at a structure that would also allow me to focus more on the training of the team, and less on the finances of the club.

I decided to start looking for potential sponsors for the team. I had many business friends in the city, and was hopeful that one or two of them would support my efforts to raise the standard of football in the country. I wrote letters to about two hundred Dar Es Salaam-based businesses, companies and organisations. I went to meet the Advertising Department representatives of several companies which in the past had sponsored sports events, and I received a few phone calls from companies who wanted to know what the deal would be. Of course, I also sent out messages through the media. I spent numerous hours visiting financial and marketing managers, discussing how we could figure out a deal that would benefit both the club and the company, but most of the time the main obstacle was transparency. Sponsorship fatigue had already set in, as years and years of misuse and embezzlement had turned most companies away from involving themselves with sports. Almost every company representative told me that their experience was that sponsorship money never reached the people or the purpose that it was intended for. I couldn't argue with that, but I did propose the alternative of sponsoring us in kind rather than financially.

Some companies later on expressed their interest in helping us with materials, as you will read later on.

Another factor that made some companies reluctant to sponsor a specific club was the Tanzanian people's narrow-mindedness when it came to their purchasing habits. Quite a few companies told me that sponsoring Safari Sports Club would mean giving up half the country's market, because Ndovu Football Club fans would refuse to buy any of the Safari-sponsoring company's products . . . and vice versa of course! In a country of over forty three million people, and where every customer thinks hard and long about every purchase before putting down his or her few Shillings, it was essential for every company's survival that they hold on to their established customer base. At first I found it hard to believe that someone would actually stop buying their preferred brand of coffee, beer, soap or water, just because the company had decided to sponsor the 'other' club. But as I started to hear the same story from different sources, it became clear that this was fact, not fiction. I could only sympathise with the companies' predicament, and decided to start focusing my efforts more on companies whose products everyone needed.

Because of the recent lack in sports sponsorships in Tanzania, the rules governing financial and material support were minimal. In fact, the Football Association of Tanzania, conveniently abbreviated as FAT (which was a pretty accurate and realistic description of the cats that ran this association) had only one single rule. Since the Premier League was sponsored, in some way, by one of the major breweries in Tanzania, teams were not allowed to enter in a deal with any of its competitors. At the start of the league season, every team received one complete outfit with the sponsor's name emblazoned on it, and this outfit had to last through the eleven-month season. I never had any idea whether there were other benefits to the clubs, despite the fact that large amounts of sponsorship money were regularly quoted in the newspapers. So, I refrained from approaching the rival breweries. In my letters to the various companies, I urged any interested parties to deal directly with me. I informed them that I would have to have the initial discussions with them, so that I could clearly spell out my plans for the club and the lines of communication. Once the basics had been sorted out and agreed upon, I would then bring in the members of the Executive Committee, who were of course the only ones who could enter into any kind of formal agreement. This process would allow all of us to know exactly where we stood, and it allowed me to have control over what the sponsorships would cover. The wait for responses from companies was an exciting one, as I firmly believed that someone, somewhere, would at least look into the advertising potential of teaming up with the biggest club in the country.

In the meantime, our team was shaping up nicely. We had full attendance for all our practices, and we could now start concentrating on building a team and teaching some tactical patterns, using the skills and abilities of every individual player. The players were keen learners, and soon we went for our first out-of-town assignment, a weekend in Morogoro where we would play against fellow Premier League teams Gari and Mbitwa.

As the leading club in the nation, we received many requests—and sometimes orders!—for pre-season friendlies. My fellow coaches and I tried to build a training program that included some matches, but things didn't quite work that way in Tanzania. Safari Sports Club is a big crowd-puller, no matter where in the country the team goes, and with this comes of course the potential for some individuals to make a quick buck. We would have liked to play maybe five or six pre-season matches in order to build and develop the team, but in all we must have played close to twenty matches. Some of these were valuable because of the decent opposition, but we also played a number of games against teams that looked and played as if they had been put together that same morning. In Tanzania, such teams usually have the word "Combine" in their name. Imagine Manchester United or Arsenal FC playing a pre-season friendly against Kensington Combine, a team made up of the local pub's most loyal customers. You get the idea. Obviously, what mattered to the regional Football Associations that organised our matches was not the quality of the game, but rather the amount of money they could rake in from the gate receipts. When we asked the officials after each game how much our cut from the proceeds was, the answer was always the same : nothing! In each case, the 'organising committee' (for want of a less flattering word) had had so many expenses in preparing for the match, that after the game there was nothing left from the several millions to share with the two participating teams—or at least not with us. Those who had decided to run for office in the Safari Sports Club leadership may of course also have benefitted from these matches. After all, quite a few pre-season 'friendlies' were played near the homes of candidates for a seat on the Executive Committee . . .

A rented bus that had seen much better days, probably around thirty years earlier, ferried us to the inland town of Morogoro, situated about 190 kilometres from Dar Es Salaam. The journey over the potholed highways took almost seven hours, and we arrived at our dilapidated guesthouse with a contingent of about 24 players, accompanied by some fans who had tagged along for the free ride. However, when we reached Morogoro, we discovered that there were about five 'officials' present there as well. Who they were or where they came from, we didn't know, and neither did we know in what capacity they were there or which function they came to fulfil. But soon enough that became clear, and I suppose now that I could have guessed their interest.

The guesthouse that we stayed in was terrible. The rooms were filthy, the beds were broken, the mosquito nets were torn, and there was hardly any electrical supply to speak of. The water in the sink was brown and had small bits of fauna swimming in it, and the showers were so dirty that any self-respecting person would refrain from setting foot in them. It was clear that our hosts, the Morogoro Regional Football Association, had refused to spend any money on our visit, but we were sure that the next day they would certainly be at the stadium in order to share the gate receipts amongst themselves and fill their plastic bags. The players were less fussy than myself, largely because some of them were used to these conditions. But it was hardly ideal preparation for a match. Dinner was no more than a pauper's meal with dry porridge and some shrivelled vegetables. And just a small bottle of mineral water, not even a cup of Chai Bora! We spent a long, sleepless night in this guesthouse, and I could hardly wait for the end of the three-day trip, so that we could return to the comfort of our home in Dar Es Salaam. In the morning, I decided to get in my car and check around the town of Morogoro for a better guesthouse or hotel. I found a small hotel on the outskirts of the city, and discussed the cost with my fellow coaches. We decided that it would be better to move to this hotel, to foot the bill ourselves, and to give the players a better experience. We naively agreed that we would use the money from the match ticket sales to pay the cost of our accommodation.

Later that day we played against Gari, a rival Premier League team, and walked away with a convincing 3-0 victory in spite of the fact that we played the whole second half with only ten men. One of our players, after scoring the second goal just before half time, pulled his shirt over his head in celebration, and was promptly sent off by the referee. It was a timely reminder of the appallingly poor standard of refereeing in this country. After all, this was a practice match in which we were trying out our tactics and team formation. The referee spoiled the purpose of the game by depriving us of a player for a laughable reason. But still, we managed to score a third goal against eleven players, which boosted our confidence and showed us that the players' resilience and determination were also in good shape.

After the game we coaches agreed that I go and get our share of the gate collection, so that we could pay for the players' accommodation and meals. Imagine my surprise (at that time) when I found that the so-called and self-proclaimed club 'officials' were already in the accounts office and waiting for Safari's share of the collection. I decided to say nothing and wait until we left the office. We were given about 10% of the collection, the rest allegedly going to all sorts of obscure football associations and committees from the Morogoro region. My gut feeling however told me that some individuals were taking home some much-needed pocket money in unobtrusive plastic bags . . .

Outside the office I asked the 'officials' for the money, so that I could go and settle our bills. But you can guess what the reply was.

"We are not giving you the money. We were sent here to collect the gate takings from these matches."
"So who sent you?"
"Mr Malazi."
"How come he never told me or the other coaches?"
"Because this is none of your business. Anyway, I am going to be the club's Treasurer after the next elections, so this is my job."
"Ah, so you have been elected already? I didn't even know that there had been elections . . ."
"That's just a matter of time. Meanwhile, I am in charge of the money."
"Look, I need to settle some bills here. Can I have the money please."
"No. I need this money because I paid for some expenses for the players from my own pocket and now I need to recover my money."

To my knowledge I had paid for all the players' expenses myself, so I asked:

"Which expenses did you pay for?"

"That's none of your business either."

"Fine. So you will settle the hotel and food bills for the players as well."

"Oh no I won't."

"Well, just consider this : if you keep all this money, then I will not settle any bills. They will then reach Mr Malazi, and maybe he will find out that you said that he sent you here to collect the money."

"And so?"

"Well, would you like him and the other Elders to know that you came all the way to Morogoro to take the club's money and run with it? I thought that you just said that you want to stand as a candidate in the next elections. I don't think that it would look good if you start stealing the club's money even before the elections . . ."

"OK, so here's the money. But I will give you a list of my expenses, and I want you to refund me."

"With Mr Malazi's approval, I will pay you back every Shilling that you have spent on the team."

"Well, if it needs Mr Malazi's approval, then just forget about it."

"OK. Good night."

I went to the players' hotel, settled the bills and met with my fellow coaches to discuss the next day's match against Mbitwa. We agreed that all the players needed to get a chance to prove themselves, and we completely changed the team's line-up from the first match. But again, the outcome was very positive as we earned ourselves a 2-1 victory. Considering that this was the first game for this set of players and against strong opposition, we were pretty satisfied with our performance. It was clear that the players were getting more and more used to the style of play that we wanted to implement. They worked tirelessly in the field, some of the strikers spent as much time trying to win the ball back as they did playing it forwards, and the team ethic and organisation were very encouraging. The tactical patterns started to show, and when I found myself on the sidelines to pass on some instructions to one of our players, one of the opposition players came over to me and said : "Coach, why are you suffocating us?". I smiled and thought to myself : "This is working".

In order to show my appreciation for the players' efforts, I decided to give each one of them a hefty bonus from my own pocket. Sometimes it is the small things that mean a lot. This time there was no argument about the gate collection, and we made our way back to Dar Es Salaam knowing that we had a good team in the making. This team was going to be able to perform well if it could be left to mature and grow as a unit. What we needed now was the continued support of the fans and everybody involved in the running of the club. Was I asking for too much?

A couple of days after our matches in Morogoro, I received a phone call from a fellow coach.

"Hello Peter! How are you?"

"Very well, thank you. How about you?"

"Fine, thanks. Listen, I wanted to ask you something."

"Yes?"

"I watched both your games over the weekend, and I was very impressed with the smooth passing game that your team now plays. My own players just can't do that. I was just wondering, how did you manage to teach them this in such a short period of time?"

"Well, it all comes down to hard work and to training with a purpose."

"Right. Any particular exercises that you can recommend, so I can try to get my players to play like that too?"

"Well, my favourite exercise, and one that works very well, is the one where I put eleven wooden barrels on the field, all spread out like opposition players. I then ask my players to pass and dribble their way through these barrels without allowing the ball to ever touch any of them. The players do this for hours and hours, and really learn to pass the ball away from the opposing players. Why don't you try that? It's fairly simple, and it allows the team to make progress very fast."

"Sure, I am going to try that in our next training session."

The next afternoon, the same coach called me again.

"Peter, Peter, what do I do now? Fifteen minutes ago we started to do the exercise you recommended, and now the barrels are leading by two goals to nil!"

I had no further advice to offer . . .

TWENTY-ONE

By the end of January, Safari Sports Club found itself in a very strange and unusual position : there was peace and harmony, there was a united set of players, coaches and Elders, and we felt that soon we would even be able to get a sponsor. Probably most importantly, there was no Executive Committee full of selfish 'leaders' who would cause all sorts of conflict and mistrust within the club. A state of peace and harmony in a Tanzanian club was quite unheard of. In fact, the big question was for how long this positive climate would continue to reign at the club. The answer came rather quickly.

The final verdict of the High Court in the leadership battle was that the club needed to organise by-elections. The actual term of the former leadership had not yet expired, but the Court found that the club was in such a poor state of affairs that it ordered for early elections to be held. Three of the former office holders had already passed away, and the others had simply disappeared over the horizon. Thankfully, the reinstated Treasurer retired to his stationary store. He'd had enough of the pressure and I am sure that he also realised that he would be watched much more closely for as long as I was at the club. The Assistant Treasurer went back to his up-country home region, probably with a bag full of cash. I never saw him again. The nature of the game in Tanzanian football was very much like that : become a football administrator for a couple of years, try to make as many 'savings' as possible during your time in office, collect all your plastic bags with bank notes, and then simply say 'Kwaheri' and walk away before the Courts come knocking on the door.

The Elders' Council had done a pretty good job of keeping the ship half-steady, but nobody could expect these septuagenarians to run the club on a permanent basis. And they themselves did not have this interest either. They had already served as club administrators in the 1970s, and they now deserved to spend their remaining years in peace and tranquillity. Time then to elect a completely new leadership, preferably one that would agree with my development and strategic plans. The next few weeks and months would tell whether we were going to be lucky enough to become the first club in Tanzania' history to have, at the very least, an attempt at a semi-professional set-up.

We were ready to welcome fresh blood and to let the *Wazee* take a back seat. At least, my fellow coaches and I thought that we were.

The Elders called a members' meeting where the many candidates would get a chance to connect with the voting public and put forth their intentions. I made it a point to attend that meeting as well. I was given a couple of minutes to talk to the members, and I told them that the team was gearing up well for the upcoming league championship.

"The Elders and the coaches thank you very much for the way in which you have been helping us and attending our matches and practices. The players are working hard, and in this sort of atmosphere I am convinced that Safari Sports Club will perform well in the league. With the elections coming up, nobody really knows what the future will bring, and it is therefore that I ask each one of you to think twice about the people that you are going to vote for. We need competent leaders, people who have the interest of the club at heart, people with a vision for the future, and who want to contribute towards the development of the club. We are tired of conflicts, financial scandals and a lack of success in the field of play. So make sure that the people that you vote for are able to lift the club to greater heights! *Safari juu*! (Go Safari!)"

"*Safari juu*!"

"We need leaders who will not only give us words and promises. We need leaders who will lead from the front, who will bring fresh ideas, who will bring sponsors and investors and who will make the first contributions themselves. We need leaders who have an eye on the latest developments in the world of top sports. Football today is science. We can not achieve anything by simply doing things the way they have been done here for the past few decades. We have to move on with the times and we must use everyone's skills to do so. Safari juu!"

"*Safari juu*!"

At this point I thought that it would be good to offer some socialist rhetoric to the audience, which consisted almost exclusively of elderly people who had lived through Tanzania's socialist years under Mwalimu Julius Kambarage Nyerere. I doubt that anyone knew that I was quoting another famous national leader—my next words might even have been borrowed from Mwalimu Nyerere's own speeches.

"My friends, the time has come for us, members and fans of Safari Sports Club, to muster all our strength to rebuild this glorious club. All of us must display our passion for the club that binds us, and our new leaders must step forward and show us the way. All of you must offer what you can contribute. The strong must offer their strength. The wise must offer their knowledge. The rich must offer their money. If you are able to provide us with material support, then please do so. If you are a doctor or a nurse, then please apply to become our team doctor. If you can offer or bring in sponsorship, then please speak with us. You will vote for a new leadership soon. Do not vote with your stomach. Do not vote with your heart. Do not vote with your wallet. Vote with your wisdom and in the knowledge that a strong leadership will see us make giant strides. There are no shortcuts in the football business. *Safari juu!*"

"*Safari juu!*"

I had done what I could. All that was left to do now was wait and find out whether my words had had any impact on the voting actions of the members. I realised that there would be an intense campaign of vote-buying and vote-selling, and that the members would call their price as they liked. Historically, the candidates with the deepest pockets stood the best chance of being elected. Someone once said that history often repeats itself.

The elections were due about a week after that meeting, but the aspirants already started to show themselves during our training sessions. One day we had a relatively modest gate collection, and some of our players needed money to pay the rent for their room in the city. Amongst the fans I spotted one of the members who was aiming to become Chairman of the club, and I decided to ask him to make a small contribution so that the players could be helped. He was sitting in the middle of a group of people, dressed in a smart suit and a tie, and looking rather well off. But he told me that he didn't have a single Shilling. He'd probably spent his last coins on the men sitting around him and hanging onto every word he said. I wondered then how this man, who couldn't help one or two players, was going to help the whole club if elected . . . The future would tell!

During the election campaign, one candidate suggested that he would consider allowing a woman to sit on the Executive Committee. He felt that there were certain roles in football administration that better suited women than men. As soon as he made his suggestion, all hell broke loose. The more conservative members of the society, which was the vast majority, completely opposed what they called a ridiculous and offensive idea, and the candidate in question was eventually forced to withdraw has candidacy altogether . . .

Election time came. One by one the various posts in the Executive Committee were filled with complete unknowns, and I was curious to find out who they were. I tried to ask around, but very few people actually had any information on any of the incumbents. I had to wait for our first meeting. I was looking forward to developing a good relationship of cooperation and shared vision with the new leaders, but now I know that this was nothing more than an illusion. The new leaders didn't take long to show their true colours . . .

Two days after the elections the new leaders came to the Bandari ground to introduce themselves to the players and to make a lot of promises. They also asked me how this daily raffle worked, and I showed it to them. We conducted our usual raffle that day, and I showed the results to the leaders.

"This raffle has allowed us to look after the players and to provide them with their training allowances and refunds for other expenses."

"So how much do you get per day?"

"It depends, but it is usually between one hundred and two hundred thousand Shillings."

Little lights started to twinkle in the eyes of the leaders . . .

"Really?"

"Yes, really."

"And what happens to the money?"

"As I just told you, we pay the players, but we also have other expenses like the training ground, security, water, training gear etcetera. At home I keep accounts, and I have a record for every Shilling that we have collected and spent. I can show you these accounts if you want me to."

"How much do you give the players?"

"This depends on their training attendance and their effort, but on average they receive two thousand Shillings per day."

"That's far too much!"

"Well, we can discuss this elsewhere. Meanwhile, do you like the idea of a daily raffle?"

"Yes, it's a good idea."

"I'm glad you like it. It certainly works, but I would also like to discuss with you other ways of raising funds and becoming financially stable as a club. We have big plans, and these will cost some money. Can we discuss my suggestions one of these days?"

"Yes, of course."

"Thank you."

In the beginning of February I took a short trip abroad. I was away for about two weeks, but even during my travels I was working out more proposals for sponsorship and establishing contacts with sports stores to see if we could make deals on sports gear or training equipment. Safari Sports Club was never far from my mind . . . I had left the raffle tickets and instructions with my fellow coaches, asking them to continue with the raffles and to look after our most important asset, the players.

Upon my return to Dar Es Salaam, a few surprises—and bad ones at that!—were waiting for me.

TWENTY-TWO

ON MY FIRST DAY BACK from my trip, I drove to the Bandari ground for practice, and found . . . nobody. I asked the people at the shop opposite the ground, and they told me that there hadn't been a practice there for about six or seven days. Apparently, the practices had shifted back to the TCC club ground in Chang'ombe.

I went to the club and found my fellow coaches and a number of our players, as well as some strange faces. Everybody was looking quite miserable.

"What's going on here?"

"You'll never believe this."

"Tell me anyway."

"Well, just after you left the Chairman came to tell us that there would be no more practices at the Bandari ground, because he wanted to put the team in camp."

"Why does that stop us from training in Temeke?"

"Because the camp is at a hundred meters from here . . ."

"Oh, and what kind of place is it?"

"It's a small, dirty guesthouse. It belongs to the Chairman . . ."

"What???"

"Yes, you heard me right. It is one of those famous 'moja saa' guesthouses, where couples rent a room for an hour or so. You know what I mean, it's what happens here between people who aren't too happy with their spouses or who are visiting Dar Es Salaam from upcountry. The Chairman has decided to put the whole team in his own guesthouse. And he is charging the club one hundred thousand Shillings per day for putting the players in his guesthouse."

"So instead of contributing from his own finances, he actually cashes in on the club by putting the team in his own guesthouse and by charging this huge amount of money. Are the guesthouse and the food worth that sort of money?"

"Absolutely not! The Chairman has put the players in his guesthouse because he can't get any other long-term customers. In fact, hardly anyone ever spends even one night there—it's really a halfway house for those who can't take their date home. Forcing the players to stay there is the only way for him to make the place profitable. And for each meal the players receive the same food : *ugali* (porridge) and *maharage* (beans)."

"No meat?"

"No meat."

"And what do the other officials say about this?"

"Well, the Chairman gives them some money as well, so they keep quiet."

"And what happened to the raffle?"

"We're not doing raffles any more. In any case, very few fans attend the practices here."

"I don't believe this! So who is financing the team now?"

"Nobody. That's why the players are hungry and weak. Some of them are training with injuries, but there is no money for medication."

"What are they doing to our team?? Wait a second . . . where are our players?"

"What do you mean?"

"Well, there are quite a few players missing, and who are these new ones?"

"Oh, well, the new leaders decided to sack some of the players and to bring some new ones."

"Why?"

"*Sijui bwana.*" (I don't know)

"But we have been working with a squad of thirty players all through January, and now some of these players have left!"

"Yes, I know."

"And what did you say when the leaders decided to do this?"

"We told them that this would seriously disturb our preparations, and that some of the players that they sacked were needed in the team."

"And what did they say?"

"They told us to coach the players that we were being given, and if we disagreed we should leave the club."

"This is unbelievable. How can they treat you like this?"

"Yes, they said that we are just employees of the club, and we should not ask any questions. We are only here to train the players, and the leaders will decide which players will play for the club."

"Are any of the leaders here?"

"No, we haven't seen them for a couple of days now."

"This doesn't look good hey . . ."

So in a matter of days we had lost our income from the raffle, some of our best players and our training ground, and we had got some players who didn't feature in our plans, a pathetic guesthouse to stay in, no proper food or facilities, and most importantly very low player morale. What's more, the league was about to start. We could only expect the worst.

A few days later I bumped into the Chairman in one of the upmarket stores in the city, and I asked him what had happened. But basically I received the same reply:

"Just mind your own business, the team is in the hands of the leaders now, so just do your job as a coach."

"Fine, but the players are hungry and weak. And we need new boots for some of them."

"The players are always complaining. Stop listening to them and get on with the job!"

"And another thing, could we coaches get our letters of appointment from the new committee please?"

"You will get those *kesho* (tomorrow)."

"Thank you."

I learned that week that *kesho* does not necessarily mean 'tomorrow', but rather 'any time really in the future, if ever' . . . It pained me to see our players come to practice dressed in rags, wearing torn shoes or slippers, and carrying their training gear in a plastic bag. They needed help, and I decided to increase my efforts. Now that the players were going to spend many long hours in this wonderful guesthouse, I thought that it would be best to keep them occupied and challenged. Since most of my players had not even finished their secondary education, I felt that giving them some mental stimulation would be useful. I spoke with some senior students at my place of employment, and I soon found four volunteers to teach English and Mathematics to the team. We sat together for a couple of hours, we devised a curriculum that would be manageable and helpful, and soon the players had two hours of class per day. One hour of English conversation, and one hour of Mathematics. The players loved to learn and were very grateful for the opportunity. Another friend of mine, a medical doctor, agreed to come and speak with the team once a week about health-related issues. Health and hygiene are major challenges in Tanzania, partly because of the poor sanitation services and partly because of the careless lifestyle of many people. Because of the appalling poverty, the low standard of education and the traditional polygamist cultures, many young people of Tanzania didn't put a high value on a human life or on their personal health and safety, and often abandoned themselves to hedonistic and lethal pursuits. I was not really prepared to invest so much time and energy and helping young adults develop their skills and giving them a shot at a better life if they were going to be sleeping around and getting infected with the world's most brutal and untreatable diseases. Of course I wasn't naïve and I knew exactly what these young players got up to in their free time. Dar Es Salaam is a big city, and players of the country's biggest clubs would never have difficulty in finding some intimate entertainment.

As soon as the sun goes down in Dar Es Salaam, the *'mia mbili'* culture appears in many districts. In the Kiswahili language, *'mia mbili'* means two hundred, and that is the amount of money in Tanzanian Shillings that local and expatriate males in the city have to pay for an hour's worth of female company. Only twenty cents of an American dollar and the lady is yours! I was told that some of these ladies lived in abject poverty and had to sell their bodies in order to support their families back home, but the vast majority were in fact working women who simply wanted to make a quick buck by cajoling any male client who had a few dollars to spare. Prostitution is of course illegal in Tanzania, at least officially. But the *'mia mbili'* culture is certainly not an underground phenomenon. There is little that the authorities can or are willing to do about it, and in fact it's a public secret that many well-to-do and many not-so-well-to-do citizens don't shy away from engaging in this activity. Now that my players occasionally received some small allowances, it was very easy for them to get intimate with a *'mia mbili'* lady. I am not suggesting that they all did this, but I was not going to take any chances. These ladies certainly knew who the players were, and would certainly consider them easy targets. So rather than pretending that it didn't happen, I asked the doctor to help the players protect themselves and behave responsibly. We tried what we could, and all in all the players responded quite well . . .

I also decided to step up my campaign to find a sponsor or a benefactor who could assist us. I spoke to as many business people as I could find, and one day a good friend of mine agreed to support my cause. He was a keen follower of Tanzanian football himself, and thus he was aware of the problems that most teams here are confronted with. Corruption, embezzlement of club funds, in-fighting, the list goes on. In spite of his knowledge, I managed to convince him to at least give it a try and to advertise his company through my club. We both knew that we put our friendship on the line by engaging in a deal that would involve a number of less reliable characters. My friend told me that he was comfortable dealing with me directly, and he asked me to be the main point of contact within the club for him. He confided in me that he had had negative experiences in the past, mainly with sponsorships for golf tournaments, but my presence made the difference for him. He was ready to trust the *mzungu*. Nevertheless, he decided to start on a very small scale and then see what sort of response the company would get. On behalf of my players, I was happy with whatever he wished to contribute, and together we agreed that he would start by printing a set of T-shirts with the company name and the club's name. These T-shirts were to be distributed amongst the players and technical staff of the club. My friend made a commitment that if the response was favorable, he would assist the team financially as well. We were looking at millions of Shillings to be pumped into the team's preparations for the league, into players' salaries and into the purchase of training equipment . . .

At this early stage however we were only sure of the T-shirts for the players, and since this concerned a simple donation between two friends, I didn't see the need to inform the leaders. I wanted to show my friend that he could trust me and that the players would directly benefit from his assistance. We agreed that I would simply pick up the T-shirts and give them to the players . . . Little did I realise then that a couple of T-shirts would make the leaders declare war against me . . .

One morning my friend called me and informed me that the T-shirts were ready.

"When are you coming to pick them up?"
"Is tomorrow 11 o'clock fine with you?"
"Yes."
"OK."
"Can you bring some journalists, so that the company gets some exposure through this donation?"
"Sure, I'll call them right away."
"Fine. See you tomorrow then."

I called three or four journalists and told them that the next day there would be a presentation to Safari Sports Club. They asked me how much was involved (as if the only way of helping a team is to donate cash . . .), but I told them that they would get all the details the next day. We agreed to meet at my friend's company office the next morning, eleven o'clock *mzungu* time.

During the presentation of the T-shirts, my friend told the reporters:

"I was approached by the Safari Sports Club coach who asked me to help the team in any way possible. It is true that he is a good friend of mine, but even so my company wants to get involved in the local sports scene. We feel that it is important that local businesses back our clubs and athletes, as they represent our people and our nation. They receive very little support from the government or from their associations, and so they are left to survive through their own means. My company is a leader in the local IT market, and we want to be associated with other winners. It is hoped that this donation is the start of a long-lasting cooperation between the club and my company. Today we are presenting a set of T-shirts, and if all goes well, then we shall soon enter into a financial agreement with the club. We are looking at becoming Safari Sports Club's official sponsor and restoring the club's lost pride."
"How much money is the sponsorship worth?"
"I could give you the value of the T-shirts, but that is not important right now. When we talk about a financial sponsorship, then we talk about several millions of Shillings per year."
"How many millions?"
"The details will be worked on once we get to that stage."
"So today you are not presenting any money to the club."

"That's correct."

"Oh, I see . . ."

The journalists were clearly not used to hearing about a sponsorship that did not include an amount of cash, but this was fine with me. There were a lot of people that we needed to educate, and the reporters were some of the main ones.

The next day some of the local papers reported on the donation.

Safari Sports Club land a sponsorship deal

**BY
MAIL REPORTER**

Safari Sports Club have landed a potentially lucrative sponsorship deal with Dar Es Salaam-based IT company "Kompyuta World". Team coach, Peter Mulder, told this reporter yesterday that everything about the contract will be revealed shortly.

"We wanted to announce it officially today, but there are some final touches to be made and therefore we thought it appropriate to make it public in a few days", said the overjoyed coach. However, Mulder did not reveal the amount involved and the duration of the contract.

During the press conference, "Kompyuta World" presented Safari Sports Club with a set of T-shirts bearing the club logo and the sponsor's name.

By lunchtime I had already received three different phone calls from three different club officials. They all had the same question, and it was clear that neither of them knew that the other officials were also calling me.

"How much money did you receive?"

"I didn't receive any money, only a set of T-shirts."

"Are you sure you didn't get any money or a cheque?"

"Yes, of course I'm sure."

"So what is there for me in this sponsorship?"

"Excuse me?"

"You heard me. *Mimi nitapata kiasi gani cha hela*? (How much of the money do I get?)"

"There is no money involved. I was given T-shirts for the players. There may be a financial sponsorship at a later stage."

"Why didn't you tell me about this donation? I should have gone to receive the T-shirts myself."

"This was a friend of mine giving me something for the players. It isn't a big deal."

"Well, you should have told me. I want you to give me the T-shirts!"

"I beg your pardon?"

"You must give me the T-shirts. I don't want you to give them to the players."

"I'm sorry, but I promised my friend that I would give them to the players, and that is what I am going to do. I don't break my promise."

"We'll see about that!"

This conversation reflects what was said to me by three different officials. All three claimed that they should have been the one collecting the T-shirts, and that they shouldn't be given to the players. We were going to fight about a set of T-shirts, would you believe it?!

TWENTY-THREE

THE SECRETARY GENERAL OF THE club, who was one of the people who had called me, then decided to take his frustration of not getting any money to the newspapers. He complained bitterly that I had received 'big sums of money' from a local company, and that I had completely by-passed the leadership.

"Kompyuta World" sponsorship makes leadership cry

**BY
OUR CORRESPONDENT**

Members of the Executive Committee of Safari Sports Club have bitterly complained that they did not receive any of the T-shirts donated by "Kompyuta World" yesterday. During a press conference held at the IT company's offices in Dar Es Salaam the day before yesterday, the media was informed that very soon a big sponsorship agreement will be signed with Safari Sports Club. In order to mark the start of this cooperation, the company presented the club's coach, Peter Mulder, with a set of 30 T-shirts to be worn by the players and the technical staff.

In an interview over the phone last night, several members of the club's Executive Committee complained that they had not been involved in the discussions and that they had not even seen the T-shirts.

The Secretary General, Mr Shenzi, told this reporter that he had not heard anything about the discussions.

"I know nothing about this, I have only read the reports in the newspapers. I have told our coach that he must give us all the information", a clearly frustrated Shenzi said.

The Chairman of the Executive Committee, Mr Massawe, also claimed that he knew nothing about the sponsorship deal.

"I wonder why our coach has not mentioned anything to the Committee. Maybe the company simply gave him these T-shirts because they are his friends. If they want to make a sponsorship deal that involves money, they can only discuss with us. After all, Mulder is just our former player who has been helping out with coaching. He doesn't even have a letter of appointment from us!".

The reporters called me and asked for my side of the story, but I felt that it had already been printed the day before, when my friend's words were quoted in reports about the donation. I didn't feel the need to add anything to that. At least I understood now why I had never received my letter of appointment. The Executive Committee clearly wanted there to be no formal relationship with someone who was just trying to develop and improve the club. I started to understand that we were on a collision course, and that sooner or later things would come to a head . . . unless of course the Executive Committee was only going to last as long as its predecessors.

A bit later I received another call from the Secretary General, who told me that he was summoning me to a meeting with the leadership. I had to report at the club house the next morning, and bring all the T-shirts that I had been given. I wasn't born yesterday, and had a pretty good idea what they wanted from me. When I went I found about ten people there. There was the Secretary General, the Assistant Secretary General, the Vice Chairman, the Publicity Officer and some other people whom I didn't even know. As I walked into the room, I could hear them talking about the club's constitution, which dated back many years. I overheard the Secretary General saying to his friends that "we need to revise the constitution soon, so that we can get rid of all those fools that don't contribute any money to the club". I had already heard from some members that there was talk about issuing new membership cards in exchange for significant sums of money, but I had not heard the members being called 'fools' before. I pretended that I hadn't heard it this time either. I did not see nor receive any Chai Bora at this meeting.

For good measure I had taken only two T-shirts, just to show the leaders that they were making a big fuss about nothing really.

"Can you explain what you have been doing?"
"The story appeared in the newspapers, which you have read. Three of you called me yesterday to ask for the money and the T-shirts, so I believe that you all know that I have received these T-shirts from a friend."

At this point they all looked at each other, probably trying to figure out which three people had called me . . .
The Publicity Secretary said:

"Let me tell you something about how things are done around here. When a donation is made, or when a sponsorship is agreed upon, the first people to gain from this is the leadership. We are not in the Executive Committee because we have nothing better to do. We have fought hard to be elected, and we now deserve our share of the pie. Of every pie. We want you to give us the T-shirts. First all the Committee members have to have one, and if any remain after that, then you can give them to the players."

"I know that you want the T-shirts. You already told me that yesterday on the phone . . . But you must know that I have promised to my friend that I would give them to the players, so that is what I am going to do. I'm sorry to disappoint you."

"Why do you look for sponsorship for the team?"

"Well, we are in need of a lot of things. I started looking for sponsors way before the elections, and am still continuing to do so. Ever since the elections, I have not seen any official trying to do the same. If you can find a sponsor for the team, then I can rest. But you are not doing anything. Meanwhile, by causing a fuss about these T-shirts, I am afraid that you might be scaring away potential sponsors that I have been talking with. After seeing the reports in the newspapers, my friend told me that he may review his opinion on sponsoring Safari Sports Club in a more substantial way . . . Would it not be a shame to lose what I think will be a very helpful deal?"

"Well, we will let you know when you can give the T-shirts to the players."

They never told me when to hand out the T-shirts, so one day I decided to give the T-shirts to the players. I called the captain and asked him to tick off the names of the players when they received their T-shirts. Each player, as well as my fellow coaches, the manager and the acting team doctor, all got one T-shirt each. They were very grateful. Unfortunately there were no T-shirts left for the leaders . . .

Only two days later, one of the players came to me and told me that his T-shirt had gone missing. I couldn't replace it, but imagine my surprise when the next day the Vice Chairman was wearing this T-shirt when he came to meet his buddies at our training ground. He must have taken it either from the player's room or from the washing line . . . I knew that the officials didn't—or just couldn't—believe that I hadn't received anything more than those T-shirts. The concept of a donation instead of a financial agreement was totally unknown and incomprehensible to them. I sensed their suspicion whenever we got anywhere near one another.

In the next day's paper, the Secretary General was quoted as saying that he would ban the players from wearing these T-shirts.

> If I as a leader of the club can not have such a t-shirt, then I can not allow the players to wear them either. Our coach has already asked the players to wear the T-shirts when we go to our matches, but I will make sure that this does not happen!

He must have been reminded by other members of the Executive Committee that it was only a matter of time before their coach landed the proverbial 'golden egg', so "just lay off, let the players wear the T-shirts, and let the coach do all the hard work for us". The ban never materialized.

Needless to say that, after the publicity that surrounded this simple donation, my friend decided not to put any money into the club . . . and who could blame him? He told me, and the press, that he would continue to support the players with donations in kind and with training equipment, but no money would be forthcoming. It is also my firm belief that other potential sponsors were following this saga, and at the end decided that it wasn't worth getting themselves into a similar mess. I certainly heard a lot of comments to that effect, and the Executive Committee did not do itself any favors here.

One positive outcome though of this episode was that the leadership at least recognized the need to look for money. The team was short on equipment and outfits, and the start of the league was approaching fast. We were soon also going to travel to Zimbabwe to honor our Africa Cup match against Chapungu FC, and I was wondering how this trip would be financed. I would find out soon. One of the Committee members had the bright idea to go to the newspapers and tell them that the club had approached the Football Association of Tanzania, to ask for the club to be given half a million Shillings. I have explained before that the FAT officials excelled at helping themselves to the goodies whilst conveniently forgetting the duties that they were elected to perform. The Chairman of the Football Association, a man who had spent most of his life selling soap and cashew nuts from his small downtown store, and who was now driving a big convertible Mercedes-Benz SLK Class Roadster, turned the request down. Five hundred thousand Shillings, or five hundred US dollars, that was a large amount in anyone's pocket. Surely he had a sick niece or a dying aunt somewhere also, and the next fully-sponsored FIFA Congress was months away. No, sorry, he could not part with this money.

A few days later, there would be more to the sponsorship story. Two overseas companies that I had written to earlier replied to me, and told me in no uncertain terms that they were looking at sponsoring my club and establishing a name for themselves in Tanzania. We were talking about huge companies here, which didn't have to worry about ten thousand dollars more or less. In fact, the figures that they quoted me were mind-boggling, and at first I thought that the amounts were quoted in Tanzanian Shillings, rather than in US Dollars . . . The offer was by far the biggest sponsorship that any club in Tanzania, and probably even in East Africa, had ever received : five hundred and eighty million Tanzanian Shillings, or around six hundred thousand US dollars from the two companies combined! This sort of assistance could speed up our development at a phenomenal pace. Five hundred and eighty million Shillings! That could have gotten us started on establishing a youth academy for the club . . . It's very difficult to comprehend how much money this is in Tanzania. And all we had to do was promote the companies' names? Sounds easy, doesn't it? Well, not so for the Safari Sports Club officials.

As soon as I received this news, I informed the Chairman of the club. Imagine my surprise when I heard him ask me:

« *Mimi nitapata kiasi gani cha hela*? » How much is in it for me?

This man was unbelievable! I had just brought him the news that his club was going to get a gift from heaven, and all he could think of was his own profit! I told him that I wanted to meet with the leadership in order to discuss this offer. Mr Massawe said:

"The other leaders don't need to know about this. They will only cause trouble. Let me handle this by myself. You keep this offer a secret, and I will reward you . . ."

"I'm sorry, but there is no way that this can be a secret. This sponsorship is for the team, not for individuals. I want to have a meeting with the whole Executive Committee."

"If the other leaders know about it, then they will want some money for themselves too."

"And you just want it all for yourself? Look, either I have a meeting with the complete leadership, or I write back to these companies and tell them that the sponsorship deal is not on. What will it be?"

"Let's meet with the other leaders then . . ."

We agreed to meet the next afternoon.

The next morning, one of the local Kiswahili newspapers carried a big headline story : *Safari kudhaminiwa kwa sh. milioni 580* (Safari Sports Club to be sponsored for 580 million Shillings). It was obvious that the Chairman had already spoken to his fellow committee members, and somebody had spilled the story to the media. I received phone calls from left, right and centre, with basically all the officials asking me the same question:

« *Mimi nitapata kiasi gani cha hela*? »

The Executive Committee eventually agreed to meet with me about this issue, so that we could work out how we would go about negotiating a sponsorship deal. Once more, I went to meet the leaders at the club house, and they were there in full force, with cups of Chai Bora also present in abundance. Five hundred and eighty million Shillings makes people move, apparently . . . Especially if these people think that these millions could be theirs . . .

I summarized for the panel of interested ears what the companies had suggested. In a nutshell, they wanted to have a massive impact on the development of the club, as they were aware of the fact that I had already tried to send some of our best players for trials overseas. These companies wanted to support the club as well as the individual players, and they insisted on us setting up a development structure that included the youth. They were talking about an academy not unlike the many youth football centres that the major European clubs had already been setting up, both within their own country and abroad. Of course they also wanted to bring their products into the Tanzanian market. They also mentioned the fact that education was one of their main objectives, and they were happy to hear that a highly-qualified teacher was going to be their main contact. With the sponsorship, which was to run over several years, we would be able to get our own team bus and our own premises. The companies felt that an investment of this size could be recouped within a few years, and especially so if we managed to send a few of the players for professional careers overseas. Some of the terms of the agreement would be conditional, such as winning the league and showing continuous progress in the development projects. This really was a gift from heaven, and I had no problem at all showing my enthusiasm to the highly attentive members of the Executive Committee. When I came to the end of my presentation, I told them that I was looking forward to their questions . . .

"If I may finish with a suggestion . . . Since these potential sponsors have contacted me in response to my letters to them, can I be given the go-ahead by the leadership to enter into negotiations, and brief them about the developments?"

Immediately the Vice-Chairman stepped in and said:

"Sio kazi yako, bwana." (literally 'That is not your job, man', meaning 'That is none of your business').
"Excuse me?"
"Sio kazi yako."
"And what does that mean?"
"He says that this is not your job."
"Oh. And so what does he suggest we do?"

(murmurs in Kiswahili)

"Listen, this is what we have decided. Where are these sponsors from?"
"One is from Western Europe, the other is from the Gulf."
"OK, listen. We want you to reply to them, and tell them that they should invite four of us to Europe and to the Gulf for negotiations. We will meet them there, and discuss how we can come to a deal."
"Well, shouldn't we first try and get more details about what exactly they are looking for?"
"No, they must send us air tickets, and we will then sort everything out. They must also send us an initial payment of ten thousand dollars, so that we can get legal advice here and prepare for the trip and the negotiations."
"Well, I think that you are pushing it a bit. I still believe that it is better to first find out the finer details about what sort of deal they want to seal with us, and for us to inform

them what we can offer in terms of exposure for their companies and their products. Why don't I take care of that first?"

"*Sio kazi yako!*"

"Fine. I will leave everything in your hands then. Here are the names and the addresses of the two companies. Good luck."

TWENTY-FOUR

NOBODY IN TANZANIA TODAY REMEMBERS what came of these extraordinary offers from Europe and from the Gulf. All I did after this meeting was to send a message to the two companies, informing them that they would soon hear from the club's leadership. It was quiet for a while, but after about two months I received a letter from one of the two companies, informing me that they had recently received a letter from just one of the leaders, telling them that he required fifteen thousand dollars in his personal account before he would even start negotiating a sponsorship deal. Needless to say that the offer was cancelled right there and then. I wrote back to the company and apologized for the inconvenience that had been caused. I assured them that in the future I would deal with them myself rather than putting them through the embarrassment of receiving letters like the one they had received from this Safari Sports Club official.

A couple of days later, another sponsorship offer was wasted. During a reception at one of the local embassies, I met with someone from the Belgian Overseas Development Service. This man knew that I was involved in a local club, and asked me why I didn't seek assistance from my Embassy.

"How would that work?"
"Well, we have grants available for local development projects. They are called micro-projects, and are meant to help Tanzanians establish themselves and others in the professional sector."
"And how does that fit in with a football club?"
"Well, the grant could be used to develop the club house or to employ somebody to make club merchandise like posters, flags, T-shirts and so on."
"Sounds like a good idea. What is the amount of these grants?"
"They have a limit of one million Shillings."
"Well, that would be a good start. The club house needs a lot of work, and I would love it if we can create some jobs for skilled people who can help us. I have always been in favor of a club reaching out to the community and having an impact. I will talk to the club's officials about the existence of this development fund."

So the next time I saw the Secretary General, I told him the whole story. I asked him if he'd be interested in this kind of 'sponsorship'.

«*Mimi nitapata kiasi gani cha hela?*»
"Nothing. The Embassy will never provide cash, they will only pay for services provided by those people that the club would employ. You'll never get to see a Shilling . . ."
"Then that's not a sponsorship."
"Well, if the Embassy is prepared to pump one million Shillings into the club so that it can develop and so that we can create job opportunities, it can help us, whether you want to call it a sponsorship, a donation or whatever."
"So what do they require?"
"They need you to fill out these forms, and they need the building plans of the club house."
"Well, I can provide these. Are you sure that we can't get any cash?"
"I am sure. But it comes down to the same thing : the services that will be provided will need to be paid for, and it doesn't make any difference whether the Embassy pays for them directly, or whether they give Safari Sports Club the money and we then pay for the services. The Embassy probably prefers making sure that all the money reaches its destination."
"Well, I will get the building plans, and then I will go to the Embassy and talk to the person in charge."
"I'm not sure if that is the best way to go about this . . ."
"That is what I am going to do."

Nothing ever came of this opportunity either. I know that the money was readily available, but it wasn't meant to go to a club official or to anyone else who didn't deserve it. It was meant to go to those people who would provide the club with a development service. Somehow, the club officials didn't seem to be interested in a one million Shillings donation to benefit the development of the club . . . Surprised?

A few weeks later I found out why it was impossible to have the club house upgraded : some of the club officials had leased the complete building to a businessman, and had swindled the rent money. Obviously, this businessman was not going to move out of the house, and the lease had to be kept a secret. Thankfully for the club and its faithful members, it wasn't. Many questions were being asked about the officials' right to lease the club house, and about the whereabouts of the money received for the lease. I am sure that the investigations continue to this day . . .

It was at this stage, and because of all the frustrations, that I decided to stop looking for a sponsor. It wasn't going to work because of the greed of the officials, who would do anything to make sure that any donation or financial assistance would not reach the players or its intended destination. So what was the point of me putting more time, energy and money in looking for outside help? I was only embarrassing myself and putting myself in a difficult situation with the people that I contacted for sponsorship. In some cases there was even the risk of compromising personal friendships, and I wasn't prepared to go that far. Not with the odds stacked so strongly against a positive outcome.

Fate had it that a bit later a sponsorship deal was finally struck. One of the many local companies that I had written to reacted to my letter, and informed the nation that they wanted to enter into a three-year sponsorship deal with Safari Sports Club. When I heard the news, I was happy for my players, but of course I had serious doubts about whether this sponsorship would actually benefit the club and its players, and not just the officials. I decided not to interfere in the negotiations, as this was *sio kazi yangu*—not my job. But I did call the sponsor and met with him one evening, just to ask him to ensure that the money that he was spending on the team would actually reach the players. I was very adamant on this, and made a simple suggestion.

"Would it be possible to open a bank account for every player?"

"Why would that be necessary?"

"Well, it would allow you to pay their salaries directly into their account, without having to depend on the officials to do so. Is it not preferable to have fewer middlemen when it comes to cash?"

"Well, yes, maybe."

"And also, this would allow us to teach the players how to save money and how to budget for their needs. When we give them their salary in cash, once a month, it will be spent within the next two or three days, if not on the first day. You know how they are unprepared to deal with amounts that are bigger than a few thousand Shillings. They've never had such amounts."

"Yes, I understand."

"What I have observed here is that when somebody gets paid, suddenly a long queue of relatives show up, and they all need some money for all sorts of ailments, expenses and debts. And for a drink of course. Our poor players will not make it home with their salaries. And of course, there is also the safety issue. Walking around with thousands of Shillings in a plastic bag in Dar Es Salaam simply isn't a good idea. You become a target very easily."

"Let me think about your suggestion. I'm still not convinced that we should transfer money into bank accounts, it's a lot of administrative work."

"Well, yes, but it's only once a month, and you can ask for a standing order at the bank."

"Then how will you penalize players who haven't shown up for practice or who haven't put enough effort?"

"I am sure that if they are going to make a few thousand Shillings per month, they will show up and they will work hard. Our task is not to punish them, but to educate them. And there is no better learning incentive here than cash!"

"That's true."

"Lastly, I also think that if we are going to raise the profile of this club, then we must be professional in all areas, and avoid that salaries are paid in cash, out of a plastic bag, on the training ground. Let's be a pioneer for Tanzanian football. At the end of the day, this will reflect very well on your company, and you will get all the credit for these innovative ideas. I will simply be grateful to have healthier, happier and better fed players."

"OK, I will get back to you on this."

I also asked him, on behalf of the coaches, to include the provision of training equipment and training kit, so that we could make our practices more professional and more efficient. He agreed to all this, and assured me that we would see a big difference in the team as of now. Somehow, I wasn't too sure . . .

This sponsorship received a lot of coverage in the local press, but it soon became very clear that it was causing more problems than it solved. Neither the coaches nor the players received regular payments. Bank accounts were never set up. I had advocated from the start that salaries should be transferred into the players' accounts straight from a specially created sponsors' account. My advice was not accepted. Instead, cheques were given to the officials, who had their own way of spending the players' salaries. Conveniently, some players were suspended for 'lack of effort' or 'indiscipline', and consequently they stopped receiving their salaries. However, the size of the cheque from the sponsor to the officials remained the same . . . You can make your calculations for yourself . . .

One of Tanzania's main mobile telecommunications providers approached me and asked if I could provide them with a copy of the club's constitution. They wanted to get a better idea of the club's development plans, and they also wanted a clear picture of the organizational structure. I forwarded the request to the Executive Committee, but no constitution was ever passed on to the potential sponsor. When the press boys came to hear of the interest by the mobile phone company, they also enquired with the Secretary General. According to him, "the Executive Committee was in the process of revising and redrafting the Constitution" which, it was claimed, dated from 1936, the year that the club was formed. So this was simply a case of bad timing. Apparently, the running of the club was not always done in accordance with the established procedures and principles, and it was wise not to make this too obvious with any potential investors. I wasn't too surprised at this, I must admit.

Now that money seemed to have become plentiful in the club, we suddenly had several thousand more fans . . . amazing how cash, or stories about cash, create such an overwhelming interest in people. During and after our training sessions, more and more self-proclaimed supporters approached me and asked me for money. All of a sudden there seemed to be an awful lot of sick relatives all over the country, and if I had kept accurate records of all the requests, I would probably have found that some fathers and uncles died three or four times in the space of one month.

It must be said that families in Tanzania are enormous. Most of the teammates and players that I dealt with had several fathers and several mothers—they not only count their biological parents, but also their parents' siblings. So the father's elder brother is called *baba kubwa* and the father's younger brother is called *baba ndogo*. The same applies to the mother's brothers. Then we need to take into account that many families have stepfathers and stepmothers, who of course also have their own siblings. This gives us an idea of how many *wazee* (grandfathers) and how many *bibi* (grandmothers) there are in just one family . . . It thus becomes almost plausible that one player's "father" dies more than once in a short space of time. Once I had figured out the family structures, it became easier to see through the deceit. And of course, more than one of these beggars either smelled like alcohol or tobacco mixed with some substance. When they came to ask me for money, I knew very well that it was not going to be spent on a funeral . . .

Eventually I got tired of the harassment and the never-ending stories about dead and sick relatives. One evening when I was talking with a reporter after our training session, I told him that the begging by some of these people had become rather annoying. I explained that I had seen people abuse the kindness of others by buying cigarettes or beer with the money that they had received from a kind heart, and that everyone needed to learn to be responsible with their money. Of course, the next day the newspaper shouted in big letters that Mulder called the club's fans 'beggars', but I didn't mind. The message was clearly received, and people backed off a bit.

The terms of the sponsorship contract got twisted this way and that way. A satisfactory amount of training gear was never provided. On several occasions there were threats to withdraw the sponsorship. This deal did not benefit the club in any way, and in fact it did more harm than good to the team. It created divisions amongst players, coaches, officials and members. And I can't even imagine that the sponsor himself got a lot of positive mileage out of his supposed investment. Who'd like to be associated with a club that isn't being run properly, that only makes it into the papers because of its internal problems, because of the misappropriation of funds, and because of its members' meetings that end up with some people being punched and kicked? It was clear from the start that none of the club's officials had properly read the contract proposal before signing it, otherwise they would have objected to the fact that this sponsor wanted the club to refrain from wearing any apparel that bears marks of any other brand, product or company name in matches, practices or any other event. In other words, this sponsor insisted on being the sole sponsor for the club, even though no provisions were made to cater for ALL the club's needs. Where were the team bus, the teachers, the medical insurance, the land for our own training ground, the funds for the development of the club house? I could go on for another three pages about the club's needs, but I won't do so. They were well-known. It has always struck me as extremely odd that the club's officials signed this contract, even though it didn't even refer to them once. I've said before that I wasn't born yesterday, and so I know that they can only have signed this deal, which was very much in the favor of the sponsor and not in the favor of the club, by receiving an incentive for their signature. Who will argue with this?

When it became clear to the general population that this sponsorship deal was mainly a public relations exercise, more and more rumors started to spread across the city. There were suggestions that the promise of millions of Shillings was merely a smoke screen for less honorable activities. Through the grapevine, I heard that behind the 'official' business of this sponsor, there was a less appealing side to his activities. The team shirts that we were given advertised various types of soap and washing powder, but the main part of the business was, apparently, not quite as clean. It was suggested that the club was being used to whitewash large sums of money that had been generated through the sale of 'medicine'. I speak euphemistically here. The port of Dar Es Salaam was an easy transit point for all sorts of products that made one forget his or her problems, or that made one braver and sexually more potent than usual . . . By regularly funneling cheques through a series of bank accounts, it was very hard to track the eventual destination of millions of Shillings . . . although more and more members of the public seemed to have a pretty good idea of what this destination may have been.

It is a great credit to the players that throughout all this time, they continued to work hard and keep their fighting spirit in readiness for the league. I commended them for not giving up, even though I was sure that this thought crossed the mind of some of them. They had been told about salaries and better times, yet in the end nothing had changed for them in terms of their conditions. We coaches also tried our best to keep the morale high, and a strong bond between the coaches and the players was formed. We managed to have some fun during the practices, which again increased the team spirit and the feeling of unity.

During a game of six-a-side:

"Listen guys, football is a game of triangles. Raymond, what's a triangle in Kiswahili?"
"*Pembetatu.*"
"Thanks. When playing football, you must try to create *pembetatu.*"
"What do you mean?"
"Look, when you have played a pass, you mustn't stand still. You have to take up a new position, so that you give your teammate the option to pass the ball back to you. You can play a one-two, and in the process, you eliminate an opponent."
"So where does the *pembetatu* come in?"
(drawing the action in the sand) "If you look at the movement of the ball and yourself, you will find the shape of the triangle."

"Oh yes, I see."

"Teacher, teacher, this is not a *pembetatu*, this is a samosa."

"Fine, if you want to consider this a samosa, then that's OK. Now go and make some samosas in the field!"

Somehow, the samosa story stuck, and learning was achieved . . . I had just been reminded that not all of my players had had the privilege of attending geometry classes, but they sure knew what samosas were.

On another occasion the whole team started to laugh with one player who explained that he wanted a return pass because he was in a situation of "one against the two". All the players imitated him, humorously mockingly:

"One against the two? One against the two?"

One day, after practice, I was surprised to see the Chairman and the Vice-Chairman at the practice ground. It was extremely rare that any of the officials came to the ground, and you had to seize the opportunity with two hands and both your feet in order to ask a few questions.

"You know, I think it would be a good idea to provide the players with a qualified teacher for their English and Mathematics classes. They have a lot of free time in the guesthouse, when they could be doing some intellectual work. It will help them in developing their minds so that it becomes easier for them to cope with the more complex tactical demands of the game, and it will also improve communication within the team. For the past few months some of my own students have been helping out, but they are not always available, and I also want to avoid exposing them to the *'moja saa'* and the *'mia mbili'* cultures that seem to pervade the guesthouse. They are minors, and I don't think it's appropriate for them to see the antics of these irresponsible adults. A full-time teacher will be able to keep an eye on the players' progress, and will also be able to supervise and control them during their downtime. Having such a person here won't cost the club much, but it can bring great benefits."

"*Sikiliza, bwana, sio kazi yako.*"

"And what about our letters of appointment?"

"*Kesho.* Now, what we wanted to ask you, will you be able to travel with the team to our away matches during the season? Can you get permission from your employer?"

"Well, a letter from you certainly won't harm my chances, but so far I have not received anything. I will probably be able to travel with the team to the venues that can be reached within a few hours. However, I doubt that they will allow me to travel to the western and southern parts of the country, when the team will be gone for one or two weeks. Fortunately, our Africa Cup matches fall during the holiday weekends, so I should be able to attend those."

"Well, if you are not going to travel, then we want you to go and watch Ndovu Football Club during all their home matches. We want to make sure that we beat them this year!"

"I can do that, but please remember that the league is not won against one single team. We need to win all our matches in order to become champions. Every match is worth three points, no more and no less, regardless of whether we beat Ndovu Football Club or Kariakoo Zindi from the south . . .

For us, the matches against Ndovu Football Club are the most important ones. We want a full stadium and we want to beat them."

"We will do what we can. Remember that we need your support. Can we get a few pairs of football boots for the players?"

"We must go now. *Kwaheri*. (Bye)"

. . .

Let's just say that it was worth the try. The words "We want a full stadium" stayed with me for a while, and on the day of the big match my suspicions were confirmed.

TWENTY-FIVE

Our first assignments in the Mainland League were in the Lake Zone, about 1500 kilometres and three days' travel by train from Dar Es Salaam. Because of my work commitments I wasn't able to travel with the team, but I followed our progress very closely. During the team's absence, I attended several matches at the National Stadium in Dar Es Salaam, so that I could get to know some of our opponents in the Premier League. I took very copious and detailed notes of all the teams that played in Dar, and the newspapers regularly printed photos of me sitting in the stands and writing frantically in my little notebook. Studying the opposition was not something that had been done much before, and I was just flattered to help the various media houses earn more income through their fascinating stories and photographs.

We came back from the west with two wins and a draw, five goals scored and no goals conceded, an excellent start considering the problems that the players and coaches had been facing in our build-up, and considering the fact that in this country it is never easy to win away from home . . .

Upon the team's return, one of the officials who had accompanied the team explained to me exactly how our team had been able to win two of the three matches.

"Did all our players put forth their best efforts?"

"No, not really."

"Did our strikers make good use of the chances they had during the matches?"

"No . . ."

"Was it because our defenders did a good job in preventing the ball from going into the net at the other end?"

"Nope."

"So it must have been that we controlled the midfield well and dominated possession?"

"I didn't think we did."

"Well, in that case, our goalkeeper must have been absolutely outstanding."

"He's had better matches."

"Ok, so what was it? Favors from the referee?"

"No, the reason why we got the results that we got was that we found this great witchdoctor who provided the team with the necessary *juju*."

No credit to the players then. No, the *juju*, East Africa's equivalent of Southern Africa's *muti*, had done its job, and the thousands of Shillings spent on the witchdoctor had been well worth it . . . How could I have forgotten that the witchcraft and the midnight chanting against the opposition were so much more important than the many hours of sweat, blood and tears that we had put in on the training field? I was later told that this witchdoctor had received one hundred and twenty thousand Shillings per game, while the players' share of the gate averaged six thousand Shillings per game . . . For the team, not per player! It was pointless trying to go and knock some sense into the leaders. The belief in *juju* was so imbedded in the society that any attempt to question it was actually seen as an insult. Better to stay away from the dark arts, lest they try them out on me! The players confided in me and told me some of the stories from their journey, and it was quite clear that most of them did not agree with this practice either. They knew what they had learned during the many hours of pre-season practice. Rather than verbally agreeing with their opinions, I simply told the players that I was proud of their achievements, and that they should carry on from here. Which they did.

Two days later we left for Zimbabwe, but not quite on a jetplane. No, our generous sponsor had hired a ramshackle bus that was going to ferry the team from Dar Es Salaam, through Malawi and Zambia, to Zimbabwe . . . and back. A three day journey each way, and all that in order to go and play a football match of ninety minutes. Even though the scenery in East and Southern Africa is absolutely stunning, one does eventually tire of the bush, the plains and the villages. And worst of all were the endless and dusty roads. Three days in a bus is a challenge for anyone, and in this case we happened to be these anyones. Space on the bus was limited as we were also carrying bags of mielie meal (porridge flour) and beans. We had heard many stories of visiting teams suffering from food poisoning after eating the food that had been provided by the local hotel, so we took all the necessary precautions to avoid that our players would spend the weekend in the toilets. We even brought our own bottled water with us. No, we were not going to take any chances—this was not the right time to find out how wonderful the Zimbabwean hospitality was.

The team arrived exhausted and with stiff limbs, and when we reached the hotel, things got even worse. In accordance with the rules that govern Africa Cup tournaments, the host club has to provide 'decent' hotel accommodation to the visiting team, and cater for all of its 'reasonable' expenses. Our expectation of course was that we would stay at the Intercontinental or the Hilton Hotel, but instead, we were taken to the Pink Flamingo Inn and Nightclub. This was no more than a guesthouse of dubious reputation, smack in the middle of a very busy part of Gweru town. The reception area looked like a typhoon had just raged through it. The rooms were small and without air conditioning, and that evening we found out that the beds were inhabited by thousands of small but nasty bugs. We also realized that many of the rooms were occupied, for at least an hour or so, by rather corpulent men accompanied by ladies in very, very short skirts. From time to time, during the course of the night, I heard knocking on the door of my room, but I wisely decided to pass the opportunity to get to know some of the locals a bit better. And as if that was not enough to disturb our sleep, that same evening the guesthouse also hosted a wedding party that continued until well after the sun came up the next morning. I was sure that this wedding feast was sponsored by the host club! We got very little sleep but we learned an awful lot about the music of the Bhundu Boys and Thomas Mapfumo, to name a few. That afternoon however, we were still good value for a 1-3 victory that all but guaranteed our passage to the next round.

As with all return journeys, our trip back to Dar seemed a bit quicker, and when we arrived in the city I gave the players two days' rest before we started preparing for our first game in the Nyerere Cup tournament. I was looking forward to this match, because we had been drawn against Manchester United FC. Of course, Mr Scholes and Mr Giggs were not going to show up, and neither was Sir Alex Ferguson. No, we were going to play against the Manchester United FC from somewhere in the sprawling townships on the outskirts of Dar Es Salaam. I selected a number of our fringe players for this titanic clash, which we won by seven goals to nil. Not many football coaches can boast with a 7-0 trashing of Manchester United in their resumé, but I can. And I do of course. Round two, here we come.

Our next few games were at home, and we won each and every one of them. We hardly conceded any goals, but I was a bit concerned about the lack of killer instinct in attack. It has always been my belief that if you can win by five goals, then you have to win by five goals. I am a strong proponent of attacking football, of putting continuous pressure on the opposition, and of making them regret that they came out to play against my team in the first place. Just consider this : a team from the regions comes to Dar Es Salaam to play against Safari Sports Club. Nobody really expects that team to win on our home turf. They are allowed to lose by one or two goals. The players go home and their wives, girlfriends or parents ask them:

"How did you play?"
"Ah, we lost 1-0." or
"Ah, we lost 3-1."

Then that is no big deal.
But if that same player goes home and has to face his wife, his girlfriend or his parents with the answer:

"Yayaya, we lost 6-1."

then that is a different situation altogether. Nobody wants to admit such a score. It hurts. And it is embarrassing. That is what I want from my teams. That they make the opposition wish that they hadn't come out to play against us.

So even though we won our league games, the scores were usually quite low, with 3-0 being the biggest victory that we could record. I tried to find an incentive for the players to score more goals. So I went to see the Chairman of the club . . .

"You know, we have been playing pretty well so far, but I want to see more goals. Can I make a suggestion?"

"And what is that?"

"Can we give every player a bonus of a few thousand Shillings if the team manages to score four or more goals?"

"No way! The players are getting too much money already?"

"What makes you say that?"

"Well, when the team wins the players share 30% of the gate collection after expenses. With all these victories, they have been getting too much money (and he probably thought to himself : "And I have been getting too little from what remained after that . . .")."

"So what are you saying?"

"We have decided to reduce the win bonus. From now onwards, players will share 20% if they win, they will share 10% if they draw, and they will get nothing if they lose . . ."

. . .

Can you believe it? I was standing there listening to a Chairman who told me that his team was winning too many games!!! And therefore he had decided to cut the win bonus. Talk about incentives and standing behind your team . . .

I have always been very focused on the three points that are on offer for every league match. I keep statistics on all sorts of football and match data, but there is no statistic that is more important than points. You can count the corner kicks, the free kicks, the ball possession or the goal scoring chances that you enjoy during a match, but at the end of the season there is only one important statistic, and that is the one that tells you how many points you have collected. All the other statistics are a means of ensuring that the most important statistic balances in your team's favor. When your data tell you that every match you have an average of eight corner kicks and you never score any goals from them, then you know that you need to work on that aspect of your team's play. Improving your team's attacking from a corner kick will result in more goals, which will result in more points.

Our return match against Chapungu FC was next, but we were soon informed that our opponents were 'unable' to make the journey to Tanzania. Of course, after that 3-1 defeat at home, their chances of progressing were very remote indeed, and in my opinion they decided not to honor the game in order to save out on the expenses. I couldn't blame them, and I was glad that we moved on to the next round without having to play. Less fatigue, less injuries, less yellow and red cards, and more time to prepare for the other assignments. In the next round of the Africa Cup, we were drawn against Vital'Ô, the cup winner of Burundi.

Meanwhile, the majority of our players were called for practice with the senior Tanzanian national team, the Taifa Stars. The team was going to participate in the East and Central African championship, a completely useless competition that has always been riddled with poor organization, biased refereeing, mismanagement and corruption. In recent year, this annual competition had also been marred by an increase in violent confrontations between rival fans. Political and social stability was still a pipe dream in the central parts of the continent, and warring factions liked to hijack the sports competitions in order to get some leverage for their cause. I was not keen at all to see my players participate in the tournament. They would stand to gain little from the experience. The journey to Rwanda was long and hazardous, the conditions in Kigali were less than appealing, and the chance of sustaining injuries was more than realistic. So I thought I should make a suggestion that would somehow safeguard the health and the safety of my players.

The Football Association of Tanzania was of course determined to send a team to Rwanda, because this would also allow some of the Association members to travel and pocket some substantial allowances. I knew that I would be unable to stop them from participating. However, I soon realized that the Tanzanian team was going to be ill-prepared for such a tournament. The team would only have two or three training sessions before its departure, and the attendance rate in those training sessions would probably not even reach fifty percent. I felt that I had a way to save the nation's face in the competition whilst at the same time weakening one of our main opponents. My thoughts went back to a story that my grandfather had told me, many years earlier.

In 1964, the Belgian national team played an international match against Holland. The "Derby of the Low Countries" was always the highlight of the year, and in this particular year, the starting eleven of our national team included ten players of Anderlecht SC, the leading club in Belgium. The goalkeeper, who hailed from Standard Liège, was the only 'outsider' in the team. However, just before halftime, our goalkeeper got injured. He was substituted by, you guessed it, the goalkeeper of Anderlecht SC . . . So for the remaining forty-five minutes, our national team was completely made up of players from the same club. And the trick worked, because we achieved a rare victory over our northern neighbors.

I went to see one of my journalist friends in the Dar Es Salaam city centre, and told him that Tanzania should take care of its reputation. Everyone knew that the team would be ill-prepared and the laughing stock of the competition. The national team coaches didn't only have to deal with the internal rivalry between the players of Safari Sports Club and those of Ndovu Football Club—there was also the added demand that the team includes Mainland players and players from Zanzibar. Cooperation between these various groups was usually as smooth as the understanding between the Flemish and the Walloons in Belgium, or the Catalans and the Castellanos in Spain. I suggested that Tanzania follow Belgium's example and send a club team to Rwanda, to go and represent the nation. At least a club team had already had some training since the start of the year, the players would know each other well and should be able to play some decent football. Furthermore, it wouldn't be hard to find a team that had enough Tanzanian nationals—they all did! I easily convinced the reporter that such a team would stand a better chance of at least being competitive, and the next day he published the suggestion. The article quickly drew all sorts of reactions and comments. In order to further my case, I suggested that the national champions be sent to Rwanda. This could have been presented as their reward for winning the league the season before, but of course it would have been more of a punishment, and a way in which I tried to weaken one of our main opponents for this year's league title. I believe that the Association actually got quite close to agreeing that this was indeed a great suggestion, but eventually they succumbed to the demand that various clubs and regions were represented. So I lost seven key players for two weeks, and Tanzania lost all its matches in Rwanda. It had been worth the try, and I was sure that after that particular competition ended, more than one person thought that the Association should have listened to me . . .

TWENTY-SIX

THIS EPISODE INADVERTENTLY LED TO a major crisis within the Football Association of Tanzania, as well as in the national government. When the Taifa Stars returned from the disaster in Rwanda, the Minister for Sports, Culture and Youth demanded that the Football Association explain the team's poor performance and the allocation of government resources. Of course there had been lots of speculation in the preceding months, most of it bordering on fact and based on pretty solid evidence, that almost all the funds were being misappropriated. However, this latest poor showing in a regional tournament had hurt the pride of the Minister, and a thorough investigation was quickly concluded. I was also convinced that the Minister had been reading my own comments in the newspapers, and that his curiosity had been picked by some of the truths that had started to come out of Safari Sports Club. As far as the Minister was concerned, the camel's back had been broken and he promptly sacked all the Football Association officials, secretaries and tea ladies. The whole bunch was indicted and taken to court. A very brave move by the Minister, and one that I applauded. Some of the parliamentarians did not approve of this action, most probably because they had their own interests hidden somewhere in the corridors of football power. The Minister stood firm though, and insisted that everyone involved in the FA be held accountable. However, the seasoned football follower will immediately realize that the sacking of the members of a football association automatically leads to a FIFA suspension. FIFA does not allow or tolerate any government interference in the matters and dealings of the national football associations, and Tanzania was no exception. As soon as the dismantlement of the association was announced, FIFA sent an envoy to come and find out what had been going on. Typically, this envoy only met with the FAT officials, and thus only heard their story. The suspension by FIFA was a foregone conclusion. Tanzania was not the first country to be suspended, and neither would it be the last. Historically, each and every suspended country has changed its mind and reinstated the sacked officials. I was pretty sure that Tanzania would follow suit, but I also wanted to seize this opportunity to inform the nation that such a suspension was not necessarily a bad thing. There were many ways in which we could help Tanzania raise the standard of its football, and this was the right moment to mention some. I slightly adapted that famous Kung Fu saying : "There is a right moment for everything, just make sure you seize it when it appears".

I felt that the suspension had a number of advantages, not least that it would allow everyone concerned with Tanzanian football to concentrate on the domestic game and on setting up some development structures. I therefore decided to add my own views to the story, and to encourage all the stakeholders in Tanzanian football to fully exploit the opportunity that the ban had availed.

The easiest and fastest way to influence public opinion was of course talking with my loyal reporter friends. They were only too keen to share my views with the public, and printed every word I told them.

Mulder welcomes FIFA ban and inspires all football leaders

**BY
OUR CORRESPONDENT**

Following the announcement that the Federation of International Football Associations (FIFA) has suspended Tanzania from all international competitions, many football fans in the country have been wondering what the government's next steps will be. Opinions are divided. There are football followers who believe that the government should listen to FIFA and reinstate the FAT officials with immediate effect. Others side with the Minister of Sports, Youth and Culture, and would like to see a full investigation into the antics of the FAT officials.

Highly respected international football coach Peter Mulder sees the suspension as a chance to right a few wrongs,

and to look at the bigger picture in the country's football development. He believes that we must look at how we can raise the standard of football, not just on the field, but also in the administration offices.

When asked what should be done to improve our soccer, Mulder said that the most important factor is that we have to take care of our youth.

"Everybody seems only interested in Safari Sports Club and Ndovu Football Club, but what about our 12 and 14 and 16 year olds? I have seen in Europe how young players are being trained and prepared for professional football, because I have been part of the system myself. It is important that we prepare the young players, just like several African countries are already doing", Mulder explained.

He added that another thing we need here is serious leaders who are concerned with improving football and not with improving their bank balances.

"We have too many leaders who are hungry and who don't care about football at all, he said. I could give you names, but you know them. Sooner or later however, they will have to pay for their thefts, because you can't keep on fooling the football lovers forever. Just look at what has happened to the FAT people."

He also said that transparency is needed.

"Why don't we ever get to see the accounting books of the clubs and the FA? Why can't they simply show us how their millions are being used? Transparency will attract sponsors, both local and foreign, and with good sponsorship we can develop proper training facilities, medical care for the players, and many other. In order to be successful in football these days, you need money. Lots of it", he said.

"Football administration in this country is poor. The standard of football has been declining, not a single team has shown promise for the future, clubs continue to sign players for one year and then get rid of them, team building is not happening, the national teams have been a joke and an embarrassment, the FA has not organized a single seminar or coaching course, the future is bleak."

Mulder added that in a way he is happy that the country has been suspended by FIFA. "This allows us to stop wasting money on international assignments that we are not ready for", he said. "It is time now to put our house in order, to get competent people to lead the FA and the clubs, to sort out proper rules for the various leagues and to draft a long-term development plan. I really hope that the government does not give in to FIFA's demands", he added.

All this of course despite the fact that my own club was still involved in the Africa Cup tournament. But I was prepared to forego the chance of progressing in the Africa Cup if it meant having the opportunity to really devise a long-term plan for the development of football in Tanzania. I truly felt that a more comprehensive view on developmental structures was needed, and at least there would now be some money that could be diverted from international assignments to youth development. It sounded simple enough . . .

I was invited by the country's main television channel to talk on their weekly live sports show. I seized the opportunity to dig a little bit deeper into the current state of affairs, and to try and alter the course of Tanzanian football administration.

"So, Peter, can you tell us a bit more about the current state of affairs in Tanzanian football?"

"Sure. I feel that Tanzania has been presented with a unique opportunity to put itself on the football map and to finally have an impact on the way football is being run around the world."

"What exactly has happened?"

"Well, Tanzania has been banned by FIFA! We should thank them for the chance that this international ban is giving us."

"What do you mean?"

"I commend the perseverance of both the National Sports Council and the Tanzanian government on this issue. Both have been instrumental in the recent developments and in taking a stand against corruption. Now we need time to put our house in order, and if we are not going to waste time, money and energy on international assignments, we can devote ourselves to introducing a serious sports development policy that can do wonders in the years to come."

"So how has FIFA managed to ban our country?"

"A delegate of the world's football governing body recently visited Tanzania in order to find out what the story was behind the troubles facing the Football Association of Tanzania. After a government-sponsored enquiry in its financial practices, the previous leadership was sacked, and is now facing criminal charges. An interim leadership has been put in place, but FIFA now claims that this was done in an unconstitutional way. FIFA has its own set of rules, which state that they will only recognize leaders who have been duly elected, and that elected officials can not be suspended or sacked by national governments. In fact, FIFA doesn't allow for any government interference in national football matters. It says that all football-related conflicts can only be referred to FIFA itself, which is the only body authorized to rule on these issues."

"That's a bit odd, isn't it?"

"Precisely. I wonder how FIFA can possibly insist that individuals who have pending court cases be given the responsibility to lead the country's football association. It baffles me. Maybe it's a reflection on the kind of people that run the world's governing body. We should not allow these self-proclaimed football administrators back into office until they have been cleared of all charges . . . which is highly unlikely to happen."

"As an experienced and passionate football man, how do you feel about this?"

"Well, personally I feel that the FIFA delegate, whose credential nobody bothered to check, was in no position to tell the nation what to do with its present football conflict. Normal procedure is that a delegation should comprise of at least two officials so as to ensure objectivity and transparency. Such a delegation visits a country on a fact-finding mission, writes a report to be presented to the FIFA secretariat in Zurich, and then the appropriate decisions are made there. It is not possible for a delegate to decide on a course of action without FIFA's input and approval."

"How does this story reflect on FIFA itself? Are they not abusing their power by overruling a national government?"

"Over the years, the FIFA leadership has done everything possible to put their puppets into positions of power. It is a public secret that FIFA elections are completely fraught with corruption and bribery. This has been reported by many journalists and authors over the years. In the case of Tanzania, FIFA has an interest in seeing the sacked FAT officials remain in office. A disturbance would mean an end to the swindling of money through Tanzanian footballing projects that have never been and that will never be. Of course FIFA has been paying the Tanzanian Football Association a lot of money for so-called development work, but this money has never reached its published destination, and has instead been credited to private bank accounts. The money is just being passed on from one account to the next, and governments are not supposed to interfere in this cycle."

"So how should Tanzania react to this current situation?"

"An interim leadership has been put in place. This leadership needs to make sure that it is transparent and that it involves the people in its decision making. Any business or company that respects itself shows its customers and shareholders how the books balance, what happens to the revenue, and how the organization is being run. That's why they have shareholders' meetings and annual general meetings. The Football Association of Tanzania should be no exception to this. I urge them to give us regular accounts of the money collected from games and other sources, and a detailed list of expenditures. Only then can this body, whose image has been severely tarnished by past mismanagement, regain the respect of the nation and of those who may wish to contribute towards the development of football in this beautiful country."

"It sounds like Tanzania has a choice to make."

"It does. As long as these corrupt practices are allowed to happen, football in the developing world will never become a professional game. It is just a lame excuse for financial deals between people who don't have the game at heart. And this is where Tanzania can take a pioneering role in world football. Now that we are facing a leadership crisis, FIFA will probably give Tanzania an ultimatum. Reinstate the previous leadership or face an indefinite ban from world football. This is where we ask ourselves the question : what does Tanzania stand to lose from a ban? It is sad but true that our teams, both the national teams and the club teams, cannot make an impact on the international stage. Apart from the odd exception, all our teams are eliminated in the preliminary stages of continental competitions. So let's settle for the second option, and accept the ban. Such a ban will certainly make world headlines, and with the right kind of input from responsible people at the top of the Tanzanian football administration, the international football world will sit up and take notice. And hopefully a ban for Tanzanian teams will open the proverbial can of FIFA worms that may expose the way in which some small people in Zurich believe that they are bigger than national governments. In this way, Tanzania can become a leader in the revolution which will eventually open the doors to a more transparent and equitable world football administration. Or to use FIFA's own hypocritical motto, it's all "for the good of the game"."

"So what message do you have for Tanzania?"

"Tanzania, stand up and be proud of your belief in what's right! Let us work on the youth, let us start setting up some football academies, and let us help our talented youngsters develop into potential world-beaters. Other countries have done it before us, and there is no reason why this country shouldn't do it either."

"Peter, you have already convinced me, and I am sure that all our viewers will be equally persuaded that our leaders need to do something positive. Let us hope that they heed your advice. Thank you very much for joining us in the studio this afternoon."

"Thank you very much for having me, it was my pleasure."

I had said what I wanted to say, and hoped that at least some of my advice would find its way to the higher levels of power. The future would tell.

TWENTY-SEVEN

AFTER SIX OR SEVEN MATCHES in the league, Safari Sports Club was leading the log and finding the going rather easy. At that moment it became very important for us coaches to keep the players focused, so that complacency didn't creep in. In order to keep the sharpness and the motivation, I took the players to the local water parks and on boat rides on the Indian Ocean. We had some training sessions on the beautiful white beaches, running under the palm trees and playing small-sided games in the soft sand. The variety kept the juices flowing, and we continued our winning streak. We didn't always play well, but as long as we kept accumulating the points, there was no cause for alarm. As soon as I had the impression that the players were taking their tasks a little bit too lightly, I immediately let them know.

I had also become aware of the importance of the referees in our league matches. In every match there were many decisions that could easily be challenged, but it was clear that trying to argue was a pointless exercise. No, we had to outsmart them. I had kept very strict records of the yellow cards that our players had received thus far, and decided to strategically plan for the next cards to be gotten. I was convinced that opposition teams could very easily bribe referees a week or two before meeting us, so that a key player who was already on two yellow cards would receive a third card in the match before our game, and thus be forced to miss that clash. So I looked at the calendar and made a plan to carefully time our next yellow cards. It may sound like something that's hard to do, and it should be, but in Tanzania it wasn't. I found it extremely easy to plan our yellow cards and our suspensions, and thus avoid missing key players in the toughest games of the season. I would be the first to admit that purposely getting a yellow card in a particular match goes a little bit against the spirit of sportsmanship. However, in the knowledge that this was the only way to avoid being penalized by the guaranteed corrupt behavior of referees, I also believed that our course of action was the lesser of two evils. Four of our players received their third yellow card of the season two weeks before our derby match with Ndovu Football Club, and they were suspended for the match prior to the titanic clash. I had simply asked three of them to stand over the ball when a free kick had been awarded to the opposition, and not to retreat until the referee had given them a yellow card. I knew that we were taking a risk, but it was a risk that I was willing to take.

The fourth one had been under instruction to waste time by kicking the ball away after it had gone out of play. Again, I knew that we were taking a risk, but again, it was a risk that I was willing to take. All four times the plan worked to perfection, and I was glad that we had taken the risk. As for our captain, whom I believed would be targeted in our next match and who might well have gotten a red card, I left him out of the squad altogether, probably to the consternation of the referee who had been tasked with sending him off one week before our match with Ndovu Football Club and who was now not going to get his Christmas bonus . . .

Another tactic that I frequently employed during our training sessions was to have my starting eleven play as a starting ten. It was common for at least one player to be sent off during a league or cup match, and since we played at least thirty percent of our game time with only ten, I found it useful to also train with ten against eleven. This helped the players cover the spaces that would be created by a dismissal. At other times, I set up my starting eleven against a team of twelve. Again, more resistance, more situations to deal with, more problems to solve, and thus more learning achieved. I constantly reminded myself and my players of the wise words of France's World Cup-winning coach, Aimé Jacquet, who said that 'entraînement difficile égale match facile"—difficult training means easy match. The players responded very well to these innovative training methods, and in fact they enjoyed them more than any trainings they had ever had. Now that they were advancing well in their tactical understanding of the game, I started preparing my plans to introduce them to the concept of the 'twelfth player'. But one step at a time. Fitness, tactics, technique, team building, formations, nutrition, education—it was all systems go now!

That particular match in which we received the four yellow cards was a home match, and even though we won, I wasn't happy with the players' efforts and performances. And I told them in no uncertain terms. With some bad luck we could have drawn or lost that game, and it was time to step in.

Two hours before our next game, I called each player individually to me. In my hand I had three notes of one thousand Shillings each.

"Captain, I am holding three thousand Shillings in my hand. Please take what you want."
"I can take as much as I want?"
"Yes, go ahead."

How much do you think the captain took? He took the three thousand Shillings. That was to be expected, wasn't it? And every other player after him also took three thousand Shillings. There wasn't anyone who wanted to leave the room with one or two thousand Shillings, or with nothing at all. So I told them:

—When I told you that you could take everything that was offered, you all chose to take the full three thousand Shillings. I knew you would, and I am glad you did. Now think about our next game. Somebody is offering you three points. I want you to go out there and do everything you can to make those three points yours. Why should you be satisfied with one point if you have the chance to take all three?

—Yeah, that's true! We are going to fight for the three points.

That afternoon we beat one of the title favourites 3-0, and it could have been more. We controlled the match from start to finish, and the score flattered our opponents. After the final whistle, I told the players to go around the field and thank our fans, who had gathered by the thousands. The stands of the National Stadium were filling up nicely of late, as more and more people wanted to witness our version of the *tiki taka* style of play. We hadn't quite reached the dazzling heights of Barcelona FC's style of play, but it was certainly good enough to head the standings in the Tanzanian Premier League.

More than an hour after the end of the match, the Safari Sports Club fans were still blowing their trumpets and dancing in the stands—and we players and coaches kept on feeding them with more smiles and waves. One of our most passionate supporters, who never missed a single match and who crept closer and closer to the team bench as the season progressed, was Abdallah. He was a huge man of about 60 years old, of Arab descent, and with a frame the size of an oil barrel. He was one of the most cheerful and funny characters I ever met during my time in East Africa, and he was known as Mzee Masharubu—'Grandpa Moustache'. That afternoon, Mzee Masharubu danced and sang as if there was no tomorrow, and we all joined in and let our hair down for a few moments. Mzee Masharubu's sister, who was also a die-hard Safari Sports Club fan, and who was just as large as her brother, was also there. Coincidentally, she also had a significant amount of facial hair between her nose and her upper lip, so she was known as Bibi Masharubu—'Grandma Moustache' . . . We had fun and hoped that the good times would last.

The next Wednesday we played our second round fixture in the Nyerere Cup tournament, and we steamrolled all over Toto Africa, a second division team from the Lake Victoria region. They put up some reasonable resistance in the first half hour, but as soon as we scored our first goal, the game was over as a contest. We eventually ran out 5-0 winners, and I knew then that the football followers in Tanzania had to start taking notice.

The team was doing well. We were leading the league and looking stronger and stronger with every match. Before every game that we played in Dar Es Salaam, I asked our fans through the media to dress up in the team's colors of red and white. As the days progressed it was clear that the National Stadium showed more and more red, and I felt very good about the way the league was shaping up for us. At the halfway stage of the season, the table showed that we were exactly where we belonged.

Premier League Top 5 Standings						
Club	Played	Won	Drawn	Lost	GF	GA	Points
Safari SC	15	10	5	0	42	9	35
Mbitwa	15	9	3	3	36	14	30
Ndovu FC	15	8	5	2	30	13	29
Ashura FC	15	8	3	4	31	16	27
Zindi	15	7	1	7	24	13	22

Word was going around that this club from Dar Es Salaam was making good progress. One morning my cell phone rang, and the screen read "Unknown number". I answered the phone, and the voice at the other end of the line introduced himself as a director of Futbol Mundial. For the uninitiated, Futbol Mundial is a football-related show whose reporters and camera crews travel around the world in search of the hottest stories. They always seem to have their ears close to the ground, and find the most inspirational football stories to report on.

The director had heard about our dominance in the league and about the noise that Safari Sports Club's white coach had been making in the media. He felt that there was a story that deserved to be told.

A few days later a crew of three reporters, two cameramen and a sound engineer visited two of our training sessions. They mingled with the players as they were going through their motions, and they positioned themselves rather precariously behind the goalkeeper during a shooting exercise. Thankfully nobody got hurt ... We also conducted some interviews and visited the dilapidated clubhouse and guesthouse.

Our visitors told me that they had never seen a Premier League club that was as poorly accommodated as ours, and I could only agree with them. But I told them that hope springs eternal and added that maybe their report would create some more interest.

And it did. The show was screened around the world a few days later, and soon after I received a number of messages from overseas acquaintances who were all excited after seeing me on their local television channels!

This visit was soon followed by another, this time from a South-African crew that was responsible for the series "Africa's Sporting Heroes". They did a double feature in Tanzania : one on the country's super middleweight world champion boxer, and one on myself. In fact, the two stories complemented each other well. The boxer had been raised in a large family somewhere in the slums on the outskirts of Dar Es Salaam, and with a little help from European sponsors he had eventually captured the world title in his weight division. He was a raw example of the potential of Tanzanian athletes. My own story showed the sheer number of people who had the same potential as the boxer, and who would also be empowered to reach dazzling heights if only more support became available.

The recognition that these two televised documentaries brought was a major boost to the players and the fans—they suddenly all wore their pride on their sleeves! Both programs were repeatedly shown on the local television channels, and I even received a phone call from the Minister, who thanked me for putting his country in such a positive light.

"Karibu tena, Mister Minister". You're welcome.

The leaders however could not be convinced to contribute their bit, not even after seeing the potential of their club being showcased on worldwide television.

Soon it would be time for the big city derby match against our traditional rival, Ndovu Football Club, and so things were starting to warm up. The club officials were getting a bit agitated, and I learned there and then that the anticipation of having a wad of cash in one's pocket apparently causes restlessness and itchiness . . .

More and more officials, some known to me and several completely unknown to me, showed up at the training ground. The city derby always guaranteed a full house at the National Stadium and a lot of money from the gate collection. This was not the time for officials, whether official or not, to absent themselves from the city. No, this was the time for them to show how much they cared about the club and the players, and how much the team's achievements gave them sweet dreams or sleepless nights, as the case may have been. As far as I was concerned, it was time to ask for a refund for the expenses that I had incurred before and after the elections, when I had paid for the raffle tickets, the players' transport, medication, rent and other expenses. I also asked for my letter of appointment. The club officials promised me that after the Ndovu match, I would get my refund and my letter . . .

Meanwhile, the High Court in Dar Es Salaam found that the sacking of the whole National Football Association Executive was unconstitutional, and ruled that they be reinstated, as per FIFA's demands. The international ban was lifted immediately, but the government pledged to continue its fight against the blatant abuse of power within the football corridors. I was glad that they would, but also a little bit relieved that we could give our run in the Africa Cup tournament the best possible shot.

TWENTY-EIGHT

A DAY LATER, ANOTHER BOMBSHELL. A member of the Executive Committee told the national press that they had no confidence in the coaches' ability to prepare the team for the big match, and that the Committee had decided to bring in a new coach. This decision was most probably made following a suggestion from the sponsor, who until now hadn't had any impact on the club's development. And wouldn't you know it? Before anyone could say Jack Robinson, a new coach, completely unknown to me, was unceremoniously drafted into the club, and suddenly appeared on the team's bench, right next to my two assistant coaches who were soon to be dismissed! I could think of less offensive ways of telling somebody that they are not needed anymore . . .

There had been some speculation in the media about the possibility of our coaches being replaced. The newspapers had mentioned an anonymous Zambian coach in order to get the gossip started, and apparently there were also at least two local aspirants. One of them, a well-established coach who had been working as a technical adviser to the Football Association of Tanzania, was reported to have asked for a monthly salary of one million Shillings, or one thousand US dollars on top of a travel allowance. The average monthly income in Tanzania at that time was around a dollar a day, so this was a non-starter from day one. Surely our sponsor, with all his millions, was not going to sacrifice such a large part of his sponsorship to a coach . . . The papers also suggested that a former Safari Sports Club player, and now a national team coach, was being sought as our new coach. This man had been part of the club for many years, and knew exactly what was going on. He politely declined the offer, and told the Executive Committee that he might be interested the year after . . . Hats off to him for not wanting to replace coaches who had been doing such a good job and who did not deserve to be dismissed.

The official reason given for this sudden news, which appeared in most of the local newspapers the next morning, was that my two assistants had shown signs of ill-discipline. No details were provided, but my suspicion was that they might have said something negative about the leadership to one or two of the players, and that the story had reached the leaders through the grapevine. I always had the suspicion that some of the players were 'planted' into the squad in order to keep their ears to the ground and report any signs of unrest or criticism to the leaders. Without ever actually becoming paranoid about it, I did consider this possibility and always kept the players at an arm's length.

Throughout my trials and tribulations at the club, starting with that career-ending injury and continuing to this day, I never told players stories about the leadership that I would not tell the leaders directly. The practice of *mizengwe* and *majungu*, loosely translated as 'gossip' and 'trash talk', was however very common in the society that I had become a part of. I spent many hours listening, or pretending to listen, to stories about people that I hardly knew. I did not want to be rude and tell people that I wasn't interested, but I certainly never picked up the same habit. I've always been of the mentality that if I have something to say about someone, I will tell that someone, and there is no need to involve any others. Unfortunately, gossip and rumor-mongering are practices that occur in almost all societies and cultures that I have been privileged enough to get to know. They are not just confined to East Africa. It was probably because I had never told *mizengwe* about the leadership that the Chairman told the newspaper that the *mzungu* would continue to coach the team together with the new *mwalimu*.

However, I was concerned about this sudden change in coaching staff, and I wanted to let the leaders know. I felt that the continuous changes were potentially detrimental to the development of the team. I asked the Secretary General if I could go and meet with him in order to express my concern, and he asked me to drop by his home the next morning. When I arrived there, I was told by one of the kids in the house that he was not around. I failed to track him down all day, and I was also unable to meet with any other members of the Executive Committee. When I came across a television crew in downtown Dar Es Salaam, and when they started interviewing me about the build-up to the city derby, I decided to make my feelings known. Television was one of the few partially reliable means of communication in Tanzania, and certainly a means that would bring the matter to the attention of those who were playing hide and seek with me. I had noticed that interviews were never edited, but rather shown in their entirety on the evening news. So I spoke my mind, in Kiswahili, and let the nation know that I was concerned about the recent developments. Of course, there was some psychological warfare involved too. I didn't mind pretending in front of the cameras that all was not well at Safari Sports Club, in the hope that those rooting for Ndovu Football Club would start thinking that their victory in the derby match was a foregone conclusion.

"We are at a few days from our match with Ndovu Football Club, and even though I fully respect my new colleague, I am concerned about the impact that the change in coaching style may have on the team's performance. We are leading the league by several points, we are still in the cup tournaments, we are scoring lots of goals and conceding very few, and at this rate we will soon be lifting the silverware that our fans are hoping for. I am puzzled as to how the Executive Committee has come to this decision. Some of our players were very close to the outgoing coaches, and I hope that they will not be affected psychologically. But the future will tell whether this was the right move at the right time."

Anyway, we played our last match with my two fellow coaches on the bench. Our guests were CDA, or Capital Development Authority. This club was based in Tanzania's capital city, Dodoma, and was the least supported team in the Premier League. Some said that this was due to the fact that Dodoma was no more than an artificial town, which the government had created in order to try and shift the migration problem from Dar Es Salaam to the inland hamlet of Dodoma. The experiment had utterly failed, and the only human habitation one could find there were the members of Parliament, who would spend three months of the year in Dodoma, and the rest of the time on their farms or flying around the world, presumably in order to attend all sorts of very important conferences. My own explanation for the lack of fans for CDA was that nobody would be able to spend ninety minutes in the stands, and shout "Come on you Capital Development Authority!" (along the same tune as "Come on you Spurs!") or "One nil, to the Capital Development Authority!" (not unlike "One nil, to the Arsenal!"). The club's name would not even fit on a scarf or on a sticker!

We dazzled our opponents and won our game 3-0. Nobody quite understood why my colleagues had to leave the club. Up to this day I believe that it was the wrong decision to do away with the two coaches who had, after all, helped me build the team and gotten it to where it was at that time : at the top of the Premier League championship, in the quarter-finals of the Nyerere Cup, and still competing in the Africa Cup tournament. This was not the right time to disturb a team and to change coaches. But at Safari Sports Club, everything was possible. A few days after the change of coaches, I was told by a reliable source that the new coach had been brought into the club by the Secretary General, who had promised this coach a job at Safari Sports Club if and only if this coach was prepared to part with 20% of his salary each month, and give it back in cash to the Secretary General! In the eyes of the Safari Sports Club leaders, this must have been as good a reason as any other to attract a new coach . . . Unknown to me, there may have been other deals, possibly involving the sponsor himself. After all, he had his many millions to somehow funnel and flush through the system.

I still hadn't received my letter of appointment and was never contracted to Safari Sports Club, so I took the change in technical staff in my stride. Did I have a choice? No. It was a case of either accepting the change and work with the new coach, or leave the club in solidarity with my fellow coaches. I discussed this issue with them, and we agreed that, for the sake of the players and the team, it was better that there was some continuity in terms of the technical staff. It was better that I carry on and keep the players focused on the job ahead. By now I had become the only continuous presence at Safari Sports Club over the past few months. I had already survived three coaches, an Elders Committee, a suspended leadership, a reinstated Treasurer and Assistant Treasurer, and an elected leadership. After only a few months I had become one of the longest serving people at the club . . .

One morning, my cellphone rang. When I answered it, I found a French-speaking voice on the line.

"Hello, is that Peter Mulder?"
"Yes it is. Who is this?"
"René Lukunku."

René Lukunku was the Head Coach of our fiercest rival, Ndovu Football Club. He was a Congolese national who had spent the last year and a half coaching our main title rivals, and I was a little bit surprised to receive his phone call.

«Salut René, comment vas-tu?»
«Très bien, merci, et toi?»
"Ça va bien, merci. How can I help you?"
"Well, I was wondering if you and I could meet up somewhere one of these days. As fellow coaches, I'm sure we have a lot to discuss. I'd just like to exchange some views and get to know you a bit better."
"Well, I think that's fine. Are you in town this weekend?"
"Yes. Can we meet at the church?"
"The church?"

There were a good number of churches in Dar Es Salaam, but I doubted that too many of the Ndovu Football Club officials spent significant amounts of time in any of them. As far as I was aware, most of them were of the Muslim faith, and those who had been raised as Christians, such as Mr Lukunku, didn't strike me as the pious type . . . But of course, I might have been wrong.

"Yes. The church is the drinking hole where Ndovu officials and fans like to gather. It's a bar just off the road to the Kinondoni Textile Market, and they sell beers out of a container."

That clarified it!

"Ah! I think I know that place. I didn't know it was called the church."
"Well, that's what we call it . . ."
"OK. Shall we meet there Friday evening?"
"Friday evening eight o'clock sounds good."
"OK, see you then!"

"Oh, and please don't tell anyone that I called you."
"Euh . . . ok. *A vendredi.*"

The next day I welcomed our new coach, Nestor Nizigiyimana, to the technical staff, and told him that I looked forward to working with him. I had no problem at all cooperating with him. After all, he was probably just another pawn in the games of the Executive Committee, and I was quite happy for him to take the lead role within the coaching set-up. Nestor, a national of Burundi, had been hired from an up-country club, and fate had it that his first match in charge of Safari Sports Club was against his former club, which he had left only a few days earlier. There were reports of unrest in the southern town where his former team was based, as he had apparently left overnight, without informing the directors of his club, to come and take up his post at Safari Sports Club. Again, this was very possible, and quite common, in Tanzanian football. I told him that we should sit down and draft our technical program as soon as possible, and he agreed to bring his ideas the next day. On match day our players did a commendable job. I thought that the trick with the three thousand Shillings had worked again, and we won 2-1. We were now firmly rooted at the top of the log.

The day after the match, Nestor told me that he always knew that we would win that match.

"How could you know? That was a strong team."
"I know all the players, and I spoke with them when they arrived in the city."
"I see."

I refrained from asking him how big the plastic bag was that the General Secretary had given him prior to his 'meeting'.

Two days later, I met René Lukunku at the church. He arrived around forty-five minutes late, not bad for a first meeting, and not unexpected either. One does get used to cultural differences, and the complete lack of consideration for other people's time is so embedded in the East African culture that I soon learned to play "Snake" and "Solitaire" on my mobile phone, simply to pass the time whilst waiting for those who invariably showed up late. Games like 'Angry Birds' and 'Tetris' would never have become popular if we didn't need something to do while waiting for Congolese football coaches . . .

On this particular evening, I had taken some test papers from my students with me, and marked these whilst enjoying a cup of Chai Bora at the church . . . When René finally arrived, he introduced me to two gentlemen that he had brought with him. They were peripheral officials of Ndovu Football Club, and as soon as their beers had arrived, he cut straight to the chase.

"Thank you for making time to meet with us."

"Sure! I always enjoy discussing and sharing with fellow coaches. We're in the same job, in the same country, and as far as I am concerned, rivalries only play themselves out on the football field. Outside the field of play, we are friends, isn't it?"

"Absolutely!"

"So, what brings you here?"

"Well, earlier in the week we had a long meeting at our club's offices, and it was agreed that Safari Sports Club is definitely our strongest rival for the league and for the cup. We all realize that your influence in this is undeniable. It is clear that you have brought a strong sense of purpose and discipline to the team, and we admire that. We also realize that you are facing quite a bit of resistance from the leadership of Safari Sports Club. We have followed the stories about the failed sponsorships, and we have seen your team at work in your home matches. We're not sure whether we will be able to compete with you this year, yet we need to qualify for the African Cup tournaments because we have a duty to travel to various countries on the continent."

"Why is that?"

"Well, some of our officials conduct business with partners in other African countries, and so, if the team can play in the continental cup tournaments, everything becomes a whole lot easier."

"Everything like what?"

"I can't go into the details, I don't even know them myself, but it all has to do with getting goods from here to foreign markets."

"I see . . . And what do I have to do with all this?"

"Well, our Executive Committee was wondering if you would consider joining Ndovu Football Club and help us to the league title and the Nyerere Cup."

"Are you serious?"

"Yes, we are. We have discussed some ideas to weaken Safari Sports Club, and the one that will have the biggest impact is to take you into our own camp. What do you say?"

"Well, I'm flattered that you say that, but it really is impossible for me to switch allegiance at this stage. We are halfway through the season, we are leading the log, I have embarked upon a program of development and progress, and I would like to see this through. I am not the kind of person who quits halfway . . ."

"We would make sure that you are happy with us."

"What do you mean?"

"Well, how much does Safari Sports Club pay you?"

"I am not working for money. I work as a volunteer and give my coaching and teaching time to the club."

"Well, we would be able to reward you rather handsomely. You know that we have funds."

As a matter of fact, I did. The Chairman of Ndovu Football Club's Interim Committee, which had been in charge for donkey's years, was also the driving force behind Tanzania's National Lottery. We never heard much about the lucky ones who had won millions in the Saturday draws, but we certainly knew that a lot of Tanzanians tried their luck and bought tickets. Yes, Ndovu Football Club did have access to funds.

"I'm sorry René, but I need to see my project through. I need to get through at least one cycle, one full year, and see how much can be achieved. We are challenging for the league title, we are on course to win the Nyerere Cup, and we are doing better than expected in the Africa Cup tournament also. I am pursuing exactly what I set out to do in my first year, and I couldn't possibly change course at this point in time."
"We don't only offer you a nice salary. We will also refund you all your expenses, and we will make sure that when we have a match upcountry and you need to be away from home for one or two nights, you will have nice company . . ."

I tried to remind the meeting that we were still in church, and I decided to bring this conversation to an end.

"This is a non-starter. I have given myself a challenge and I will complete it. Come what may, I will finish the season with Safari Sports Club. What happens after that, nobody knows. But thank you for your interest. I hope that you understand my position."
"No problem. It was worth the try, but we respect your decision. May the best team win next week!"

Indeed. Our next assignment was our own version of "El Clásico" against Ndovu Football Club . . .

TWENTY-NINE

Now, I HAVE NEVER BEEN someone who gets all excited about big derby games. During my youth I experienced several Belgium versus Holland matches, and Royal Antwerp versus Beerschot games in the city of Antwerp. You will remember that the first match I ever watched live, at the invitation of my grandfather, was that city of Antwerp derby. Of course I understand that each team wants to be the number one club in the city and become the noisy neighbors, but at the end of the day, every league match is played for three points. Do you get extra points for beating your city rivals? I don't think so. To me, as a coach, a victory against the local rival is as sweet as any other victory. Yes, it does give the fans bragging rights during the days after the match, but the league continues and a win is, eventually, worth nothing more than three points. On the other hand, a defeat is always painful, no matter which team beats you.

Because of my injury, I never experienced the Dar Es Salaam derby as a player. But of course, I knew that for the people of this city, the whole football season revolves around this game. I soon learned that for most fans of either Safari Sports Club or Ndovu Football Club, beating the local rival is much more important than winning the league title. I have never understood this, as it has always been my aim to qualify for international tournaments and to win cups and titles. What is the point of beating your local rival if a few weeks later you finish the league without any prizes? I rather keep my mind set on the bigger picture, which is the national championship, and not on one or two games against the city rivals . . .

But anyway, it was obvious that for the fans a lot was at stake in the next game. My club officials were also eagerly awaiting the derby, but for different reasons. I am convinced that they were praying that we didn't win the game, so that the players wouldn't receive any of the gate collection, which was anticipated to run in the millions . . .

On the Monday before the derby, and when I arrived at the TCC grounds for practice, I found all the players sitting outside the locked gate in the grass. We were refused entry in the club, because the ground fees of the previous week had not been paid. Of course, there were no club officials in the neighborhood, and so we set out on foot to look for an alternative football ground. Any open space would have done, we just needed to practice in preparation for the next weekend's cliffhanger. After an hour or so, we found a gravel pitch next to the National Stadium, and decided to have our practice there. We trained there for two days, and I also took the team to the National Stadium itself, where we did a lot of running up and down the thousands of stairs. Great exercise, not something Tanzania had seen before, but the players understood the benefit of hard training. It was of course also a matter of improvising and using the scarce training resources that we had at our disposal. When the press got to hear about our forced move onto a dangerous patch of gravel and small stones, some reporters came to visit us and wanted to know why a club of Safari Sports Club's status had to train on a dangerous gravel pitch. Where were the leaders in this time of need? What had happened to our famous sponsor? What were his millions doing? Where were these millions? It was clear that the reporters were also starting to realise that not all was well at the club. We coaches did nothing to discourage them from reporting on our trials and tribulations. Maybe some exposure and some pressure from the media and fans would make the officials realise that they needed to take a different direction in their leadership, or things would go wrong.

Our new coach had no idea what he had gotten himself into, but I quickly brought him up to speed and welcomed him to the great Safari Sports Club once more. I gave him some background information on where we had come from a few months ago, and together we agreed that we could do no more than try and make the most of our training sessions. I suggested once more that we sit down together and work out our program, and once more he told me we would do so 'soon'. I seem to remember that he said 'kesho' . . .

Our training sessions on the gravel fields were of course quite restricted, and it soon became clear that Nestor liked to talk. A lot! His command of Kiswahili was average, and he usually spent at least half an hour just talking to the players, who were sitting down in the dust and who clearly didn't understand most of what he was talking about.

One afternoon, his talk went on for two hours. He had made the mistake of allowing the players to express their complaints about all sorts of issues, at the expense of our training time. I eventually told him to stop talking as I wanted to go through some set piece routines with the players. There was little time left before our big match, and there was a lot of curriculum that we needed to cover. With the players that I had, I could not be satisfied with doing each routine once or twice. It took hours for them to finally understand or execute what I was looking for, even though most of the routines were pretty simple. After the session, I told Nestor that he shouldn't allow the players to start thinking about money and buses and fields at this critical time. They needed to focus on the work ahead, and it was up to the leadership to provide in the players' needs. I explained to him that I had already given the leaders an extensive to-do list, and that there wasn't much more that he and I could do. "Let us focus on our work and get the team ready for next week", I told him.

Besides the set-piece routines, I also tried to work with small-sided games, in an attempt to get some combinations and some samosas going. Nestor did not understand these exercises, and insisted on making the players run laps and play eleven versus eleven. Whenever he interfered with a small-sided game, he messed up the set-up and confused the players even more. I realized that our coaching philosophies were in stark contrast with each other, so I suggested to him that he take charge of the physical sessions, and I would lead the technical ones. At least I got the players to work a lot with the ball in small spaces, they did a lot of high intensity drills, and the enjoyment was there for all to see. They loved their afternoon sessions and started dreading the morning ones. And so we marched on towards the weekend.

On the Wednesday before the game, we heard from one of the Executive Committee members that a camp venue had been booked for us. The whole team was taken from the Chairman's pathetic 'one hour' guesthouse to a military camp right on the beach outside Dar Es Salaam. According to the leadership, we suddenly needed a safe and secure base where the players could train and rest in the comforts of a military installation. There were four military checkpoints between the main road and the gate to the boot camp, and one thing was for sure : no reporter would be able to disturb our peace and enforced solitude.

Upon arriving at the barracks, the players took the little gear that they had to their dormitories, and I will never forget the expression on their faces when they first saw their new abode. The rooms were spartan, as blank and empty as could be, with only four bunk beds against the walls. No desks, no chairs, no cupboards and no sink. Just walls, a floor, a ceiling and those bunk beds. No mattresses either. Our players were going to spend the next few nights sleeping on wooden boards. I didn't ask anyone, but guessed that this was meant to 'toughen them up a bit' . . . The dining room and the recreation rooms were not much better. The wooden benches tucked under the long wooden tables would soon become our classroom equipment from where we 'taught' the players the tactical parts of our match preparation. A cockroach here, an army of red ants there, and amidst all this a team of very hungry players. We were informed that they were able to eat anything they wanted for the next four days, provided they chose *ugali* (porridge) and *maharage* (beans). I truly felt for my players, but was powerless to do anything about the situation. Getting into the barracks was much, much easier than getting out!

The morning after our arrival we held our first training session in our new home base. We all walked to the football field, about half a kilometer away through the bush and the shrubs. When we arrived at the field, we were very reluctant to start training there. The soil of the field was stone hard, there were tractor tracks that had created ditches deep enough to break one's foot, and there were sea shells and crabs scattered all around the field. I call it 'the field' but in fact it was no more than a sun-drenched open space with two wooden goalposts on either side. No lines, no markings on this 'field', and the distance between the two goals was probably twice as long as it should have been. Any half-decent pilot could have landed a passenger plane over the first goal and brought it to a complete stop before reaching the other goal. Maybe we were going to train on an airstrip, who knows?

Training had to be limited to a bit of running and some technical work such as short passing games and foot volley. We could not risk injuring any of the players with our important assignment looming on the horizon. The press corps were kept at bay, and during the three days building up for the big match, I was the only person who left our Alcatraz at the end of each day. Some reporters called me up and asked how the team was doing, and I reassured them that everything was 'absolutely perfect'. No need to give the opposition any kind of advantage . . . and I preferred to keep my complaints to myself until after the match, in case we didn't win.

Despite the importance of the match in a Tanzanian context, no special measures were taken at the club. The players were given no special incentives, and some of them had to carry on training with their injuries. Not the best way to prepare for 'the match of the year', if you ask me . . . But the club officials knew that there was a lot of money on its way into their hands, and so why should they disturb the players and encourage them to win this match? There was a huge conflict of interest, and the rest, as they say, is history.

The epic encounter was played in front of a packed house, as expected. Thousands of fans thronged the stands, sat on the track around the field, and hung off lamp posts and trees outside the stadium. Nobody wanted to miss this clash, and it turned out to be a nail-biter.

The first half was a classic affair with both teams trying hard to draw first blood. After about thirty minutes one of our strikers was fouled just outside the penalty area, and I immediately jumped up and reminded our players of the many set pieces that we had practiced in training. An opportunity presented itself here, right in front of forty thousand spectators and the television cameras. Even though my players signaled to me that they remembered the routine, I could not be sure that they would also execute it. It wouldn't have been the first time that a coach's teachings were 'forgotten' in the heat of the moment, or that a technically gifted player got 'creative'. But on this occasion, the task was carried out impeccably.

During our many matches leading up to this day, I had noticed that defensive walls in Tanzania had a habit of jumping. Maybe this was what the old Tanzanian coaching manuals suggested, and I hoped that the Ndovu players would also carry out their task to perfection. Thankfully, they did. As our captain struck the free kick low and hard, all five Ndovu players in the wall jumped up in breath-taking synchronicity, and the ball hit the net just inside the far post. One nil, game on. The red and white half of the stadium, including a number of government personalities, burst out in joy and dance. The yellow and green half went silent. And so did our friends of the Executive Committee. One nil, that was not good, because that looked like a victory. This day, of all days, had to bring defeat, so that the gate collection could remain in safe hands and in small plastic bags . . . Fortunately for them, there was enough time for Ndovu Football Club to hit back before the break.

At the half-time whistle and with the teams deadlocked at one goal each, we retreated to the dressing room to regroup. For some reason, the key to the dressing room could not be found, and neither could the stadium official who had that key. This was of course all part of the greater picture, and possibly all at the instruction of our own leadership. Eventually we decided to just have our team talk in the corridors. Upon seeing that Nestor was going to share all his coaching wisdom and talk about all sorts of technical patterns that weren't going to materialize in the field of play, I decided to try and calm down the younger players. I asked them to stick to their task, to keep playing simple football and not to let themselves be bullied by the senior players on the opposition team. I was confident that we could defeat Ndovu Football Club, and told the players the same.

We had a little team huddle and went back to the field, but were told to wait a couple of minutes because a cycling race was going on on the running track that encircled the field. The person in charge of the half-time entertainment had booked an acrobat troupe who performed for almost ten minutes, followed by what must have been Tanzania's first ever cycling race. Four cyclists, each one on a used ladies' bike, were cruising around the field, to the cheers and the jeers of the crowd. They had been told to go for ten rounds, and nobody was going to stop them even though it became clear that they were going to need a lot of time to cover this distance. The race leader soon lapped the other three cyclists, but even that was not enough to crown him the national champion. No, they were going to complete the race, and we were going to wait . . .

Eventually the race ended and we took to the field for the second half. The quality of our play somehow dropped, and before the ninetieth minute arrived, Ndovu Football Club had found two more opportunities to score.

Safari Sports Club lost the local derby by three goals to one. In the second half we had been outplayed and outclassed by a much fresher Ndovu Football Club, and our lead at the top of the table was now under attack. It was our first loss of the season, and I was well aware that the loss of an unbeaten record is usually followed by more points lost in quick succession. Nerves had gotten the better of our young players, and some of them almost froze when they walked out for the second half in front of a boiling stadium. The noise from both sets of fans was deafening, the atmosphere was absolutely electric, and whilst I totally enjoyed the occasion and thought back of some of my best moments at the Royal Antwerp Football Club, it was impossible to get some kind of composure in the younger and less experienced players. I didn't blame them in my post-match comments. Instead, I blamed the boot camp and the lack of proper support from the leadership.

As soon as the match ended, or maybe even before the final whistle, they all disappeared. My guess was that they made a short stop in the accounts office high up in the main stand of the stadium, and then made off with their heavy plastic bags. It took us several days before we would see any of the Executive Committee members again . . .

This match also presented us with another novelty : the sponsor who gets into the dressing room before kick-off and who tells the players not to be scared . . . You can just imagine those eighteen players eagerly awaiting the clash with their rivals, the adrenaline is flowing, they are trying to forget their nerves, and there comes the sponsor with photocopies of an article on fear and pressure . . . He gave every player a copy of this article, in English, not even realizing that some of the players were hardly literate. According to our wonderful sponsor, the best way to forget about pressure was to read an article about it a few minutes before a crucial match. I somehow had a different opinion on that. And I somehow had an opinion about people coming into the dressing room before a match. I believe that the dressing room belongs to the players and the technical staff only. Anyone who wants to have a word with the players or the coaches should do so well before the team reaches the stadium. My teams usually go through a fixed set of routines, and I don't want anybody to disturb those. But no, according to our sponsor, the best way of forgetting about pressure is to be told by an outsider that . . . you should forget about pressure . . .

"It is just something that you put on yourself . . ."
"Oh yes, thank you for reminding me. I am ready to go onto the field now and totally ignore the pressure . . ."

The sponsor's intervention contributed to our performance. Instead of putting up some serious incentives for the players, he came to remind them not to fear the opposition . . .

After the match, the usual accusations started to fly. The leaders publicly accused some of our players of having accepted bribes by the opposition, and while this can never be proven, I believe that the reasons for our defeat were to be found elsewhere. The conditions in which the players had to prepare themselves left a lot to be desired, there were no incentives, and the officials did everything in their power to show that they were not interested in a victory at all. After all, a victory would mean that they would have to give a large percentage of the money to the players, and obviously that would have been a shameful waste . . .

A bit later I understood even better why the leaders needed the money. I was told by a very reliable source that the Vice-Chairman had by now collected enough money to pay dowry for his new wife . . .

We lost, the officials collected their money, and I decided to ask the Chairman for my refund once again. When I finally found him four days later, he told me to call him after two days. The Executive Committee was due to meet. And so I did.

"Mr Chairman, have you decided on my refund and on my letter of appointment?"
"Call the Publicity Secretary."
"Can't you tell me what you have decided?"
"I said, call the Publicity Secretary. He will tell you what we discussed."

And so I called the Publicity Secretary.

"Do you have an answer for me regarding my refund and my letter of appointment?"
"What are you talking about?"
"The Chairman told me that you discussed my refund and my letter of appointment in yesterday's meeting."
"We never discussed these items."
"But he told me you did."
"We never!"

I then called the Secretary General.

"Did you discuss my issues in yesterday's meeting?"
"Yes we did."
"Can you tell me what was decided?"
"Why don't you speak to the Chairman?"
"I did. He told me to ask the Publicity Secretary, who told me that my issues were not discussed."
"Oh. Let me talk to him . . ."

A few minutes later, I called the Publicity Secretary once more.

"The Secretary General just told me that you did discuss my issues . . ."
"Yes, it's true. I must have dozed off in the meeting, but now I remember everything . . ."
"Sure . . . And so what did you decide?"
"We talked about your issues at length, and we decided that for your refund you have to wait until the next derby match, and we will further discuss your appointment in our next meeting."
"For what reason can't you give me this refund now? You collected almost ten million Shillings last Sunday!"
"That money is finished. We had a lot of expenses to prepare for the match . . ."
"And when will your next meeting take place?"
"*Kesho.*"

Once more, the word '*kesho*' had to be understood in its broadest possible sense . . . If ever you need to give an example of 'the right hand not knowing what the left hand does', then feel free to use the above conversation.

THIRTY

THE DERBY AGAINST NDOVU FOOTBALL Club somehow marked a turning point in the fortunes of the team. The first half of the season had gone extremely well for us, and we finished the first round on top of the league. It proved my point about the fact that every game is worth three points and nothing more. Despite the fact that we had lost 'the biggest match in the history of mankind', nobody was able to take away the league top spot from us. I made it very clear to my players that our position in the league was a million times more important than the result of one single match.

Our next assignment in the Nyerere Cup tournament was against AFC, a relatively strong team from the town of Ashura. During the days building up to the match, I spent quite some time with the players trying to get them over the disappointment of the previous weekend (probably more the disappointment of not getting their share of the gate collection than the disappointment of losing to our city rivals), and I was hopeful that we would be able to recover and move on to the next round in the Cup. As it was though, AFC arrived in town on a mission, and they surprised us with their clever play. They scored halfway through the first half, and spent the rest of the match kicking the ball out of play as often as possible. Their goalkeeper should also have won an Oscar for play-acting. Every time we attacked his goal, he looked like he got shot by someone, and started rolling on the ground for minutes on end. His time-wasting tactics went unpunished by the referee, and were thus quite effective. The actual playing time in this match must have been well below fifteen minutes, out of a possible ninety, but the trick worked for AFC and we were out of the Cup tournament. Or were we?

I feared that the timing for our match against Burundi's Vital'Ô was very unfortunate. We had just lost two big matches in a row, and while we expected to beat our Central-African neighbors, it was hard to tell the players' mental state of mind. This time we didn't have to travel on a bus—instead we got a two-day long train journey in the company of two club officials. We assumed that we were in good hands.

The hotel in Bujumbura was of a decent standard and we did get some sleep over there . . . In my pre-match talk I reminded the players that it was in international matches that they could expect overseas scouts to be on the lookout for talents, and I encouraged them to give their best efforts. I would have been happy with an away goal and a draw, but the players somehow managed to compose themselves and before halftime we had already scored twice. In the second half we took our foot off the pedal a little bit, also because suddenly a tropical downpour started and the field became very muddy and slippery. I thought that the referee would abandon the game, even more so because this would have favored the home team. For some reason he didn't, and we returned home with a safe lead. I started to look at the teams that we might meet later on, and there was now a good chance that we would be drawn against one of the continental giants. I started to get excited about the prospect! But of course, we still had to ensure qualification for the next round . . . and that was by no means a done deal, what with the African referees and the *juju*! Before our departure for Dar Es Salaam, we suddenly found out that the two officials who had accompanied the team had already left town, and that the plastic bag with the team's financial resources had left with them. There was no money to buy the train tickets back to Dar Es Salaam. We tried to get a loan from our Burundian hosts, but they were in no mood to pay for their rivals' expenses. We approached the representatives of the Confederation of African Football, but not surprisingly, they had their own financial issues to deal with. Our last resort was to go to the Tanzanian Embassy in Bujumbura and plead with them to get us the tickets. After a lot of talking and a couple of phone calls, the Embassy official told us that we would find the tickets ready at the train station. We thanked him and made the two-day journey back to the coast. Along the way I tried to tell myself that I was living an interesting adventure. The stunning scenery of Northern Tanzania certainly helped us enjoy the journey a bit more. The train ride from the west to the east of the country is one of those epic trips that everybody should make at least once in their lifetime—easily comparable with the Transsiberian Express, the Orient Express or the trip from Cuzco to Machu Picchu in Peru!

At the start of the second round of the league, the problems brought into the club by the leaders started to affect the team more and more, and our performance went down—drastically. We started to draw and occasionally lose games that we should have won, and slowly but surely other teams were catching up with us. But one thing was for sure : I would never ever blame any of the players for this turn of events. They always tried their best under the difficult circumstances, and they were the victims rather than the culprits within the mess that had been created.

Our slump in the league also coincided with the departure of some of our key players. They decided not to wait for further successes in our continental campaign, and went to look for a brighter future overseas. Even though some of them managed to find teams in Europe and in the Middle East, the club never benefited from their transfers. It was claimed many times that transfer fees had been paid, but that they had been eaten almost immediately by those who received them . . .

Our return match against the Burundians was a meek affair, more of a case of 'going through the motions', and after a barren draw we had qualified for the quarter-finals of the Africa Cup. I eagerly awaited the results of the draw in Cairo.

Our next league game was a date with Kariakoo Zindi, a team based on the south coast of Tanzania, and famous for being the home of another Tanzanian football phenomenon, *uzalendo* (or 'favoritism' for the home team). I had already heard harrowing stories about 'home advantage' in Tanzanian football, but I always told my players that no matter what the referees did or said, they should continue playing football. Many a team in Tanzania resorted to the practice of abandoning a game when they disagreed, and most often rightly so. It was not a rare occurrence that games ended with severe and thorough beatings for the referee and his assistants. The injustices suffered by the away teams did not justify the violence, but one could very easily understand why some fans, officials and players lost their self-control when confronted with blatant favoritism or *uzalendo*. However, walking off the field automatically means forfeiting the match, and it was my belief that these referees would one day reap what they had sown. A top team can rise above the frustrations, and can still be too good for the opposition, no matter how much the referees try to help the opponent.

Because of my work commitments, I couldn't make the trip with the team, but of course I heard all the stories upon the team's return home. At this stage in the season, Kariakoo Zindi had developed a nationwide reputation for being assisted by the famed *uzalendo*. They had been promoted the previous season, and would normally have been expected to struggle and to be involved in the relegation battle. But that never happened. While they had lost all their away games, most of them by margins of at least two or three goals, not a single team had been able to beat them at home. A number of games played in Zindi didn't go the full ninety minutes, as several teams became so upset with the referees' handling of the matches that they decided to abandon the game before the end. Our story was no different . . .

But let me first tell you about the trip to Zindi. It takes a two-day boat ride down the Indian Ocean coast to reach the nearest fishing village. Hardly the ideal preparation for a football match. But so be it, the team got onto the boat and disembarked somewhere not too far from Zindi. For the next part of the trip a truck was to be rented, but there was no money foreseen for this. Believe it or not, but the team manager had to ask the players to contribute from their own pockets, and promised them that after the game against Kariakoo, they would all be refunded. They managed to collect just enough money to rent the truck, but it broke down at about twenty kilometers from Zindi. Of course, the money had been paid, and was not refunded by the truck owner. The players and technical staff then had to walk the final twenty kilometers to their destination, knowing that the next afternoon there was a game on the cards . . .

In my mind it would have been acceptable for the players to travel by boat and truck if the club was really going through some difficult times. But here we were talking about one of the country's two biggest clubs, and the trip took place just a few days after our big match against Ndovu Football Club, which earned the club several million Shillings. And to make matters even worse for the players, when they reached Zindi, they found that the whole leadership had flown there . . . Up to this day I don't understand why seven officials needed to travel so far away by plane and at such a cost, when there wasn't even enough money to rent a truck or bus for the players . . .

The next day the game started, and of course, it didn't take long for the *uzalendo* accusations to start flying. After what was seen as a biased decision by the referee, the Safari Sports Club Chairman came down from the stands and called his team off the field. Initially the players responded, but eventually they decided to return to the action and try to play football. However, this soon became impossible, as the referee continued to penalise our players for non-existing fouls, and for calling them off-side on more than thirty occasions. A bit later Kariakoo scored their goal from an obvious off-side position, and the Safari Sports Club players had seen enough. They challenged the referee and his assistants, two of the players were given a red card, and suddenly an army of fans invaded the field. Stones, chairs and sticks were thrown around, and the match came to a halt. There was no way that this game could restart, and so it was left to the Football Association to decide on the outcome of the match. As expected, the game was awarded to Kariakoo Zindi . . . This meant that Kariakoo received the three points plus two goals, that Safari Sports Club had to pay a hefty fine, and that the Football Association officials walked home with their plastic bags.

I don't want to comment on the status of football in Zindi because I have never attended a football match there, but I know from very reliable sources that 'serious efforts' have been made to ensure that the club continues to play in the Tanzanian top division. Somewhere in the area there lives a very powerful and influential chief, and the story goes that the fat cats of the Football Association of Tanzania benefit immensely from this man's wealth. On condition of course that his team is kept in the Premier League . . . It is undeniable that problems have occurred there, and it has even come to the stage where some teams have decided not to waste their time, their energy and their money anymore and to forfeit their away match against Kariakoo. They are quite happy to pay the fine, which is less than the travel and accommodation expenses of a complete team. And if you are sure that you are going to return home without any points, then what is . . . the point?

The next day most of the club officials flew back home, while the Secretary General decided to spend some more time in his home region. He said that he had some 'family business' to attend to . . .

Two days later, a newspaper reported that the team was stuck in Zindi and that it had run out of money. The leadership had already flown back to Dar Es Salaam, and our poor team manager, who wasn't much better off than the players themselves, had to get creative and raise some funds in the Zindi community. He sent the players around town to go and ask individuals for money, so that a truck could be rented to return the team to the port, from where another two-day boat ride would bring the team back to Dar Es Salaam. I have never heard of any other Premier League or other team whose players had to become beggars in order to be able to return home. But with Safari Sports Club, anything was possible . . . "And where was the money from our sponsor?", you might ask . . .

Needless to add that the players had a very uncomfortable return by boat. They were never refunded the money that they had lent for the truck rental, and they never received any match allowance.

Next up was an away game in Tanga. Given the fact that this town is only about five hours by road from Dar Es Salaam, I decided to go to this match and see for myself how bad this *uzalendo* really was. When I told some of the officials that I would be driving to Tanga and stay for the night, they all jumped up and claimed to be my best friends.

"Can I get a ride from you?"

"Yeah, OK."

"I'm bringing a friend as well."

We agreed to leave at 8 am on Saturday morning, as the match would start at 6 pm. When I arrived at the meeting point in town just before eight o'clock, there were about twelve people there waiting for a ride to Tanga.

"Hey ho, I can only take three people."

"We'll sit in the back."

"Oh no you won't, I am taking three more people and that's it. Ibrahim, get in please!"

"But you are my friend. Let me sit in the back."

"I'm sorry, but I won't put ten people in this car. First of all, that's illegal, and secondly, ten people would be too heavy."

"*Hawu mzungu!*" (But, white man?)

"*Pole sana!*" (Sorry!)

We arrived in Tanga in good time, and found the team at the guesthouse where they were staying. I asked for my room, and the guesthouse manager needed to talk—in Kiswahili—to the Assistant Secretary-General.

"Do I give him a room with or without television?"

"Without television!"

"All the other officials have television!"

"I said, you give him a room without television, you douchebag. I don't want to pay for a room with a TV for him. If he wants a TV, then let him pay the difference himself."

175

What they didn't know was that by now I had learned enough Kiswahili to understand conversations like that, but I decided not to argue. What would I have needed a television for anyway? But again, what did all the leaders need televisions for?

We went to play the match, which we lost 2-1. The players put up a brave fight, but the poor condition of the field and some opportunistic goal scoring by Tanga United cost us the match. Again there were cries of *uzalendo*. I wasn't too impressed by the referees' handling of the match myself, but as I told you before, I took it in my stride and asked my team to rise above that. I never have, and I don't think that I will ever violently debate or contest a referee's decision. At the end of the day, even these referees only get away with so much, and one day their cheating catches up with them. They were waiting for cash in a plastic bag, somewhere in Tanga . . .

One of our players sustained a serious injury during the match, and as there were no officials to be seen immediately after the game, I put the player in my car and took him to the hospital. Nestor and I stayed with the player for about two hours, until it was decided that he would have to spend the night in the hospital. During all this time, none of the leaders ever bothered to check on our player's condition. An obvious case of history repeating itself . . .

A few hours later Nestor and I went back to the guesthouse, and at around 10 pm the officials arrived with the money bag. A plastic one, of course. They all disappeared into a small room and started to count. The players and I were watching the news and a movie in the dining room. The office door remained closed for about three hours, until the Treasurer called the team captain into the room and gave him some pocket money for the players. I was told that the players had demanded their refunds from the trip to Zindi, but they were not given. The captain came out of the office, visibly unhappy and agitated, and told the other players that they would only be getting six thousand Shillings each. The players started to shout and complain, and who could blame them?

A bit later Nestor was called into the office, and he remained there for about thirty minutes. Then, to my great surprise, I was also called in. When I entered, I found the whole leadership lying about in sofas, their eyes staring at the bank notes on the desk. They had already downed several cups of Chai Bora each, and it looked like the night was still young for them. After I had been in the office for about fifteen minutes, the Treasurer told me that they hadn't collected enough money to refund me anything. Why was I not surprised? He added that the next morning he would put some diesel in my car, to compensate for the three people that traveled free of charge with me.

While I was in the office, one of the guesthouse managers entered, and presented the Treasurer with the accommodation bill. The manager obviously realized that she needed to get her payment sooner rather than later, knowing very well that there would be nothing left for her the next morning. The Treasurer paid her, and after she left the Chairman suddenly got agitated and told his Treasurer:

"Bwana, before you hand out any more money, can you put our share on the side. I don't want to end up with nothing, and seeing the rate at which you are handing out money, soon there won't be anything left for me."
"OK, I will remove your share."

What he removed looked like a handsome sum of money to me . . . Nestor looked at me, and I could tell that he was thinking the same thing as myself. Meanwhile, no mention of our injured player.

The next morning, before returning to Dar, I went to check on the player, and made sure that he had transport to come back home. The leaders decided that he should go back on the team bus. Conveniently, that left more places for them in my car . . .

THIRTY-ONE

IT WAS NOW AUGUST. WE were languishing in second position, having been overtaken by the eventual champions. We were still heavily involved in the fight for one of the three top spots in the Mainland League, but the signs were not good. The draw for the quarterfinals of the Africa Cup was imminent, and as far as we knew, we had been knocked out of the Nyerere Cup tournament.

The lack of direction from the top started to affect the focus and the discipline of the players, who had not received any allowances for a number of weeks now. Some of them started to ignore our internal rules and instructions, and even inside the field of play all was not well. During our league match against Ashura FC, we managed to do enough to lead 1-0 at half-time, and the signs were that we would get a well-deserved victory for our efforts in another difficult away match. In the last minute, one of our young strikers had the option to pass the ball to an unmarked teammate who would have had the easiest chance of his life to score, but instead he chose to shoot himself . . . and missed. This angered his teammate so much that the latter ran straight to the youngster and started to beat and kick him . . . in the field of play! I ran from the sidelines to where the 'action' was, and managed to separate the two players, who promptly received a red card for 'dangerous play'! So we had a bleeding nose and two suspensions, and a whole lot of conflict resolution to deal with . . . The good thing was though, we held on for that 1-0 victory.

The draw for the Africa Cup tournament gave me exactly the team I wanted : Zamalek FC from Egypt. This club was one of the standard bearers in African football, and as I stated a long time ago, I wanted to measure myself against the strongest teams on the continent, and not just in Tanzania or in East Africa. As soon as I heard the news, I started to spend hours in front of the computer, trying to find any information and statistics that I could find on the team, the players, the system of play and the coach. I was determined to prepare my team as well as possible, and I was not going to leave any stone unturned in my search for details that could give us even the slightest advantage. I also contacted an old acquaintance who was now living in Cairo, and asked him if he could provide me with video tapes of some of Zamalek's most recent matches. My friend, whose identity will remain concealed forever in order to protect the guilty, sent me three tapes that contained a wealth of information on the tactics of Egypt's most successful club. One thing that struck me immediately was that in international competition, Zamalek hardly ever won its away matches. This information told me that their home ground, which holds around 100.000 very vocal fans, had to be a nearly impregnable fortress. I felt that if we were to have any chance of beating them, we had to make a difference in our home game. And so I started planning.

One of our leaders had a more pragmatic approach. After one of our training sessions, the Publicity Secretary called me and informed me that he had an idea.

"What do you suggest?", I asked him.
"I think we need to take our players to Lybia for a camp."
"To Lybia?"
"Yes."
"But why?"
"Well, they have never seen an Arab, and they will be afraid of them when they meet them in the field! So I think we need to take them to Lybia and show them what Arabs look like."
"And we have money for that?"
"I'm sure we can find some . . ."

The idea never materialized.

Two days later, the newspapers carried the news that Safari Sports Club had been reinstated in the Nyerere Cup competition. One of the four semi-finalists, the Correctional Services Football Team, had withdrawn from the competition for apparent financial reasons. At least, that was the official story. What I found out later was that the Prisons team withdrew as part of a deal that had been made a year earlier, when it had received some 'help' from Safari Sports Club in its pursuit of the Premier League title. Well, we got a second shot at glory in the cup, and I was determined not to see it go to waste. We were drawn against Malindi FC of Zanzibar, while our conquerors, AFC, were drawn against the Police team (which was, obviously, not facing the same financial difficulties as the Prisons team).

Our midweek cup game took place in Zanzibar, and we did what we had to do. It wasn't a pretty match, and the only thing that mattered was that we had reached the final of the Nyerere Cup. I was going to take my team to Wembley, so to speak, and I was proud of having achieved this in my first season as a coach. Ironically, AFC lost its semi-final and we had booked ourselves a date against the Police team.

We had recently started training twice a day at the National Stadium. Over time I had struck up a good friendship with the stadium manager, and when I approached him and asked if we could train in the stadium, he kindly agreed. This privilege was an advantage for us, because soon it would be time for the return match against Ndovu Football Club at the same stadium. The newspapers and the fans started to talk about revenge, and the momentum had begun to pick up.

Ndovu, Safari match fever grips Dar

**BY
OUR REPORTER**

Tension is mounting at the camps of the country's big guns—Safari Sports Club and Ndovu Football Club—as they shape up for Sunday's Premier League clash at the National Stadium in Dar Es Salaam. Ndovu Football Club have been undergoing intensive training in Ashura since last week under their Congolese mentor. On the other hand, Safari Sports Club, who have vowed to reclaim the league title, are training in the city under close supervision of their Belgian and Burundian coaches. Safari coach Nestor Nizigiyimana boasted in the city yesterday that his boys were responding well to his instructions and that nothing would stop them from riding high in the match billed to be a crowd-puller.

The red and white leadership has promised to give the players seventy percent of the club's share of the gate earnings of Sunday's clash in an attempt to boost their morale.

Hold on . . . what? Let me read that again . . .

The red and white leadership has promised to give the players seventy percent of the club's share of the gate earnings of Sunday's clash in an attempt to boost their morale.

I pinched myself and yes, realized that this was what had been printed. Had it been said? I'll never know. But it had been printed. Somehow, I was a little bit skeptical. I continued to read . . .

> Safari players will also get 50,000 Tanzanian Shillings each from the club's sponsor should they win the match.

OMG! This was unreal. Given the scope of the match and the potential for a victory, our players were being told that they could become millionaires overnight. All they had to do was win the match . . . and try to believe the newspaper report. Suffice it to say that I spent quite some time trying to keep their heads on their shoulders and their feet on the floor. And lo and behold, our presumed sponsor had given a sign of life!

I am sure that the final part of the article was not picked up by most readers, but to me it sounded an ominous warning:

> Ndovu Football Club, who have also boasted that they have what it takes to claim the Premier League title, were expected to meet in the city last night to draft plans that would pave the way for the team to emerge victorious in the match.

What the article did not tell us, but what I could easily fill in myself, was whom the Ndovu Football Club would be meeting with . . .

Either the story about the players' allowances had been completely invented by a journalist, or one of the leaders had spoken without the knowledge of his accomplices. Sorry, his colleagues. The promise of a huge potential financial windfall for the players struck a sore note with several officials, and a verbal slanging match started in the papers and on the local radio waves. Realizing that there was internal strife in our club, the media hounds smelled blood and added their own bits to the simmering conflicts. I suspected that our arch rivals had paid off a reporter when one morning a newspaper started to query who was in charge of the technical matters at Safari Sports Club—my Burundian colleague or myself? The 'war' between the two coaches should never have been a story, but like so many other *mizengwe* in Tanzania, it soon took on a life of its own.

The paper suggested that there was a campaign to unseat my Burundian friend Nestor and to have me in sole control of the team's trainings and matches. This was absolute rubbish, as Nestor and I mostly worked well together. We even took some of the technical decisions together. He respected my experience and my input concerning set pieces and tactics, and I respected the fact that he could travel with the team to our up-country assignments. The team needed a coach who could accompany them, and Nestor fitted the bill as far as I was concerned. We didn't argue much, as we had drawn clear lines of expertise and responsibility. But of course, the papers saw things differently. Their paymaster, quite possibly our main challengers for the League title, could easily have paid a reporter to write complete fiction about Safari Sports Club, and thus destabilize the coaching team before the next big match. Under the motto "If it bleeds, it leads", the journalists contributed their bit in confusing everyone. For them, it was better to write trash than to write nothing at all. The journalists reminded the whole country that I had already survived two reshuffles in the coaching department of Safari Sports Club. All those months ago, Mr Kimora had left the club to return to Zindi, and I stayed on. When my two colleagues, Mr Mahmoud and Mr Mwengo, were so unceremoniously dismissed and even humiliated, somehow the *mzungu* coach survived again. Was it the leadership that wanted the continuity and kept the white coach in his position, or was it maybe the white coach himself who had caused all these changes? What the journalists didn't realise—or maybe they did, and in that case it's even worse—was that their fantasy articles caused problems for other people. Many people read the papers, and many people actually even believed what was written. I have always been very fair towards the journalists, and given them the information that they needed for accurate reporting. But I cannot say likewise about how they have used, misused and abused my name. And if, as it has been claimed, this has all been done for the sake of 'selling more papers', then someone could at least have told me and given me a little commission . . .

The story simmered for a few days, and one newspaper went as far as suggesting that Nestor had been spotted in a local nightclub, drunk as a skunk and in the company of some of the senior players, as well as a couple of members of the fairer sex . . .

Some of the leaders became involved in the debate, and it would be naïve to say that this episode did not have a negative effect on the relative peace within the club. As always, the leaders felt that they had to take sides, even in a completely fabricated issue, and I could sense some cold shoulders around me. But eventually the story did what all nonsense stories do : it went away.

Our sponsor didn't contribute much to the harmony in the club either. On several occasions did he announce that he was going to get rid of the coaches and bring in a professional from Europe or South America. He never spoke to either Nestor or myself, and even the leaders claimed that they didn't know what he was talking about. But when I asked the reporters, they guaranteed me that he had called them and informed them that a professional white coach was coming . . .

As it is, the club is still waiting for that incredible coach, but you will understand that the sponsor did cause a lot of unrest amongst the players and the technical staff.

One morning my Burundian colleague didn't show up for practice at the National Stadium. I conducted the training session, and told the players to be back in the afternoon. That same afternoon, again no Nestor. And no officials who could explain his absence.

For a whole week I conducted the training sessions by myself, without any news from Nestor. Then, one day, I saw the Chairman, and I asked him what was going on.

"The coach has a problem."
"What kind of problem?"
"Something with his work permit."
"What's wrong?"
"The Immigration people have gone to see him and found that he doesn't have a valid residence and work permit."
"How does that happen?"
"We forgot to apply for a renewal."
"And what is going to happen now?"
"Ah, we know the people from Immigration. The issue will be settled in a couple of days. You just continue training the team."

The coach did come back a few days later, and it appeared that the problem had been resolved. This may sound like a trivial event, but a few months after this incident, Nestor had effectively been arrested for illegal presence in the country and for not having a work permit. I found it strange that the club leaders knew about this for such a long time and that they never bothered to settle the issue for once and for all. Or did they have a good reason as to why they didn't want to legitimize the coach's presence at the club?

Once my fellow coach had returned to our practices, I decided to take a short break and go spend a few days in a beautiful beach resort in Bagamoyo, an hour's drive north of Dar Es Salaam. Those four days gave me a welcome rest, but even in Bagamoyo I was reminded of Safari Sports Club. On my last day there, I decided to go via the fish market and pick up some *samaki* (fish) and prawns. To my surprise, I spotted Abdul, one of those people whose job in life it seemed to be to constantly hover around in the vicinity of the club leaders. He was engaged in a heated discussion with three of the local fishermen, and I thought I should go and greet him. He was surprised to see me at the market, and quickly closed the plastic bag that he was holding. I asked him what had brought him to Bagamoyo, and he said:

"Business."
"What sort of business do you have here?"
"Oh, all sorts of things."

The conversation was rather vague, but when I was back in Dar Es Salaam and told Nestor that I had seen Abdul in Bagamoyo, he told me that this man usually gets sent there to go and prepare our *juju* . . . Apparently, everyone around the club called him *'bwana samaki'*—Mister Fish.

A lot of *juju* magic would be needed the next weekend. True to the adage that old habits die hard, our leaders decided that the boot camp was still the best place to lock away the players before the return derby. In preparation for our match, the team was once again put in camp under military supervision. We trained twice a day on the same rock-hard field, and it was very difficult to do any meaningful work with the goalkeepers. They would have injured themselves just from falling down . . . The players also started to complain about sore ankles, but we just tried to keep them focused on the task at hand.

In order to properly prepare and condition the goalkeepers for the upcoming match against Ndovu Football Club, I decided to wear a yellow and green jersey during our training sessions. The jersey was a replica of the Jamaica National Team jersey, but this Reggae Boy simply tried to encourage our goalkeepers to stop anything that was fired at them by people wearing yellow and green. No tactic was too daring in order to try and get through to the goalkeepers!

THIRTY-TWO

By THIS TIME IN THE season, it had become extremely rare to see any of the club officials anywhere near the team. You could bet your life savings and your properties that they were there when the money was being counted, but they never checked on the players' health or on the team's progress in between matches. It is no exaggeration to say that people like the Publicity Secretary and the Assistant Secretary General absented themselves from the team for at least two months at a time.

I did my own bit to try and destabilize the opposition also. Mind games are part and parcel of football in Tanzania, and because of my excellent relationship with the vast majority of the journalists, it was very easy to launch my own little *mizengwe* stories. I told one of my most trusted journalist friends that I had met with some of the Ndovu Football Club players, and that they had expressed a deep desire to join Safari Sports Club sooner rather than later. They had heard from their friends at my club that we coaches cared a lot about the well-being of our squad, and that there was an opportunity to be sent abroad for trials with more renowned clubs. Of course, the players concerned were not bit-part players. No, they were Ndovu Football Club's most experienced and most dependable players, and it was not hard to believe that they had the ambition to go and make a living out of football abroad.

As soon as this story broke in the local newspapers, the Ndovu Football Club officials were all over the place. They went looking for their players, they interrogated them and put them in something akin to quarantine. They vehemently denied that any players had mentioned that they wanted to leave. Of course, I kept the story running for a couple of days, insisting that some overseas scouts were going to attend the match at my invitation, and that these players had indeed made up their mind. Some fans, those usually found on the front row in the classrooms, were a bit more clever than others, and saw right through my ruse. The club officials though could not take any chances and had to be seen to be doing something about this situation. I simply watched from a distance . . .

Match day arrived. In good old Tanzanian tradition, the pre-match preparations in the camp took so long that by the time we left with our cars and the team bus, it was thirty minutes before kick-off. The drive from the camp to the National Stadium was going to take at least fifty minutes, possibly even an hour, depending on the traffic. There was absolutely no way that we would arrive at the stadium on time. In the best of circumstances, without any traffic and with pretty fast cars, we could just about pull off the journey in under half an hour. So I needed to create or find the best of circumstances.

As I drove out of the gate of our boot camp, I spotted a police car on the other side of the road, hidden in the shrubs and bushes. Bingo! I immediately knew that two hungry police officers had set up a speed trap in order to get their Christmas bonuses from unsuspecting drivers. I quickly drove up to the officers and made them an offer that they could not refuse.

"Excuse me, gentlemen, how is business today?"

"Very slow."

"Sorry to hear that. What's the problem?"

"I think the drivers going in the direction of Bagamoyo are flashing their lights and warning everyone that we are here."

"Quite possible, quite possible . . ."

"How about you, coach? How are you?"

"Well, we're off to our match with Ndovu Football Club and I was wondering if you would like to earn yourselves a thousand Shillings each in the next thirty minutes."

"Sure! What do we need to do?"

"Can you escort us to the stadium? We're a bit late and we need to rush through the city. With the traffic, it's going to be difficult to get there on time. But you could drive ahead of us and clear the road . . ."

"Sure! But it's going to cost you more than a thousand Shillings! The stadium is far . . ."

"How much?"

"Three thousand each."

"I don't have that much. I will give you one thousand five hundred each, but you must switch on the sirens and your flash lights for that."

"It's an extra five hundred for the sirens and an extra five hundred for the flash lights."

"But that would be two thousand each. That's too much, we're a poor club."

"I'm sure you can find that money. Just ask your Chairman."

"Well, he's not here. I'm afraid I can't give you two thousand each. One thousand five hundred each is the maximum. Tell me now, because I'm running out of time."

"Two thousand each and not a Shilling less."

"One thousand five hundred each or nothing."

"Deal!"

The police escort did the trick. We sped towards and through the city at the speed of light, or at least at the speed of a noisy and flashy police car. First stop, the Chairman's guesthouse, where we met with our hardcore fans. With flags waving through the car windows and with *vuvuzelas* announcing our triumphant arrival, we drove towards the National Stadium via Mandela Road, and what did we see? A red car, parked at the corner just in front of the National Stadium. When our convoy approached, this red car pulled onto the road and drove right in front of the team bus. It started to lead the convoy towards the stadium, the gates opened, and as we drove onto the track inside the stadium towards the point where the players would get out of the bus, who disembarks from the car and starts waving at our fans? You guessed it right : our Publicity Secretary . . .

So this was the idea : abandon your team for two months, and then lead them into the stadium, in full view of the thousands of fans that are there, and just smile as if all is well with your club. If you have ever seen a better example of hypocrisy, please let me know.

The match was another classic encounter, but with our depleted squad and the poor refereeing we just weren't given a fair chance to show what we could do. For the second time that season, we lost the derby to Ndovu Football Club, this time by two goals to nil. Both Nestor and I knew that the potential of our squad was bigger than what we had seen. With the added experience of the first derby match, it was clear that the players were a bit more settled, and this was by far the most entertaining and exciting match I had seen in Tanzania in a long time. There was a real purpose to the style of play of both teams, the spirit on the field and in the stands was exemplary, and all forty thousand souls who witnessed the afternoon went home happy and satisfied. Most of all our leaders of course : another huge payday, and no need to share the gate collection with the players. We coaches also knew full well that it would be very difficult, if not impossible, to fulfill the team's potential under the current leadership. There were just too many obstacles, too little cooperation and goodwill, and whichever way I looked at it, the odds were no longer in our favor.

During the match, I remember looking across to the team bench of Ndovu Football Club, and I wondered whether things were any better there. Of course there were stories about their club also, but on that particular afternoon, there seemed to be a certain level of serenity and calmness in their area. Was this only because they were winning the match, or was it a reflection of a greater sense of unity and purpose in their camp?

After the final whistle, and realizing fully well that they had just witnessed a spectacular game of football, hundreds of fans of both teams flooded the field and swarmed around the players and coaches. In the midst of the melee, I found my way to our opponent's area and saw that René, their coach, had been lifted upon the fans' shoulders. Out of respect for the fact that he had managed to defeat us twice in a row, I fought my way through the crowd in order to shake his hand and congratulate him on his achievement. He returned the compliment, and acknowledged that it had been a tough match for his charges. We had a brief conversation and we wished each other well for the rest of the league. Respect between coaches should be a given—no need to take the professional rivalry into the private domain. We both also knew that we'd meet up soon again. After all, the Tanzanian football world is a rather small one.

Once more the gate collection was huge, and fortunately for the leaders and the sponsor, nothing needed to be shared with the players. In the aftermath of the match, the sponsor went on the record in the newspapers, claiming that our players were not strong enough for this match, that they had lacked stamina and strength, and that they needed to train harder. Had anyone told him that they had been living the life of starving soldiers in a boot camp with only porridge and beans? Where was the food and the accommodation that he should have provided? No word about that, and it was now totally clear that he had no interest in this club at all, but that he just used it to get his name in the newspapers from time to time. I also knew now that no refunds would be forthcoming for me. It was time to start forgetting about ever seeing my money back.

A few games were left, most of them away from home. It was still possible for us to qualify for the Super League, but we would have to win most of our away matches. One of those matches was the away leg against Nestor's former club, and he told me from the start:

"Don't worry, from that game we already have three points."
"What do you mean?"
"Well, these are my former players, and I will bring them to our club next season. They will not put up any resistance."
"Are you sure?"
"You will see. Just trust me."
"OK, we'll see."

As it was, Safari Sports Club went to play against his former charges and lost 2-1 . . . So much for being sure of victory against your former pupils.

The next weekend was supposed to be one of the highlights of my budding coaching career. Our date with the Police team offered me my first opportunity to win silverware, and as you will remember, this was really what competition was all about for me. I could almost smell the cup and looked forward to receiving it from the President of the Republic himself.

The Cup final lasted for just over an hour before the referee decided that he had had enough. The Police team were leading 4-3 when one of their players assaulted the referee after he had been shown a yellow card. Rather than giving the player a red card and getting on with the game, the referee called his assistants and they all walked off the field. At first we were wondering whether they would return, but when it became clear that they were not going to resume the match, we could do nothing but leave also.

The following day the Football Association decided to punish the referee and ordered a replay of the Cup final. We met the Prisons team again two days later, and we won 1-0 thanks to an early goal and a lot of resolute defending. The quality of play was not really worthy of a cup final, but that was probably not the first and last time that this occurred. Come to think of it, it was still a whole lot better than the 1990 World Cup final! Both teams had a player sent off and after the final whistle there was another brawl, but half an hour later my captain and I were finally invited to climb up the steps to the VIP box and receive the Nyerere Cup. I was holding my first prize as a coach and told myself that this was only the beginning.

The cup worked as a catalyst for more determination and more hunger. I let the players enjoy the moment. They spent almost an hour on the field, posing with the cup in all sorts of silly positions, but I wanted them to let their hair down a bit and go crazy. The end of the season was going to bring more pressures, and it was good to let off some steam here. When the celebrations were over and most of the fans had left the stadium, it was almost dark. As I looked back over the football field before exiting the stadium, I noticed something shiny in the distance. I decided to go and check what it was, and I was stunned to find the Nyerere Cup lying on the ground, completely abandoned and left like a piece of junk. All the players and officials had either forgotten or neglected to take the cup with them, and I wondered whether I had taken its value a little bit too seriously. I picked up the cup and left the stadium. I thought that maybe in the parking lot I might find one or two officials, but they had apparently already left with their famous plastic bags. So I put the cup in my car and drove home. The Nyerere Cup, the equivalent of the FA Cup, stood in my house for about a month before I was able to find out where I should take it. Since nobody from within the club showed any interest in displaying our cup, I took it back to the Football Association offices and left it with the Secretary General. I could not imagine that the FA Cup could ever end up in anyone's private home, but then, this was Tanzania, and nothing was quite impossible here . . .

Our last important league match of the season was away against Mbitwa, who were well on their way to clinch the Mainland League title. This club belonged to Tanzania's largest sugar company, and their relative isolation from the rest of the country, well-hidden in between the endless sugar cane plantations, meant that they had unlimited private access to match officials and members of the Football Association. While their players were training in the beautiful surroundings of the sugar company, their leaders were renowned for spending a lot of time in their offices, not so much dealing with the latest sugar export and production figures, but rather plotting and paying their way to the team's next victory. The system worked of course, and the team's league position was no coincidence.

In the build-up towards this match, some of our own leaders suddenly started to involve themselves in the team's technical affairs. There were explicit references to team selection, and as coaches we were being told, in no uncertain terms, which players we had to field in the next few matches. At first I wondered whether they had suddenly completed a FIFA coaching course and were now qualified enough to lead a Premier League team, but soon the true reason behind their sudden involvement in team selection became clear. As we were nearing the end of the season, the time had come to showcase some of the players who might bring in transfer money. The leaders suddenly showed their skill at planning for the next season and of course, any player who happened to be a distant (or not so distant) relative of a leader or a prominent member was suddenly given an automatic spot on the team sheet. Or at least, this is what the leaders wanted. But they had forgotten that their team was in the hands of a coach who liked to clearly distinguish between the roles of the various officials, and I never gave them the chance to interfere with team selection. I kept on going back to the wise words of Brian Clough, who once famously said that "in this business (of being a football manager) you've got to be a dictator or you haven't got a chance". Of course, this did not go down too well with the leadership, but for me it was the right thing to do.

THIRTY-THREE

Nᴇxᴛ ᴛʜɪɴɢ ʏᴏᴜ ᴋɴᴏᴡ, ᴛʜᴇ newspapers started writing about the disconnect between the leadership and the coaches again. Some of the officials had felt it necessary to go and complain about their own coaches in the national papers, and of course the Shilling signs started blinking in the reporters' eyes as soon as they heard the latest *mizengwe* episode. They gladly complied. My fellow coach decided to keep his mouth shut, as he needed to worry a bit more about his position in the club.

New conflict brewing at Safari Sports Club

**BY
OUR REPORTER**

Internal conflict is reported to be brewing up again at Safari Sports Club of Dar Es Salaam, following a misunderstanding between the club's leadership and their coach, Peter Mulder.

Informed sources within the club told this newspaper that the misunderstanding follows the recent interference of the leadership with the team's technical affairs, noting that Mulder has told the leadership that the technical matters are the prerogative of the coaches,

and that the leadership should instead focus on development and fundraising for the cash-strapped club. According to the source, Mulder recently used the media to castigate the club's leadership for trying to involve itself in team selection and to threaten that unless the leadership stopped, he was going to stop training the team.

According to the sources, the Safari Sports Club leadership has told their coach that they were not going to cooperate with him if he continued to exclude them from team selection and technical matters.

Mulder commented that he was astonished to find that the leadership have already informed three players that they will not be registered with the club next year, and he has also refused to select players that the leadership have tried to force him to select. "The task of the coach is to select the best players for the job in hand. I study the opposition, I look at the strengths of my own players, and based on the tactic to be used and on the players' fitness, I put a team together. Selection for the match is based on merit and utility, and not on the whiffs of a leader", Mulder said sternly.

Mulder also commented on the fact that the leaders are actively pursuing the signature of Ali Banyanga, the former central defender of Safari Sports Club, who is now 35 years of age. "Modern football is science and you require talented youngsters, not veterans as some people seem to believe. Recruitment, as much as team selection, is the coach's job, and I will continue to see this as one of my tasks, no matter how much the leadership tries to frustrate me", he added. He seemed to suggest that if things don't improve at Safari Sports Club, he may think about training another Premier League team, including Safari Sports Club's archrivals, Ndovu Football Club. "My main inter-est is to help develop football in the country. I am not interested in banging my head against a wall of resistance and opposition, after all I am doing all this work out of the goodness of my heart!", the Belgian warned his current club.

The Safari Sports Club leaders responded by saying that they have been legally elected and that they are in charge of all the team's affairs, including technical matters. "Mulder is duty-bound to do as we say, and even though he has helped the club a lot by going out and soliciting sponsorships, he has not provided anything for the leaders. Instead, he only takes care of the players. This is not why we stood for election", the Secretary General commented.

When this reporter approached some Safari Sports Club fans outside the club house, he learned that the fans support their coach. "We have seen poor leadership in the past, and any interference that they have in team selection only serves their own personal agenda", Mussa Madanga commented. "The leaders should allow our coaches to do their work undisturbed. If they don't have confidence in the coaches, then they should say so and ask them to leave. This is what happens in modern football—just look at the top teams in Europe, they often change their coaches. But not when the team is winning!"

Signs were starting to appear that the leaders were trying to create a rift between themselves and the coaching team, and I kept my eyes and ears open during the days that followed.

I decided that the game against the "sugarboys" of Mbitwa was big enough to make the five hour drive to Turiani. I left Dar Es Salaam early in the morning, but got delayed by an over-zealous—or hungry—policeman who decided that this was a good day to put a speed trap on the highway. As I was driving and listening to the latest great Bongo hits, the inimitable and totally infectious Congolese music, I forgot that there are in fact speed limits in Tanzania, and of course I got caught in a trap. In the middle of nowhere, probably somewhere in an area that is normally reserved for elephants, giraffes and a couple of lions, suddenly a policeman jumped out of the bushes and put up his hand, instructing me to stop my car. I complied, and he took his jolly good time to walk up to the car and start asking me some questions.

"Good afternoon officer."

"Mmm."

"How are you?"

"You know you were speeding?"

"I had no idea. I was just driving along and listening to some music. There's no traffic on the road at all."

"You were speeding. You must pay a fine."

"How do you know that I was speeding?"

"We have a trap here. Here's the proof."

So he showed me a small device that looked like a megaphone and that showed the number 148. At this point, I would like to inform the reader that I was driving a Toyota Hilux Surf whose absolute maximum speed was somewhere around 100 km/hour with a tailwind and going downhill. There was no way that I had been cruising at 148 km/hour.

"I'm sorry officer. I could not possibly have been going at that speed."

"Well, that's what the speedometer says."

"Well, maybe your speedometer is wrong. Maybe it should say 85 km/hour."

"Now don't get smart ok?"

"If you like, you can get in my car and drive it, and see if it goes anywhere near 140 km/hour."

"That won't be necessary. The speedometer is always right."

"I see. So now I have to pay a fine?"

"Yes, of course. You must pay in cash. Twenty thousand Shillings."

"I'm sorry, I don't have cash on me. Can you give me the ticket, and I'll go and settle it at the police station in Dar Es Salaam."

"No, you can't do that."

"Sure I can! That's what a colleague of yours in Dar Es Salaam told me when he stopped me last week because my indicator was not working. He told me that I had to go to the police station and pay the fine there."

"That's not how things work here. Here you have to pay in cash to me, and I will then take your money to the station."

Somehow I doubted that the last step of this procedure was common practice in these parts.

"I'm sorry. I don't have enough cash to pay you. I will just go to the police station. Please give me the ticket and I'll take care of it."

"I can't do that. If you don't have the cash, then maybe you can give me some cigarettes or some food."

"I'm sorry, I don't smoke and I didn't bring food either."

I could see that he was starting to become disappointed at not being given any cash.

"Where are you going?"

"I am on my way to Turiani."

"Why are you going there?"

"My football team has a match there this afternoon. And I don't want to be late."

"Hey! I thought I recognized you! Aren't you Peter Mulder?"

"Yes, I am. And I hope you are a Safary Sports Club fan."

"Of course! Everyone in my family is a Safari fan! It's so good to meet you! I hope you win this afternoon and that we can win the league again this year!"

"Thank you. We will try our best! Can I go now?"

"Of course! You mustn't be late. And forgive me for asking you for that fine. You are my friend, so you don't have to pay. In fact, you didn't even speed. But I hope that you understand that I had run out of things to smoke . . . Don't worry about it, ok?"

"I won't. OK, I will go now, I have a match to get to."

"Can I get a lift? I would love to see the game."

"Well, yes, why not?"

"OK. Let me go and get my children and my neighbours. I am sure they would also like to go and watch the match."

I was not keen on getting twenty people in my car, so as soon as this policeman ran off to go and tell his kids and friends to come and join us, I decided to continue my journey and took off. After all, there was only so much I would put up with.

I arrived at the stadium about twenty minutes before kick-off. Actually, 'stadium' is a nice word for what it was. It was really no more than a field that was roughly shaped like a football pitch, completely surrounded by sugar cane fields, and with a few hundred spectators standing on and even inside the lines. This match promised to be another Mickey Mouse affair.

Our team had travelled to Turiani the day before, and Nestor and I had already decided on the team line-up. By the time I arrived in Mbitwa, he had already conducted the warm-up, and I had just enough time to speak to the team and put some encouraging words into the players' minds. I told them that we were in enemy territory, that we would be playing against a team of eleven players, four referees, a powerful leadership and hundreds of blood-thirsty fans. I pleaded with my soldiers to try and refrain from reacting to the referee's antics, but I was by now experienced enough to know exactly what was coming. I knew that we would have to perform at least seven miracles to come away with a draw here, but as things turned out, we never stood a chance.

Barely twenty-five minutes after kick-off, the game was over. By that time, three of our players had been sent off, Mbitwa had scored a goal when one of their players was at least ten metres off-side, the referee and his linesman had been assaulted three times, and every time one of our players touched the ball, a foul was given to our opponents. The most ridiculous sending-off of all time happened in this match. One of the Mbitwa players kicked the ball out of play for a throw-in, one of our players retrieved it and threw the ball back into play, and then ran into the field. He was promptly sent off. Everyone looked completely bemused, even the Mbitwa players were puzzled about this one, and when I asked the referee what the red card was for, he told me that the player had entered the field of play without his permission!

When the third Safari Sports Club player was given his marching orders, a massive brawl started, and even Nestor could be seen chasing the referee and kicking and punching him as soon as he lost his footing. I wasn't proud of my colleague then, and just stood and watched this mass of Barbarians punch each other senseless. My heart bled, and I had the feeling that the end of the road was near. What on earth was going on here, and how could we ever get this sorted out?

The referee's performance in this particular match was *uzalendo* at its best, or worst, or most extreme, and ever since that day I have totally despised the way in which Tanzanian referees kill the game there. I took back everything I ever said about them 'trying their best' and 'working under a lot of pressure'. This referee and his linesmen were cheats of the worst kind, and they didn't even try to hide the fact that Mbitwa needed to win this match. They had been appointed for this match the morning of the game, which was totally against the league regulations, and meant that there were actually two refereeing teams present for this game. We played the match under protest, but that didn't help. After a kangaroo court disciplinary hearing at the offices of the Football Association, the game was awarded to Mbitwa, who became Mainland champions in this very dubious and controversial way. Nothing to be proud of, but in a way also history repeating itself in Tanzania . . . Furthermore, Safari Sports Club was fined a significant sum of money, and yet again, there was nothing left for the players.

As soon as the match was abandoned I went back to my car, and found that one of the rear view mirrors had been smashed. This was enemy territory, and I vowed never to return to this hellhole. It was a long drive back to Dar Es Salaam, and on the way home I started thinking about my ambition to help improve the standard of Tanzanian football. Was it still worth it? How much more frustration should I take? Why was it that almost all my attention had to go to dealing with problems, corruption and poor management, rather than to my coaching? After all, coaching was what I really wanted to do.

Back in Dar Es Salaam, the infighting within the club leadership was also gaining momentum. One day the nation was informed that our Assistant Secretary General had resigned with immediate effect. It was not quite clear to me why a leader with such a title was needed, but fact was that he would not be missed by the rest of the Executive Committee. The Secretary General himself told the newspapers that "the club would not persuade their former colleague to reverse his decision as he had failed in his duties since being voted into office earlier in the year". According to this official, his former assistant had been "a liability to the club", and the office was a better place without him. The former Assistant Secretary General had refused to hand over all the club documents that he had in his possession, and only a court case was going to force him to return the said documents. He claimed that he had resigned because of the "incompetence and selfishness on the part of his colleagues". Apparently, the club had already received a lot of money from the sale of two key players, and the cash had "ended up in the pockets of a few individuals in the Executive". Furthermore, because one of our opponents in the African Cup had not shown up for the return match, they had paid a fine of twenty million Tanzanian Shilling, all of which had ended up in the Chairman's pockets and plastic bags. Well, finally, at last somebody agreed with my opinion on this corrupt leadership. Maybe my influence was finally starting to be felt. When approached by a reporter, I again hinted that I might consider joining our arch rivals, claiming that they seemed more organized and more serious about the development of their club. Of course I could not be certain, but it could hardly be any worse than at Safari Sports Club. Now that the officials themselves started to go on the record with allegations and accusations of corruption and embezzlement, it was clear that I had not been mistaken.

And if further proof was needed, the next weekend the Executive Committee held a members' meeting that ended in fistfights and several participants being arrested by the police. The newspapers had a field day of course!

Safari members are arrested

BY

TIMES REPORTER

A number of Safari Sports Club members have been arrested in connection with Sunday's violence at the club's headquarters. Officers at the Kariakoo Police Station confirmed that they were holding "several suspects" but declined to give details, saying more information could be obtained from the Regional Police Commander.

Safari Sports Club Secretary General, Mr Shenzi, later told this reporter that all those involved in the fracas in which club officials were attacked would be charged with assault. He said the Executive Committee would meet today to discuss how to go about the matter.

The members' meeting called by the Executive Committee ended inconclusively on Sunday when a group of rowdy members set upon club officials with kicks and blows, accusing them of "grossly mismanaging" the club.

The Club house turned into a temporary boxing ring when incensed members grabbed the club leaders by the collar, rouged them up and prompted a premature termination of the meeting. The commotion in the club house was such a noisy affair that it brought business in the street to a halt. Tempers were flying high, with disgruntled members mouthing insults and even obscenities.

The violence broke out as one member was giving his views on the Executive Committee's report presented by the Secretary General.

The Chairman and Treasurer were knocked to the floor in the melee, which ended only after policemen detailed to provide security rushed to the conference room on the fifth floor of the club house. The policemen took almost an hour before they intervened.

In my mind, it was the Executive Committee members that should have been arrested, but of course, they had enough cash in the plastic bags to buy their way out of trouble. At least for the time being.

After the fracas of this meeting, the Secretary General distanced himself even more from the club's members by publicly stating that the violence was the work of people "who were ignorant of the club's constitution" and "who call themselves Safari Sports Club members but who are only interested in sparking and fanning chaos in the club".

I decided that I would once more try and get back at least part of what I had invested into the club. I went to see the Treasurer on several occasions, but each time he came up with the same excuses:

"I haven't received the cheque from the sponsor yet, so come back tomorrow." or
"I received the cheque, but it bounced. We have to get a new cheque tomorrow." or
"I received the cheque but I had to pay some people, so come back next Monday."

I had taken almost a year to realize that I was just trying to nail jelly against the wall. Maybe I was a slow learner, or maybe I fed off my enthusiasm for too long. But what was clear was that the odds were no longer in my favor . . .

THIRTY-FOUR

Amidst all the upheavals, hardly anybody took notice of the fact that Zamalek FC had landed in Dar Es Salaam. Led by their globetrotting and highly successful German coach, Otto Pfister, they were one of just two or three favorites for the Africa Cup tournament, and of course I knew that we would need a couple of miracles to survive against this giant of African football. As stated before, I relished the opportunity to measure ourselves against the best that the continent had to offer, and we would surely all get a reality check from the moment we crossed swords with them on the field.

The Zamalek delegation consisted of a squad of twenty-three players, close to ten technical staff and about twenty officials. They received the typical African football welcome, and were duly taken to a local guesthouse that was completely incompatible not only with the rules of the African Football Confederation, but also with the status of this top club. Of course, they refused to occupy their rooms, and when they saw that their hosts, our leaders, were not going to provide them with decent accommodation, they decided themselves to migrate to the city's top hotel. Upon checking into the hotel, they made the promise to settle all the bills themselves, but deep down inside I was hoping that they would check out and leave the unpaid bills for the Safari Sports Club leadership to sort out.

Our leaders tried to treat the Zamalek delegation in the same way that our own team had been treated in Zimbabwe, but it was nothing more than a ludicrous and embarrassing attempt. These Egyptians were experienced and had seen it all before. Several of their star players had played in the FIFA World Cup, some of them were African champions, and they were not going to feel unsettled just because the bus to the stadium broke down three times . . . It was pathetic really, and I could only guess at the treatment that we would receive when we travelled to Egypt for the return match. None of the leaders was able to think that far ahead though.

Match day arrived, and the stadium was packed. I was sure that most of the spectators had come to see the bald Hassan brothers, Hossam and Ibrahim, as well as a host of other international star players. There weren't too many opportunities to watch the greats at work in Tanzania, so the gate collection on that day was very healthy. Of course, many of our own fans also showed up. It was the first time in several years that we could actually compete with the bigger clubs from the continent, and there was a general belief in the press that we might just pull off a little surprise. During my pre-match talk I gave my players the usual dose of "they only have two legs and two arms each, just like all of you", that "the ball is round" and that "you only need a second to score a goal", but I thought it wiser to ignore the fact that within the Zamalek team, there were more than four hundred international caps represented. No need to scare my boys, right?

Nestor had had his input in the tactical plan. He felt that it would be best to attack the Egyptians over the wings, and to put solid crosses into the centre of the opposing defence. What Nestor did not realize was that the average Zamalek player was about 1,85m tall, about six feet, and that our diminutive strikers would have no chance against them in the air. Some of the Egyptian defenders were almost two metres tall and weighed about a hundred kilos—almost twice as heavy as our underfed strikers. Nestor wasn't easily swayed though. He stuck to his ludicrous idea and instructed our players to get their crosses in.

We finished our warm-up, retreated to the relative safety of our dressing room, and got ready to walk onto the field in order to be introduced to the many guests of honor and to sing the national anthem. As soon as we walked out of the tunnel, I noticed that there were hundreds of fans who had made their way onto the running track. Someone must have left a gate open somewhere, and while the President of the Republic came down to meet the players and officials, the police were busy clubbing any fan who refused to get back into the stands. Since the stands were packed already, there was no way that this crowd was going to move. Well, they had nowhere to move to. The police however enjoyed their moment in the spotlight, and swung their batons around as if they were swatting mosquitoes. While we stood in a line on the field, I quickly walked over to Mr Pfister and wished him a good game. "May the best team win", I said. "And may the odds be ever in our favor", I thought to myself. "Heaven help us", I added subconsciously.

It was time for the national anthems to be played. The military band that occasionally made an appearance at a match or at a government function was conspicuous by its absence. No band. So we waited for the PA system to play the tune of the Egyptian anthem. Nothing. After a minute or so, an official came down from the VIP box, walked onto the field and whispered something into the ear of the Egyptian Ambassador. The latter then said something in Arabic to the Zamalek officials and players, and suddenly they all started to sing their anthem without musical accompaniment. A rather embarrassing situation for the Tanzanian hosts, but certainly not one without precedent. When the Egyptians finished singing, it was our turn to present a rendition of the Tanzanian national anthem, *Mungu Ibariki Tanzania* (God bless Tanzania). Again, no music to help us stay in tune, so upon the invisible signal of I don't know who, first one, then two, then a few and then the whole team started to timidly hum the lyrics. The signing of a national anthem is of course supposed to be a solemn and serious affair. Standing straight up, right hand on chest, and keeping a straight face as much as possible. However, when you have a couple of octogenarians in the line-up, government or association officials who for the life of them can't remember the words nor the tune, then it's hard not to start sniggering. Right next to me one of the Football Association's oldest members was visibly struggling with his memory, and the words that came out of his mouth had absolutely nothing to do with God blessing Tanzania. He wasn't even close. In fact, even Psy's "Gangnam Style" lyrics bear more resemblance to the anthem than what this poor old man was pushing through his remaining teeth. The players had a hard time not to burst out in totally inappropriate laughter, and the end of the presumed song couldn't come soon enough for all of us! Eventually the torture ended and the formalities were concluded.

When the introductions had been completed and we tried to get to the team bench, we found that it had been completely taken over by fans. I never sat down during the whole match. I stood by the sidelines most of the time, arguing with the fourth official who kept on telling me that I could not stay there permanently. I asked him where he suggested I should go—there was absolutely nowhere to move to . . . With the chaos going on around the field, it was difficult to have any sort of communication with my players.

The first forty-five minutes went by, and the Zamalek defence had probably never had an easier international match. Only two crosses made it into the penalty area, and the toughest challenge that the Zamalek goalkeeper had to deal with was a back pass from one of his defenders. The bumpy field caused the ball to bounce left and right a bit, and the keeper was clearly not used to playing on potato fields. Oh no, he'd already played at the San Siro in Milan and at the Olympic Stadium in Rome. His lack of appreciation for the quality of this venue was easily forgiven. The Zamalek team had shown little initiative though to break us down, and we reached half-time with the score intact.

During the half-time break I got the chance to speak with the players, some of whom had already identified the impossibility to do any damage with our wing play and crosses. Up front my strikers were playing like short Davids against tall Goliaths, and we needed to change something. I thought of my own shortcomings as a tall player, all those years ago, and asked myself what would make me most uncomfortable as a tall defender. I decided to ask the wingers to cut inside from what I call the 70% point, and to run straight at the defenders. I knew that most of the time my players would run into a human wall, but I also felt that getting past them with our speed was the only way to penetrate that solid defense. A backtracking defender could never be as quick as an advancing striker, and we only needed to get lucky once or twice . . . so let's give that a go!

About six or seven minutes into the second half, my left winger intercepted a pass and started to advance towards the Egyptian penalty area. Twenty minutes earlier he would have crossed that ball, but he had listened well to my instructions, and took off on a rather impressive solo run. The Zamalek players did not expect this, and before we knew it he had passed two opponents. Up next was the wall of defenders—no less impregnable than the walls around the temple of Karnak! Haruna, because that was his name, clearly started to get excited, and had the good sense to draw a one-two out of our central striker, Mrisho. Something special was happening here, and I could easily sense it. Something that months and months of training had been leading up to. It was palpable, we could sense it in the air, a little voice inside my head started to speak. "Go on, son. Go on. Take them on!".

Haruna laid off the ball for Mrisho and continued his run. Mrisho, who normally liked to take twenty or thirty touches on the ball before passing or shooting, was in an inspired moment. He played a one-touch pass right into Haruna's path. And with that single one-two move, the Egyptian fortress had been breached. Surely the hardest work had been done. All that remained now was to get the ball past one of the greatest goalkeepers Africa had ever produced. As Haruna continued to bear down on goal, time seemed to stop. The noise around me stopped too. All I could see now was Haruna, running in slow motion, and keeping perfect control of the ball. In what seemed like total silence, the goalkeeper advanced by a few metres and made himself twice as big as he already was. The goal became very small, and Haruna stood no realistic chance of squeezing his shot between the keeper and the goal post. But he did. He picked his spot and stroked the ball home, as calmly as you like. The ball rolled agonizingly close past the goalkeeper and settled in the back of the net. A moment of absolute stillness and whiteness, not unlike the atmosphere just before a tsunami strikes. And then, a deafening roar that seemed to come from above, from below and from around. The impossible had happened—we had scored against Zamalek FC. We were winning an Africa Cup match against the formidable Egyptians. We were on top of the world.

For a few minutes, at least.

With unbelievable ease, and without breaking a sweat, Zamalek equalized five minutes later. Three, four quick passes, a dummy for one of the defenders, and 'Bam'! One all, and we had just gotten a taste of real champions' cold bloodedness. I guessed that that's what you get when you have the audacity to book a team like Zamalek FC in a cheap guesthouse.

Thankfully the Egyptians felt that getting the draw and the away-goal was sufficient, and the match ended with honors even. I had mixed feelings about the result. On the one hand I felt good about not having lost, but I was also realistic enough to know that Zamalek could easily have taken us to the cleaners. The way in which they scored their goal at will, exactly how and when they wanted, was frightening. This was a team that had total control not only over its own game, but also over the opponent. We still had some way to go to achieve that level of proficiency.

I also knew of course that the return match would be a formality—nobody had ever beaten Zamalek in Cairo, and some teams had been mercilessly humiliated in the land of the Pharaohs. But those were concerns for later.

At the end of the match, I was so much impressed with the level of Zamalek FC that I walked over to Otto Pfister and thanked him for the match. I cheekily congratulated him in German for managing to draw against us, and told him that I would love the opportunity to share a drink with him and talk some more about football and coaching in Africa.

"Come on over to the hotel tonight, if you like."
"Sure! Let me invite you for dinner, and let's share stories."
"*Wunderbar*! *Bis heute abend.*"
"*Tschüß!*"

That evening, I met Mr Pfister in the lobby of a hotel befitting the status of his club. The Hilton Hotel in Dar Es Salaam was the only four-star hotel, and by far the most comfortable and luxurious of all the accommodation options. Its vast gardens and two swimming pools were a haven for those seeking rest and relaxation in between their meetings or training sessions. I regularly visited the Hilton Hotel for their succulent brunch and buffet meals, and I was looking forward to an interesting evening with one of the most travelled and experienced coaches in Africa.

Before going to the dining hall, we sat down in the lobby and ordered some refreshments. We had only just started to talk about the afternoon's football match when I suddenly noticed the Publicity Secretary of Safari Sports Club. He was walking towards the reception desk with a rather large plastic bag. He did not notice us, and started to talk with one of the hotel employees. I could not hear what they were discussing, but as time passed, the conversation seemed to get more and more heated and animated. I continued to talk with Mr Pfister about the challenges in African football, but couldn't stop myself from glancing over his shoulder from time to time to see what was going on at the reception. After two or three minutes, our Publicity Secretary starting swinging his arms and pointing fingers at the employee. I could see that he was getting quite upset and angry, and suddenly he pointed at the plastic bag. Obviously his whole discussion had to do with money, and most probably with the hotel bill. I assumed that he had come to settle the bill up to that point and that he had brought too little cash with him. Now that the volume of the conversation had picked up, I could hear some numbers being mentioned, and there was clear disagreement about how much should be paid. I thought that it would be better for Otto and I to move to the dining room, so I asked him to come with me.

As I stood up and started to walk towards the dining room, the Publicity Secretary spotted me and shouted across the lobby:

"Hey, Peter! Hey!"

I turned around and waved at him.

"What are you doing here? And why are you with the coach?", he shouted.

Rather than replying across the vast lobby, I went to him and said:

"The coach and I are having dinner together. I would like to discuss with him what he has learned from his many years of coaching in Africa, and ways in which we can take our respective clubs forwards. There is a lot I can learn from him."

"Oh, I see. Why don't you ask him if they can invite us for a training camp some time? But they would have to cover all our expenses."

"I'll see what I can do. Do you need any help with what you are doing here?"

"Oh no. These fools here are overcharging us for the food that the Arabs are eating. These days you can't trust anyone around here. Why do they think that we have money to just give away?"

"Yes, I wonder too . . ."

I rejoined Mr Pfister and we headed off to the dining room. We spent a couple of hours discussing his early coaching career, how he had gotten into professional coaching in Africa, and what he saw as the opportunities and the challenges. They were some of the most valuable hours spent in my coaching career, and Mr Pfister's experience showed me that there was a road that leads to the top, even though it may be long, winding and sometimes rather bumpy. I was certainly not the only one who had undertaken this journey, but I was pleased when Mr Pfister gave me the same advice as Oscar Fullone had given many months earlier : "Follow your gut, do what you think is right, and always remember that you can't please everyone all of the time". He also encouraged me to travel to Europe during the summers and to take a number of international coaching courses, and to then adapt what I had learned there to the particular conditions in Tanzania.

It was close to midnight when we said our goodbyes, and we agreed that the return match in Cairo would be an interesting affair. I wished him a safe journey back.

The next morning, the nation woke up to a shock.

THIRTY-FIVE

Mulder sells Safari Sports Club's secrets to Egyptians!

BY
OUR REPORTER

Safari Sports Club's Belgian coach, Peter Mulder, has been accused of selling his club's tactical and technical secrets to their Africa Cup opponents, Zamalek FC of Egypt.

According to the club's Publicity Secretary, Mulder was seen yesterday in the company of Zamalek's Head Coach, Otto Pfister of Germany, at the Hilton Hotel in the city. Mulder and Pfister spent a number of hours together, and this newspaper has learnt that they discussed Safari Sports Club's secrets.

"When I arrived at the hotel to settle some bills, I found our coach in a deep discussion with the Egyptians' coach. They were clearly talking about our tactics and about the way in which we prepare our team for international assignments, and it was obvious that Mulder was giving away or selling our precious secrets. Mulder was also trying to sell some of our best players to the visiting club, and asking them to hire him as an Assistant Coach to Mr Pfister."

Apparently Mulder and Pfister had dinner together, and this reporter was unable to get a comment from Mulder before going to press.

For the past year, Mulder has been trying very hard to develop Safari Sports Club and to bring a sense of professionalism to the club, but he has been constantly frustrated by what he has regularly called 'incompetent and corrupt' club leaders.

Safari Sports Club played against Zamalek FC in last Saturday's Africa Cup match, which ended in a 1-1 draw. The return match is set for Cairo, Egypt, in two weeks' time.

HA! MISTER PUBLICITY SECRETARY HAD found a new story to get himself in the papers with. At first I thought nothing much of the story, and simply considered it a lot of hot air. But later that day the reporter who had broken the story contacted me and asked me for my version of the events.

"It is true that I met with Mr Pfister the evening after the match, and we discussed a whole lot of things, all to do with coaching in Africa and developing clubs here. Mr Pfister and I have common European roots, and we are both coaches who have come to Africa and are trying to make a difference."

"So you did not sell any secrets?"

"Of course not. That's not how football works, is it? Maybe it is, in the mind of the Publicity Secretary. It just shows how narrow-minded he really is. Since when do clubs sell secrets to one another? What secrets do we have? Mr Pfister saw how we played against his team, and I am sure he has already figured out how to play against us in Egypt. And what would I stand to gain from selling secrets, if we had any? I think I have shown throughout the past year how much I want my club to do well. If I was not serious about at least trying to beat Zamalek, I don't think we would have gotten a draw on Saturday."

"There was also a suggestion that you may have tried to sell some of your best players."

"Yes, I saw that. What a ludicrous and stupid comment. I am not a FIFA-registered players' agent. I know the rules of the game, and I can not do any illegal business unless I am a licenced agent. Of course, the person who made this comment has no idea how these things work. He should first study football before making such a fool of himself."

"Did you ask for a job as an Assistant Coach?"

"I think you know that I have a full-time job here in Tanzania, and that I am only helping Safari Sports Club out of the goodness of my heart. Why would I want to leave Tanzania, leave my job, and go to Egypt? I have started on a project here, and unless there is too much resistance from idiots like our Publicity Secretary, I will do everything I can to see it through."

"So what comment do you have for the Publicity Secretary?"

"Well, now that he has accused me of sabotaging the club, he should present the evidence. If he can prove the allegations, then I will accept the consequences. But if he can't, then he should face the repercussions himself, and I would expect the Executive Committee to oust him for bringing the club into disrepute. He can then use his free time to go and find out how top football clubs are run these days. There is a lot for him to learn!"

The next day the newspaper carried my reply, and in the following days there were many letters from readers accusing the Publicity Secretary of concocting lies and misinforming the public. The sports shows on the radio also talked about this episode, and it was generally expected that the Publicity Secretary would be sacked from the Executive Committee. At one point, even the Minister of Sports, Youth and Culture was interviewed and added his view that there should be no room for false accusations in the administration of the football clubs. Several club members asked whether the Publicity Secretary had already decided to leave the club and whether he was trying to destabilize us while we were preparing for our biggest match in recent memory. Seeing the wave of support that I was receiving, I added a bit of fuel to the fire.

In my next interview with a journalist, I let everyone know that this same Publicity Secretary was carrying the proverbial 'plastic bag' when I saw him in the hotel, and that I had heard him say that he wouldn't settle the hotel bill because "the gate collection should be for the leaders of the club, not for accommodation expenses" . . . I was pretty tempted to reveal more about this man's behavior, but I thought better of it and decided to let the Executive Committee do what it needed to do. With thousands of members and the national press watching their next move in this case about development versus corruption, they would soon have to show their true colors. In the meantime, I continued to train the team and tried to work on our defensive organization—we would certainly need that in Cairo!

The press boys continued to challenge the leadership. The journalists wanted to know how the club would deal with the Publicity Secretary and a group of members suggested that the Executive Committee organize a members' meeting to bring closure to this issue. I knew that I had the support of the members, so I backed the idea of a public meeting. The Executive Committee refused though, and stated that it had no choice but to stand by its Publicity Secretary. The tight bond that their conniving had created was not to be broken, but of course the real reason was that the Publicity Secretary knew far too much about the corrupt behavior of all the other leaders. If any one of them got sacked, he would certainly spill the beans about all the others, and complete chaos would ensue. Quite a number of football officials had ended up in jail before them, including top leaders of the National Football Association and of the National Olympic Committee. The prospect of joining these crooks in the cells did not appeal to any of the Safari Sports Club leaders, and they told the nation that they would not take any disciplinary action against the Publicity Secretary. Little did they know that they were only postponing the inevitable.

They did however confirm that there was absolutely no reason to believe that any of his allegations were correct, and they assured the nation that there was no evidence suggesting that their coach had acted in an inappropriate manner. In fact, one of the leaders mentioned that it was quite common for coaches from different clubs to get together and exchange ideas and views on all sorts of football-related things. Well, he was a bit smarter than the others, or maybe he had invested some of his loot into a TV and watched what the coaches of the English Premier League teams do after a match . . .

As soon as the Executive Committee announced its standpoint, the club members became more agitated. More and more of them were getting tired of these malpractices, and especially so because they were now required to pay even higher membership fees. They could no longer see how their money was contributing to the club's development, and they started to talk about seizing power out of the hands of the leaders.

Two days later, the leadership announced the list of players and staff who would travel to Cairo for the return match against Zamalek FC. They had chosen their own 12 players without consulting the coaches, or at least without consulting me. Only twelve players to go and play against the mighty Egyptians. Once more, a cost-cutting exercise that had absolutely nothing to do with the needs of the club but rather with the destination of the club's cash. This was getting pretty disgusting now. When I looked down the list of people who would travel to Egypt, I found these twelve players, followed by Nestor, followed by one of the peripheral members who was identified as a 'club doctor', and finally all seven members of the Executive Committee, Publicity Secretary included. And at the bottom of the list—would you believe it? Our sponsor! I didn't need any reminders that he was on his way to the north of the continent in order to conduct his real business. When you take twenty-five deflated footballs across borders, you can be taking many kinds of substances with you too . . . After all, stitching up a football is easy, and they don't normally get scanned at airports. My name was not in the list.

I wasn't blind to all this, and that evening, while driving home after practice, I started to wonder whether it was all still worth it. Was I not starting to look like a stubborn fool, working so hard to try and help people and to try and change some lives for the better, yet constantly having to spend time and energy on dealing with complete morons whose agenda was diametrically opposed to mine? I did not want to end up like a Danaid and draw water into bottomless barrels for the rest of my life. I wasn't getting any richer from my coaching work either, and I could feel that the odds were no longer in my favor. What was the point in holding on to something that went against the interests of a few and against a culture of the many? Should I not just move on and find a better place to pursue my ambitious goals?

Enough was enough. I decided to go and see the Chairman of the club the next day. I told him that I could not reconcile myself with their cowardly decision, and that I could not work with people whose little plastic bags were so much more important than any morality or conscience that they may or may not have had. I knew that this probably sounded like music in his ears, but before he could say anything, I turned around, walked out of his shabby shop and vowed to pursue my coaching ambitions in a more conducive environment. Surely there were places where the odds would be more in my favor.

That was a couple of weeks ago. I decided to take a short holiday and fly to Barcelona.

EPILOGUE

THE CIRCLE HAD BEEN COMPLETED. My mission under that fateful Safari Sports Club leadership had come to an end. Not an end that I would have anticipated a year earlier, but an inevitable one nonetheless. There was just no way that this club could make progress under such incompetent leaders. Safari Sports Club was not a place for those of us who wanted to develop the club in the only way possible, through honest, fair and civilized means. It wasn't to be, but nobody knows what the future holds.

Soon after I left the club, I got vindicated. The team, with its contingent of officials around it, flew to Cairo and got a four-nil drubbing at the hands of Zamalek FC. Not a surprise, and in fact, it could have been more. The Africa Cup adventure was over. Of course, the leaders would claim that I must have sold all those secrets after all!

They never really got the chance to claim anything. A few days after the team's return to Dar Es Salaam, the leadership dismissed Nestor, who was subsequently arrested for being in the country illegally. All these months the club leaders had refused to sort out his work permit, and eventually the Immigration Department did what it had to do. And on this occasion, there was no little plastic bag to bail him out of his predicament.

It then took only three more days before the club members organized their own meeting and ousted the Executive Committee. The members had clearly seen enough, and finally held the leadership responsible for the way in which the club had been mismanaged. There were some reports of violence during the meeting, but the main outcome was that the whole Executive Committee was suspended with immediate effect, and that control over the club's affairs was returned to the Elders' Council. During the meeting, a number of irregularities were discussed, and some of the leading members decided to lay charges against the members of the Executive Committee. The mismanagement of club funds was of course the main issue, but there was also alleged abuse of power, intimidation and something to do with a trade in illegal substances . . . The Chairman, the Secretary-General, the Treasurer, the Publicity Secretary and all their assistants had to answer charges of corruption in the courts and soon after received a three-year ban from all involvement in football matters. The sponsor was informed by the Narcotics Department that he would have to submit to criminal investigations. My earlier prediction was proven wrong : these officials would not just disappear into the sunset with a plastic bag full of money under their arm. They would have to face the ignominy of falling into public disgrace. Of course, the investigations might lead to nothing, but the fact that there are investigations in the first place is a victory for all those who want to clean up the football administration in this country. More court cases, a number of arrests, and soon enough a couple of former leaders in jail. When the cash in the plastic bags runs dry, then there's simply no way out of trouble . . .

In actual fact, their fate was sealed from the day they took office. Just like so many equally corrupt and narrow-minded 'leaders' before them, they ended up having to fight off allegations and accusations of bribery, corruption, embezzlement and theft. They lived by the old Soviet saying that 'he who does not get caught is not a thief'. Well, they got caught, and they'll have a hard time trying to avoid the quasi unavoidable. The missing dollars and Shillings may never be found, but any new leadership will know that they are being watched. It was sad that it had to come to this, but I have always maintained that you can only get away with so much. One day you reap what you sow. Just like Creon in the ancient Greek city of Thebes, the officials of Safari Sports Club ignored public opinion for too long, and ended up paying the price. Whoever rules from an ivory tower and decides to stand aloof from the feelings and the interests of the masses will come down one day. If the same can happen throughout Tanzanian football, then the future looks good. And if I contributed just a little bit to the development of Safari Sports Club and to the way in which a football club can take care of itself, then I will claim that I have been successful and that, all in all, it was worth it. Sometimes, we can make the odds favor us.

As I sit here in the Nou Camp, I don't just reminisce about what could have been, or where I want to go next. I also relive numerous wonderful moments at Safari Sports Club.

My relationship with the players was terrific. I never needed to get their respect by instilling fear in them. Instead, I deserved their respect by respecting them and valuing them for the contributions that they made towards the team's success. They trained, learned and played in very difficult circumstances, conditions that my words don't even do justice to. Their efforts and determination could easily bring tears to the eyes of the casual bystander. I thank the players for being as hard-working as they were.

I had great moments with the fans. I will forever remember the many friendly welcomes that I received when I first walked onto that training field, first as a player and later on as a coach. I will never forget the days when our fans would remain at the stadium for hours after the end of our matches, singing and dancing in the stands. Those moments made me realize that I was doing the right thing, and that the fans were enjoying what they saw. It's a pity that the enjoyment wasn't meant to last, but there are many opportunities out there.

And yes, there were frustrating moments. But who are we to complain about a lost match or a wasted chance. We can afford to get all excited or feel down when luck is not on our side. I don't know how many times I looked around me at the National Stadium in Dar Es Salaam, or at the smaller football grounds around the country, and felt the pain in the eyes of the handicapped people who usually took up their position near the team bench. We coaches complained about poor refereeing or about the *uzalendo*, but a lot of people around us had much more difficult problems to deal with.

They spend their whole life in a wheelchair or on crutches, and through no fault of their own. I made friends with fans who had been born with polio or other physical handicaps. I never walked past the fans in wheelchairs without acknowledging them and asking how they were doing. These friends never even had the option to try and make it in the sports world, and they have been hindered by their handicap from day one. They go to sleep every night with the pain of having been born with a physical defect, and their situation will never change. I fully realized that we only saw the bravest ones who had learned to live with their handicap and who weren't ashamed of it. But they are only the tip of the iceberg. The majority suffers quietly in the shadows, day and night. For a football coach or player, a defeat hurts, but the pain quickly goes away. After all, a couple of days after the match, there's another match, where all the mistakes from last time can be corrected. Some defeats, especially those suffered in a penalty shoot-out, take a bit longer to heal. I am sure that Roberto Baggio and Stuart Pearce will never completely forget their moment of failure. But a physical handicap never goes away, and requires a life-long adaptation. Some people never come to terms with their difference . . . I always made time for anyone in the city who wanted to have a chat about football. Many of the people that I was lucky enough to meet around the football grounds face tougher challenges than we do, so they have more reasons to feel hard done by. Their problems, be they physical, mental, financial or social, affect them every day of their lives, from morning till evening and even during the night. It was important to keep things in perspective, and to remind ourselves that sometimes football is a game. Just a game.

But then again, for so many, it's so much more than a game. It is a reflection of a community, a culture, a nation. It is who and what we are. It is who and what we identify with. The game brings just as much hope as frustration, just as much joy as despair to millions of people. It is what brings out the best and the worst in people. Conflicts have been created and conflicts have been resolved because of football. People have been able to improve their lives and the lives of those around them through football. People have suffered and even died because of football. It's the great leveler, the game that takes our emotions on a never-ending roller coaster. When Swaziland gets a corner kick against South Africa, the nation celebrates. When Brazil does not win the FIFA World Cup, the nation mourns. The same game, but rather different expectations. It's what makes this game so much more than a game. It's why we're addicted to it.

Was my year as a coach at Safari Sports Club worth it? Let's see.

It was a tremendous learning experience, and as stated before, it was a privilege for a foreigner to discover Tanzania's culture and customs through the medium of football. Ever since those days at Safari Sports Club, I have made giant strides as a football coach, and I have learned to appreciate the problems that this particular part of the world has to try and cope with. I have developed a big admiration for the Tanzanian football players—my former teammates and my former protégés. I don't have to try and convince anyone of the fact that there is a lot of talent in Africa, and I do not doubt for one second that several Tanzanian players could make a very good impression in the European leagues. It is only a pity that their progress is halted by club officials like the ones I had to work with. But the positive note is that, if everybody in this part of the world can work towards the same objective of improving the standard of football through honest means, then the sky is the limit! The raw material, in this case talented players, is certainly there.

Personally I developed tremendously as a coach. I tried out a lot of my own tactical strategies, I learned to better utilize everyone's strengths, and it was wonderful to see our efforts bear fruit during the matches. I knew that there was a road ahead for me. A road that started on the snake-infested fields in Swaziland, that then went right through the dusty and hard-as-rock gravel pitches in Dar Es Salaam, and that has ultimately led me to becoming the coach of the national youth teams of Tanzania and Qatar. I lived a journey that has enabled me to rub shoulders with some of the game's greatest players and coaches. This simple sport, where 'twenty-two guys run after a ball and then kick it away when they finally get it', has helped me forge a friendship with a Head of State and with Pep Guardiola. And let's not forget it, I got to speak with Oscar Fullone and Otto Pfister!

My cultural football odyssey, which had already taken me through Swaziland and Tanzania, was only just beginning. I knew and appreciated the fact that I had gotten two know two incredibly rich and valuable cultures through the medium of football, and I would not have traded this experience for anything in the world. Very few foreigners are afforded such in-depth and privileged access to what makes the local people tick, and when a friendship with a monarch is thrown into the package, then one can only feel blessed.

I suddenly realize that the match between Barcelona FC and Sevilla FC must have ended about twenty minutes ago. The stands have cleared, there are only a few other spectators left, and down below on the Nou Camp pitch, the groundsmen have started patching up the grass. In three days' time, Andrés Iniesta, Lionel Messi and company will be writing more poetry on this green background.

I get up from my seat, take a deep breath, and head down to the players' lounge. I have a quick word with Pep Guardiola, who moves swiftly from one interview to the next. I say my goodbyes and walk into the Catalan night. I smile at the thought that one does not have to be a Sir Alex Ferguson, a Pep Guardiola or a Louis Van Gaal in order to enjoy life as a football coach. Anyone who gives it a try will soon realize that this is so much more than a game.